W9-AUS-593

GV
14
.C47

THE
SOCIAL
ORGANIZATION
OF
LEISURE
IN
HUMAN
SOCIETY

NEIL H. CHEEK, JR.
Texas A&M University

WILLIAM R. BURCH, JR.
Yale University

HARPER & ROW, PUBLISHERS
NEW YORK, HAGERSTOWN, SAN FRANCISCO, LONDON

Sponsoring Editor: Dale Tharp
Project Editor: Eleanor Castellano
Designer: Michel Craig
Production Supervisor: Stefania J. Taflinska
Compositor: P&M Typesetting, Incorporated
Printer: The Maple Press Company
Binder: The Maple Press Company

THE SOCIAL ORGANIZATION OF LEISURE IN HUMAN SOCIETY

Copyright © 1976 by Neil H. Cheek, Jr., and William R. Burch, Jr.
All rights reserved. Printed in the United States of America. No part of
this book may be used or reproduced in any manner whatsoever without written
permission except in the case of brief quotations embodied in critical articles
and reviews. For information address Harper & Row, Publishers, Inc., 10 East
53rd Street, New York, N.Y. 10022.

Library of Congress Cataloging in Publication Data
Cheek, Neil H
   The social organization of leisure in human society.
   Bibliography: p.
   Includes index.
   1. Leisure. 2.   Recreation. I. Burch, William R.,
1933–   joint author. II. Title.
GV14.C47   301.5′7   76-20582
ISBN 0-06-041037-X

ACKNOWLEDGMENTS

Acknowledgements are made to the following for permission to reprint (the page number given is for the page in this text on which reprinted material appears).

Page 7. Edward Norbeck, "Man at Play." Reprinted with permission from Natural History Magazine, December, 1971. Copyright © The American Museum of Natural History, 1971. Reprinted by permission of Doubleday and Company.

Pages 42, 54, 63, 103–104. Melvin Kohn, Class and Conformity—A Study in Values, pp. 3, 76, 190, 210. Copyright © The Dorsey Press, 1969.

Page 46. Leonard Reissman, "Class, leisure, and social participation," American Sociological Review, Vol. 19, 1954, p. 82. Copyright © The American Sociological Association.

Page 49. Saxon Graham, "Social correlates of adult leisure-time behavior." Pp. 331–354 in M. B. Sussman (ed.) Community Structure and Analysis, pp. 350–351. Copyright © Thomas Y. Crowell, 1959.

Page 50. Table from p. 101 of Roger Sidaway, "Public pressure on the countryside," Forestry Supplement. Copyright © Oxford University Press, 1971, by permission of Oxford University Press, Oxford.

Page 56. Table from p. 103 of Stanley R. Parker, The Future of Work and Leisure. Copyright © Praeger Publishers, Inc., 1971.

Pages 65, 81. Harold Wilensky, "The uneven distribution of leisure: the impact of economic growth on 'free time'." Pages 107–145 in E. Smigel (ed.) Work and Leisure, p. 109. Copyright © College and University Press, 1963.

Page 65. Joel E. Gerstl, "Determinants of occupational community in high-status occupation," Sociological Quarterly, Vol. 2, 1961, p. 48.

Page 65. Table from p. 149 of Joel E. Gerstl, "Leisure, taste, and occupational milieu." Pp. 146–147 in E. Smigel (ed.) Work and Leisure. Copyright © College and University Press, 1963.

Page 69. Table from p. 69 of Stanley R. Parker, "Work and non-work in three occupations," Sociological Review, Vol. 13, 1965. Copyright © Sociological Review, Keele, England.

Page 75. Benjamin Lee Whorf, "Science and linguistics." Pp. 111–119 in Theodore M. Necomb and others (eds.) Readings in Social Psychology, p. 214. Copyright © Holt, Rinehart & Winston, 1947.

Pages 76, 82. Richard B. Lee and Irven De Vore (eds.) Man the Hunter, (Chicago, Aldine Publishing Company); copyright © 1968 by Wenner-Gren Foundation for Anthropological Research, Inc.

Pages 77. Marshall O. Sahlins, "Notes on the original affluent society." Pp. 85–89 in Richard B. Lee and Irven De Vore (eds.) Man the Hunter, p. 86. Copyright © Aldine Publishing Company, 1968.

Pages 78. Richard A. Gould, "Journey to Pulykara." Reprinted with permission from Natural History Magazine, Vol. 79, 1970, p. 64. Copyright © The American

Museum of Natural History, 1970. Reprinted by permission of Doubleday and Company.

Page 79. Table from p. 76 of Richard B. Lee and Irven De Vore (eds.) *Man the Hunter.* (Chicago, Aldine Publishing Company); copyright © 1968 by Wenner-Gren Foundation for Anthropological Research, Inc.

Pages 80–81, 87. Beate R. Salz, "The human element in industrialization in hypothetical case study of Equadorian Indians," *Economic Development and Cultural Change* Vol. 4, 1955, p. 155.

Page 87. Karl Polanyi, "Our obsolete market mentality—civilization must find a new thought pattern," *Commentary*, 1947, pp. 112, 113. Copyright © *Commentary.*

Pages 101–102. Talcott Parsons, "Age and sex in the social structure of the United States,"*American Sociological Review,* Vol 7, 1942, p. 613. Copyright © The American Sociological Association.

Page 111. Nicholas Babchuk and John N. Edwards, "Voluntary associations and the integration hypothesis," *Sociological Inquiry*, Vol. 35, 1965, p. 153. Copyright © *Sociological Inquiry.*

Pages 114–115. Table 26 of Lewis Mandell and Robert W. Marans, *Participation in Outdoor Recreation—A National Perspective,* 1972.

Page 120. Table from p. 46 of Otis Dudley Duncan, Howard Schuman, and Beverly Duncan, *Social Change in a Metropolitan Community.* Copyright © 1973 by Russell Sage Foundation.

Page 132. Charles Kadushin, "The friends and supporters of psychotherapy: on social circles in urban life," *American Sociological Review*, Vol. 31, 1966, p. 788. Copyright © The American Sociological Association.

Page 133. Mark S. Granovetter, "The strength of weak ties," *American Journal of Sociology*, Vol. 78, 1973, p. 1378. Copyright © The University of Chicago Press.

Page 134. Donald Horton and Anselm Strauss, "Interaction audience-participation shows," *American Journal of Sociology*, Vol. 62, 1957, p. 587. Copyright © The University of Chicago Press.

Page 134. John D. Kasarda and Morris Janowitz, "Community attachment in mass society," *American Sociological Review*, Vol. 39, 1974, p. 335. Copyright © The American Sociological Association.

Page 139. Murray Wax, "Themes in cosmetics and grooming," *American Journal of Sociology*, Vol. 33, 1962, p. 593. Copyright © 1962 by The University of Chicago Press.

Page 141. William E. McAuliffe and Robert A. Goron, "A test of Lindesmith's theory of addiction: the frequency of euphoria among long-term addicts," *American Journal of Sociology*, Vol. 79, 1974, p. 832. Copyright © 1974 by The University of Chicago Press.

Pages 142, 143. Kenneth Clark, "Art and society," *Harpers*, Vol. 237, 1961, pp. 74, 81, 82. Copyright © 1961 by *Harpers* Magazine.

Pages 183–184. Bennett M. Berger, "The sociology of leisure." Pp. 21–40 in E. O. Smigel (ed.) *Work and Leisure*, pp. 26, 28, 29. Copyright © College and University Press, 1963.

Pages 188–189. Edmund R. Leach, "Genesis as myth." Pp. 1–13 in J. Middleton (ed.) *Myth and Cosmos*, pp. 3–4. Copyright © The Natural History Press, 1967. Reprinted by permission of Doubleday & Company Inc.

Pages 189–190. Allen Johnson, "Individuality and experimentation in traditional agriculture," *Human Ecology*, Vol. 1, 1972, p. 157. Copyright © Plenum Publishing Corporation.

Pages 201, 202–203, 203–204, 205, 206. George Herbert Mead, *Mind, Self, and Society*, pp. 150–151, 152, 153, 158–159. Copyright © 1934 by The University of Chicago Press.

Page 210–211. Alan G. Ingham and John W. Loy, Jr., "The structure of ludic action," *International Review of Sport Sociology*, Vol. 9, 1974, pp. 41–42.

Page 215. Clifford Geertz, "Deep play: notes on the Balinese cockfight," *Daedalus*, Vol. 101, 1972, p. 26. Reprinted by permission of *Daedalus*, Journal of the American Academy of Arts and Sciences, Boston: Massachusetts, Winter 1972, *Myth, Symbol, and Culture.*

for our parents whose joyous encounters
unknowingly culminated thusly

CONTENTS

7

LEISURE LOCALES: AN EXPLANATION OF THE RELATION BETWEEN PLACE AND SOCIAL BEHAVIOR 151

8

MYTH AND REALMS OF SOCIAL CONDUCT: A PRELIMINARY FORMULATION 179

9

INTERPRETATIVE DRAMAS—PLAY, GAMES, AND SPORT 195

10

RECREATION AND ITS SOCIAL ORGANIZATION 217

FOREWORD

At last we have, in this work, a distinctly original analysis of the place of leisure in human societies. The most conspicuous originality is in the conceptualization of the varieties of "nonwork," and here there are some difficulties to which I shall return. The underlying theoretical originality is, to me, more impressive, for Cheek and Burch underscore the universality of patterned nonwork activities in human societies and make an attempt to account for that "structural universal," along with suitable attention to accounting for variation between and within societies.

Put briefly, the authors attribute the universality of nonwork to biosocial commonalities in the human species. The essential components of the explanation are these: (1) Human beings depend on a rather small number of "significant others," not only in infant and childhood socialization but also as adults. (The authors adduce comparative evidence from primate species as well as historical and ethnographic information to support the biological basis for this regularity.) (2) The importance of "culture" in the human species, particularly in learning and internalizing the normative order, accentuates affective and not merely instrumental relations within bounded groups. And this affectivity, in turn, manifests itself in uncalculating reciprocities and trust, but also in patterned expressive activities that are, in both form and function, precisely that universal segment of nonwork that the authors identify as leisure.

Later, when the evidence of the "persistence" (note, not the appearance) of leisure in highly modernized societies is under close inspection, the argument is rephrased in terms of the limits of rationalization in human societies. Here I feel on familiar ground, as some of my own recent thinking on those limits has been influenced by discussions several years ago when Neil Cheek and I were, for a year, departmental colleagues. Some of these ideas were presented in an unpublished paper for the American Sociological Association in 1973, a paper provoked by Cheek. What Cheek and Burch have done here is to examine the impact of rationalization on nonwork, leading them to distinguish among recreation (rationalized nonwork), sport (a traditional form of spectacle highly modified by rationalization), and leisure in a technical sense, which maintains the consistent small-group format, affective and expressive quality, and therefore resistance to "modernization." This is an interpretation very different from the standard argument in terms of functional systems—subclass "highly industrialized societies"—for that argument in terms of a simple compensatory balance asserts or implies that leisure is a peculiarly modern phenomenon or problem.

In effect, the authors do have a compensatory argument, but without the restriction to societies which have a high degree of institutionalized rationalization, including precise temporal restraints and demands affecting virtually all instrumental activities. Their argument is phrased in two terms that are given uncommon meanings or extensions of meanings, and, my cautions to the authors not having totally succeeded, the reader is cautioned. For the shared cognitive, affective, and expressive understanding within the universally significant bounded groups, the authors use the term taste. To account for larger social entities such as communities and societies, where intimate interaction and shared understandings do not exist, but identification and some shared values are requisite to maintenance of the collectivity, the key concept is myth. I am, of course, perfectly willing to stipulate that the cohesive values of differentiated societies, including the rationale for any system of institutionalized authority and other forms of distributional inequality as well as claims to cultural distinctiveness and political sovereignty, rest on nonrational beliefs. It is perhaps the pejorative connotation of "myth" in this highly rationalized culture that makes me uneasy. Once the meanings are clear, the terms as such do not impair the argument. Here, note the authors have explicitly moved from a biosocial basis for social cohesion to a sociocultural basis. And though they do not build all the bridges, it is a clear inference that "mythical" cohesion is subject to greater attack and innovation (including the insidious consequences of rationalization), than are the more "fundamental" affective bonds in limited groups. Law is the prime ingredient of the normative code of a "mythically" coordinated collectivity, and ceremony a prime form of nonwork.

There is, of course, an intermediate mode of social cohesion that the authors recognize in other contexts: Durkheim's organic solidarity deriving from the interdependence of functionally differentiated units within a society. Even those units that are nominally instrumental in character, such as the public administrative agency or the private corporation, are not free from dependence on "myth" (and, one supposes, that is also true of "natural" groups). Once a high degree of institutionalized differentiation is established, "natural" groups are clearly less multifunctional, and though they might survive destruction or radical change of the strictly collective (mythic) elements of the society as a totality, they almost certainly could not survive the collapse of the intermediate organized units. Yet the nub of the relevant argument presented in this book is that whether the linkage between such groups and a society is more or less direct or mediated through a variety of specialized segments of society, the groups do persist and maintain affective and expressive functions. They even survive functionally differentiated units deliberately devoted to contrived affectivity and standardized expression—here identified as recreation.

Much of this book is descriptive and statistical, as it properly should be, for the authors seek to clarify variety and differences in recreational and leisure behavior as well as commonalities. In these brief introductory comments I have emphasized commonalities, because those are more to the taste of this member of that surviving subset of sociologists that seeks the highest possible level of generalization. In the course of these remarks I have expressed some misgivings concerning the use of concepts, and there remains a further qualm. Suppose one is convinced—I am—that there are nonwork activities, involving confident display of nonutilitarian interest, that are essentially universal in social form and function. Suppose, further, that we agree that these activities exist despite two noteworthy challenges: the challenge of such desperate poverty that the struggle for physical survival might be supposed to preempt all other concerns, and the challenge of rationalized affluence that might be thought to destroy all "natural" or "spontaneous" activities by commercialization. But why, simply for want of a better term, call these activities manifestations of leisure? The word specifically denotes and commonly connotes free or discretionary time, and thus seems to me insufficiently precise for the use to which the authors put it. Thus, though I commend the authors' judgment in choosing to expound their subject in English rather than in a pretentious technical vocabulary, I could have tolerated, in this case, the invention of a new term. But I do not have one to suggest.

Perhaps a solution to the semantic problem would be to restore to dignity the term "recreation," noting the variable degrees and effects of commercialization, which has impaired but not destroyed the universal elements in nonwork. The authors do in fact use recreation in this more inclusive sense in presenting survey data on the range of activities that comprise nonwork in sampled populations. Since these populations derive from highly rationalized societies, the activities correspond with the uses of leisure in the usual sense, but they include some activities that are highly vulnerable to commercialization as well as those that we might be tempted to call "traditional," though the more apt term, it is now clear, is "universal."

This book may be perused at leisure—in the ordinary sense of the word —or as a professional duty, depending on one's intellectual interests. In either situation, I expect it to be read with some joy in its novelty, for it displays a creative interpretation of our wondrous capacity for finding the occasions and recalling or inventing the ways of not being useful.

Wilbert E. Moore

PREFATORY NOTE

It is often considered appropriate whenever two or more colleagues collaborate to jointly author a volume, such as this one, to assign primary responsibility to one or the other for particular chapters, sections, or other divisions. In many cases this is quite appropriate, for often the several authors bring particular perspectives, uniquely identifiable, to a common task. We abjure this opportunity here, for the creation of this manuscript has been a truly collaborative endeavor. Throughout its creation we have failed to keep any neat accounting of which one of us momentarily first uttered what the other was perhaps relishing cerebrally. We are true believers when it comes to an appreciation of the wonder of symbolic exchanges. Imperfect they may be, but exciting they are. Therefore, peculiarly to some, our first indebtedness is to joint inquiry freely entered, solely for its own sake. Should this declaration strike one as pretentious, then perhaps it is thus. Nevertheless, mere pretentiousness does not necessarily belie sincerity.

Intellectual labors do not exist in a vacuum. Since ours is an integrative effort, the precise sources of our original interest in the area may be clouded. Our students, colleagues, and former professors have all contributed to a sense of the worthiness of intellectual endeavor. Anonymous though they remain, our sense of indebtedness is substantial.

We would like to acknowledge with gratitude the support of the U.S. Forest Service and the Texas Agricultural Experiment Station for assistance at several phases of this endeavor. Ruth Allen, Fred Buttell, David Griest, Elizabeth Wallace, and Patrick West made contributions not always suspected. Jim and Loretta Ellett, Robert Lee, Roger Sidaway, and Judy Sidaway encouraged alternative perspectives when they were needed. And the several anonymous reviewers gave invaluable guidance, most of which we observed.

To our children, wives, and friends we acknowledge forebearance in our impatience to understand the ways in which we ourselves, along with them, were caught in that which we seek to explain.

Neil H. Cheek, Jr.
William R. Burch, Jr.

LIST OF TABLES

INTRODUCTION

We believe sufficient empirical materials exist to enable an examination of the social organization of leisure in human societies. Our effort in this volume is to array these materials in such a manner as to suggest the principal importance, sociologically, of leisure. We attempt to examine and place in a particular perspective the contributions of others. We make few claims for originality as ours is an interpretive endeavor. What may be original is our ordering of the concerns and materials. It is a perspective that enables the understanding and importance of leisure not only in contemporary societies but in other times as well. Our approach attempts to emphasize that human society has not transcended the biosocial imperatives of the species; it has built upon them. The interrelationships existing between biosocial and cultural factors, which we believe are properly the concerns of sociology, can be fruitfully examined through the study of human leisure. We eagerly await the reasoned responses of our colleagues, for it is these exchanges that enliven inquiry and advance knowledge and understanding.

We begin by accepting a commonsense notion of leisure and recreation. We examine a selected set of empirical regularities common to one industrial society at one particular time. We note that not all activities (that is, leisure and recreational pursuits) are engaged in equally by all individuals. We start a quest for an explanation of such regularities. Initially we appeal to the traditional sources of explanation in sociology for understanding other empirical regularities characterstic of populations (for example, mortality, morbidity, nativity, migration, locality, employment). Among these explanatory sources we examine social class, or the distribution of wealth in the society. Next we consider social status, or the distribution of honor and prestige in a society. Each provides a partial explanation for some of the regularities, though at times contradictory. We continue by examining life-style through the interplay of occupation and education but find it also unsatisfactory. What we do recognize is that life-style is the particular ordering of an individual's everyday round. This leads to an examination of time as an explanation of leisure patterns.

We note that time has different meanings in different cultures. It is not conceived as a commodity in all societies; yet there is an ordering of the daily round in all cultures. Regardless of how it is imbued with meaning, the diurnal cycle seems to have consequences for most forms of life. Similarly there are other cycles—lunar, seasonal, and so forth, each with its own round, if you will. Thus the significance of temporal dimensions lies in the ways in which the coming together and moving apart of conspecifics is regulated culturally as well as biologically. (This symbolic aspect is developed extensively in Chapter 8.)

Within these temporal regularities, we note there appear to be other universal bases around which all primate social systems seem to be organized: age, gender, and number. Culture enables the creation of social roles and statuses on bases other than these, but it does not therefore ipso facto necessarily supplant or alter their importance as a basis for human social organization. Hominids seem to make noteworthy and distinctive use of number. The social group with distinctive age-sex ratios, comprised of varying members, forms the basis for human society. Primary associations arise and occur between members and are sustained. This overlapping network of primary associations (strong and weak ties) remains even in complex societies (that is, societies having many potential cultural bases around which social relationships can be constructed) and retains its functional importance. How are primary associations formed and generalized to others? How are they terminated, if ever? We suggest the answer lies in the biosocial nature of the cultural animal.

We consider several kinds of bonding mechanisms that uniquely hold individuals together. Taste is a cultural mechanism that builds upon a biosocial character of the species. Once an individual learns how to relate to another individual (namely, particularistically), the circumstances of each relationship must be differentiated. Hence the individual learns several modes of attachment to others. Taste continues to remind him of how he is uniquely related to some but not to all others. Culture permits the contact between individuals outside of the social group through the mechanism of myth. In short, we are suggesting that societies are real, not merely figments of analysis or dreams. It would seem unusual in the face of what we know about societies that an institutional sphere would not have evolved and developed around the maintenance of networks of primary associations. We would expect therefore to find special locations where integrative rituals of attachment would occur and the presence of codified rituals and elaborate social structures in which the necessary celebration of exclusionary rites could be enacted. This brings us to leisure locales.

We argue that the universality of the celebration of these rites in certain settings serves to bind "strangers to strangers" because of their co-presence, although we acknowledge that locales differ in the degree to which intergroup contact occurs. Recognition by individuals that others not in their group are like themselves occurs on the basis of the biosocial properties of group composition (that is, age, gender, number, and their interrelationships). Thus, simultaneously, bonding among conspecifics occurs at two levels, the interpersonal and the generalized other. In a following portion we suggest how culture generally facilitates this in all human societies.

We examine how play, games, and sport assist in sustaining social unity. We then examine some of the impacts of rationality upon pleasure and its limitations. Finally we turn a brief look to some of the futures of sport, recreation, and leisure in human society.

Neil H. Cheek, Jr.
William R. Burch, Jr.

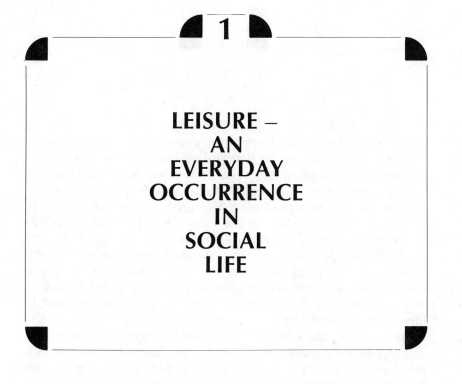

1

LEISURE –
AN
EVERYDAY
OCCURRENCE
IN
SOCIAL
LIFE

Relaxation and enjoyment—however momentary, however fleeting —are known to all humans during their lives. Where such experiences occur, with whom they occur, how often they occur, and how long they persist are not the same for all people. A great variety of factors may influence the variation of these and related aspects of relaxation and enjoyment. Those events, experiences, and places where relaxation and enjoyment transpire differ historically for one people as well as differing among cultural groups. While these differences are intriguing in and of themselves, equally intriguing is the ubiquitous occurrence of relaxation and enjoyment regardless of the differences. There are many words and concepts used to identify these events—having fun, playing, letting go, easing off, and so forth—yet all are subsumed under the concept of leisure. All societies, past and present, are known to have had or to have the institution of leisure. The term *institution*, as used by sociologists, does not refer to a particular class of organizations such as prisons or hospitals. It means the sum totality of social rules, roles, relationships, transactions, cultural beliefs, and values applying to particular classes of human behavior. Some examples of institutions in this sense would be education, health, law, religion, and work. The study of society, known as sociology, examines these institutions, their interrelationships, and the processes associated with them in a search for a theory that will apply to all societies—past, present, and future.

The study of leisure is not the sole province of any particular discipline, though many disciplines provide insight into its understanding. Thus physiology, kinesiology, sociology, physical education, psychology, and ethology have amassed observations about leisure. Curiously there have been few general works focused solely upon leisure. Most works treat selected aspects of leisure in conjunction with other variables. Seldom is the institution of leisure examined directly. This book attempts to take the presence of leisure in human societies as problematic and tries to determine its importance. The approach is sociological, though it touches on many aspects of leisure that are of interest to other disciplines.

One might suppose that since many disciplines have touched upon various aspects of the institution of leisure without having explored it extensively, the institution of leisure has been found to be of little or no importance intellectually speaking. It is our belief that such a supposition would be incorrect. Instead we believe that the institution of leisure falls at the edge of conventionally drawn intellectual and disciplinary boundaries. In particular it is our contention that leisure can best be understood by examining it as an aspect of both the biosocial nature and the sociocultural nature of human beings. The apparent divergence between sociology and biology is of comparatively recent occurrence in terms of intellectual history. Until the excesses of the eugenics movement in the second decade of the twentieth century, the two disciplines were thought by many writers to be closely allied. While sociology and biology may have remained allied publicly, the writings of scholars have tended to separate them sharply one from another. This separation is unfortunate for it may very well be that human beings and their societies can only be understood by simultaneously considering their biological and cultural character. We are thus interested, in this work, in the presence of universal properties of human societies regardless of the fashionable argument of their origin. In our investigation of leisure, we take the biosocial properties of man seriously and ask how they acquire additional dimensions as a consequence of the adaptive mechanism of culture. This perspective broadens our understanding of the social organization of human beings while providing a means for pulling together systematically the several sources of information currently available about leisure.

ASPECTS OF SOCIAL ORGANIZATION

The study of social organization draws upon a diverse set of scientific and humanistic ideas. Often terms used in one field do not have the same meaning in another. When we undertake to examine a phenomenon like leisure, which appears to fall at the intersection of a number of these related areas of inquiry, there is the danger of confusion arising simply as a consequence of different meanings for similar concepts. To attempt to reduce these misunderstandings as much as possible, we will provide some indications of our use of terminology.

A term we employ frequently is *conspecific*. We use it as in biology to mean another animal of the same species. In a somewhat similar vein we use the biological name of our species, *Homo sapi-*

ens. Our reason for the use of these terms is to remind the reader that familiar terms acquire new dimensions when considered from a different perspective. Similarly we employ some terms with which social scientists are familiar in a slightly different manner from their conventional usage. While we generally deny the wisdom of altering the conventional usage of technical terms, we believe making an exception will assist our investigation of the phenomenon of leisure. When we employ the term *individual* we mean one, single animal. When we talk about a *social person* we mean the sum totality of all of the social roles a particular individual may be called upon to enact as a consequence of his place in a society. One use of this term is close to the way in which the term "identity" is used in social psychology, but it serves to emphasize the idiosyncratic manner in which social roles are enacted by an individual. *Taken together (the unique enactment of social roles) constitutes a social person.* *Social role* follows fairly common usage and means the rights and obligations incumbent upon the occupant of a particular social status. This follows the distinction between a position in a social system (status) and the carrying out of its requirements behaviorally (role). *Social groups* are comprised of individuals who are recognized by others as members and who acknowledge reciprocally this shared definition. *Social aggregates* refer to categories of social animals possessing common characteristics but not involved in social interaction. In contrast *social collectivities* or *assemblages* constitute an arrangement of social persons for a specific and articulated purpose. *Social organization* is the arrangement of social persons and social groups and their behavior in a society. The analysis of some particular institution, such as leisure, may be carried out partially by its study, employing concepts such as the ones we have suggested as well as many others currently employed by the disciplines mentioned. For example, we use *population* in a conventional sense to mean a number of objects sharing some specified set of characteristics. These characteristics might be social, biological, or physical. We wish to reemphasize that our purpose in these slight variations in common usage is to facilitate understanding through enlarged analytical insights. The reader alone must judge if our efforts are successful. In general our task is to arouse the reader to look at familiar objects and explanations from a slightly different perspective. We recognize this as a formidable undertaking since subtle nuances are often more difficult to communicate than gross disparities. Hence we ask forebearance on what at times may appear to be imprecision in direction and reference. We see our approach as a strategy for encouraging critical thought on the part of the reader. Our purpose is to look at leisure as a complete entity not as an "add on" or adjunct to other aspects of human life and social order.

HUMAN BEING, A SOCIAL SPECIES

The human being is not only a social species, but a mammalian, primate social species. Evolution has placed the species in a position where it, as well as individual representatives of it, have species—specific biological requirements for survival. In some cases biological necessities and cultural necessities are covariant and mutually reinforceable. The human being as animal cannot survive even in an nonpolluted environment—one with clean air, clean water, nontoxic substance—without the presence of conspecifics. This is generally characteristic of all mammals, among which an extended period of dependency for nutrition exists between parent and offspring. In short, all mammalian offspring require a breast or breast-substitute for sheer survival.

Man as a cultural species also requires a conspecific in order to acquire access to the "ways" of his kind. This is no more or no less than, for example, a young carnivore acquiring the techniques of stalking prey by associating with adult carnivores. But it is different in that man does not respond to others *as* individuals but as representatives of particular symbolic categories—that is, as social persons. Hence the presence of conspecifics is essential for survival both biologically as well as culturally.

Although the human being responds to conspecifics largely as members of particular social categories, this does not mean that *within* some social categories he or she responds to all in a similar manner. The anthropologist S. L. Washburn has observed that man has apparently evolved to a point where he cares most intensely about only a very few others. This raises an interesting question about how these social bonds either prepare or do not prepare an individual for other less intimate relationships. It also raises a query regarding how, if at all, such circles of intimates are interrelated since there is some overlapping among circles by virtue of their sharing some individuals (for example, kin groups and friendship groups) partially as a consequence of life cycles, life-styles, and other consequences of social existence. It would appear that human social groups draw simultaneously from biological and cultural imperatives. In some sense it is perplexing how the human being as individual arises culturally in the face of the human being as social animal. Perhaps no more eloquent testimony to the power of symbols can exist.

Turning now to the question of human leisure, if it is to be examined from the sociological perspective, then an appropriate beginning will be to employ the natural social unit, the human group, as the basic unit of observation. Before considering these matters, let us consider, in general terms, the nature of work and play among social species.

ASPECTS OF HUMAN SOCIAL ORDERS

All social orders exhibit an economy. The nature and extent of such economies are many and varied. Among social orders of *Homo sapiens*, economies are often characterized in terms of the mode of production characteristic of an historical era. Thus we speak of pre-industrial as well as postindustrial societies. One characteristic of human economies is the degree to which diverse forms of the division of labor arise. For example, industrial economies permit—perhaps require—a more expanded division of labor than is usually found among nonindustrial economies. Basically it is a matter of specialization and specification. That is, behavior that is recognized as specific to the accomplishment of a task tends to become bundled together into a particular occupational social role. The demarcation between behavior deemed relevant to the economy and behavior deemed not relevant tends to become quite distinct, as contrasted with some nonindustrial economies. Generally speaking the former tends to be considered *work*, while the latter becomes *nonwork*.

Associated with such matters are the observed distinctions, within a social species, of individuals of different age grades and how they are articulated with the economy. Adults tend to perform those social roles essential to the economy, while nonadults tend to perform nonessential roles, if any. Economies where the rationalization of production processes has taken place tend to separate production locales from nonproduction locales. This separation is not so much in terms of place, which is a distinguishing feature of human social orders, as it is a matter of the separation of role behavior and hence social age categories. But human social life is a continuous process. Though *Homo sapiens* may separate age grades in an industrial economy in a manner different from that in nonindustrial economies, such separations are momentary in the lives of the individuals, who continue to persist in living together in small social groups throughout most of their lives. Participation in the economy of a social order does not constitute the totality of existence. It may be that the study of play among humans will contribute most to an understanding of how basic species-specific dilemmas are "worked out" beyond economies with their elaborate divisions of labor. Perhaps leisure is as necessary as nonleisure to an understanding of the human condition.

PLAY, LEISURE, AND RECREATION

It is not surprising, if our suggestion about the study of leisure falling at the interface of several existing disciplines is correct, that the terms leisure, play, and recreation are often used interchangeably. It is sometimes thought that some of the terms are utilized for the same behavior but occur differentially among social aggregates in a society. Thus children are said to play, while adults have leisure time. Both children and adults engage in recreation, though the meaning of the term is not precisely the same for each. It may be useful to have terms distinguishing childhood behavior from that of adults, but this distinction may be more apparent than real. Hence we will delay making sharp analytical distinctions.

Our purpose is to explore, in a purposefully broad manner, a variety of phenomena collectively thought of as leisure, play, and recreation. Since our purpose is to understand, we will choose the strategy sometimes known as emergent theory. Definitional terms for concepts shall be allowed to emerge as our investigation continues. At its conclusion, we will have identified conceptual formations that are appropriate and, most importantly, empirically grounded. We will begin by examining several representative definitions of play.

Edward Norbeck (1971), an anthropologist, stated:

For all forms of life, play may be defined as voluntary, pleasure-able behavior that is separated in time from other activities and that has a quality of make believe. Play thus transcends ordinary behavior. Human play differs uniquely from that of other species, however, because it is molded by culture, consciously and unconsciously. That is, human play is conditioned by learned attitudes and values that have no counterpart among nonhuman species.

Brian Sutton-Smith (1971), another anthropologist defines play

. . . as a transformation of feelings, volitions, and thoughts for the sake of the excitements of the novel affective, cognitive and behavioral variations that occur. In play the ends are subordinated; the means justify the ends. . . .

Both of these definitions selectively emphasize objective and subjective aspects of play.[1] All of the elements present in these defini-

---

[1]The study of sociological phenomena is construed variously. This is commonplace in scientific disciplines where there are often competing explanations for the same observation. In fact, to a layman, the testing of competing explanations in a controlled manner is what science is all about. Thus physics has for some time contained dual explanations for the phenomena associated with light. In sociology there are likewise a number of competing theoretical orientations in the study of societies and human interaction. These perspectives provide somewhat different guidelines as to what an appropriate observation is. In one perspective, observed behavior alone is considered sufficient (for example, noting the number of times something occurs or is done); in another perspective, subjective phenomena alone

tions will be touched upon in the following investigation. We have suggested that human societies have to deal with the biosocial imperatives of the species as well as cultural constraints like those mentioned by Norbeck. We may wish to examine how play in groups is or is not related to play not occurring in groups. We are curious about how play, leisure, and recreation are influenced by gender. Is play among females similar to that among males? Does leisure activity in which males and females participate differ from that in which only a single gender engages? Are sports the same as other forms of leisure? What is known about the relationship between childhood play and adult leisure behavior? How does culture constrain the biosocial imperatives of the species in terms of the variety of leisure activities known and the possibilities of what might exist? These and other questions will be considered. Some will be given more extensive treatment than others for our exposition is intentionally exploratory rather than exhaustive.

SYNOPSIS

We begin our examination by considering some recently obtained data regarding selected aspects of the leisure and recreation patterns common to contemporary adults of the United States of America. In Chapter 2 we are seeking the empirical regularities as they might exist. In Chapter 3 we broaden our investigation by examining data from earlier studies conducted in industrial societies, which seek to identify explanations for empirical patterns. We examine social class, social status, occupational factors, and educational factors as they affect participation in general and leisure participation

---

are considered sufficient (for example, knowing what attitude a respondent has about something); and in a third perspective, knowledge about objective and subjective phenomena are required (for example, knowing the attitude of a respondent and the number of times he has done something). Thus as we examine the institution of leisure, we will be encountering a concern about which perspective most adequately explains our observations.

A related matter concerns the problem of maintaining explanation at the level of observation. Frequently observations are made at one level and explanation occurs at another. This is a source of considerable confusion to many analyses. One encounters this fallacy each day in the mass media. An observation is made about some sociological matter and the explanation given is in terms of psychological variables. For example, each weekday a report of stock market sales is made, accompanied by an explanation that some news event somewhere in the world concerned investors hence the observed stock market activity. A moment's reflection will remind us that we can know a great deal about the concerns of an individual or individuals and still be unable to predict stock market activity. On the other hand if we know the number of shares traded the previous day, profit ratios, dividends declared, and other indices of the same level, we might be able to make a relatively good prediction. Hence we will be sharply watchful, as we examine leisure, play, and recreation, that observation and explanation are made at the same level.

in particular. Having noted such interrelationships, we expand our analysis in Chapter 4 by asking whether the regularities are solely the properties of industrial orders or whether they are but special cases of more generic patterns across all societies. Hence our concern moves to issues such as time and its meaning in various cultures. Chapter 5 begins our examination of the variables of age, gender, and number as they are involved in the kinship and friendship networks, which we find the most dominant commonalities in leisure and nonwork across several cultures. By this point we have examined a variety of empirical information and proposed explanations for nonwork behavioral regularities wherever they have been recorded. Yet each subsequent examination of previously unanswered questions has expanded our queries into new areas.

In Chapter 6 we begin to construct an alternative explanation for the observed regularities noted about nonwork (leisure) which fall outside of the usually offered explanations based upon work characteristics. Chapter 7 offers a test case of this emergent explanation by examining two cases of specialized leisure locales—parks and wilderness areas. We broaden our theorizing in Chapter 8 as we suggest ways in which nonwork and work are interrelated—when viewing each as mutually necessary for a society—but not interdependent, as is often suggested. Chapter 9 offers a reexamination of the concepts of play, games, and sport in light of our thesis. We show how, while possessing similar ties, each is uniquely essential to the formation of human social orders. In Chapter 10 we provide an analysis of the emergence of a unique social institution in one industrial society—recreation—which has differential consequences for the meanings of play, games, and sport in that society. We close out our exposition in Chapter 11 by considering what lies ahead in terms of trends for leisure and recreation in industrial societies. Our overall argument shows how existing explanations for the regularities observed in leisure and recreational behavior take on additional meaning within an enlarged conceptualization of human society, which seeks to understand the interplay of biosocial and sociocultural imperatives of the species.

2

ORGANIZATION
FOR
LEISURE
AND
RECREATION
IN
INDUSTRIAL
SOCIETIES:
SOME
CONTEMPORARY
REGULARITIES

Persons in an industrial society, who ride horseback, fish, swim, shoot pool, play poker, garden, collect stamps, repair and restore furniture, fiddle with old cars, hike, and so forth, share an important attribute of leisure in industrial societies. Most people engage in nearly all of these activities in places different from those in which they work and with persons different from those with whom they work. In industrial societies a variety of places exist where leisure activities occur. Some are essential to the activity and others are not. Some are the property of the political subsystem and are maintained through expenditures of public monies (Green, 1964). Others are the property of individuals who meet a demand from which profit is extracted (Clawson and Knetsch, 1960). The organization of leisure and recreation is reflected in the types of places where individuals and groups normally engage in such activities.

Individuals in industrial societies also share the characteristic that they do not engage in leisure activity during their remunerative work period. That is, participation occurs outside of work time. While this does not, as some writers have suggested, define leisure per se, it is a useful empirical regularity about which we shall make some observations later. In short, in industrial societies one's work time and one's leisure time tend to be segmented. To identify such regularities does not imply any necessary connections between the two events. That is, we do not know how these segmented time blocks are related in a causal sense. What we need to know is how they occur naturally before we rush to explanations.

As suggested earlier, the variety of leisure activities available in a society—which constitutes what might be called the universe of leisure—is determined by the culture. Literate cultures will tend to possess a larger number of activities than nonliterate cultures, simply as a result of the presence of the printed word. For example, games of the past, which are no longer played, can be rediscovered through reading about them and played by persons with no prior knowledge of those games. Hence the universe of leisure activities tends to be greater in literate societies. While this may be the case, we need to examine what the empirical distribution of participation is with respect to this universe in order to examine the questions of how leisure and recreation are organized in a particular society.

The social organization of leisure and recreation in a society consists of: (1) the kinds of activities in which members engage, (2) the places where such activities occur, and (3) the times when such activities occur. Once we know the what, where, and when of leisure activities, we can begin to ask questions about how leisure activities came into existence and how they vary historically.

STUDIES OF LEISURE AND RECREATION

In general the literature on leisure and recreation is broad, varied, and unsystematic. Daily newspapers carry many items about leisure behavior. In the United States, newspapers frequently devote considerable space to a variety of leisure activities known collectively as sports. They report on the performances of football, basketball, baseball, and ice hockey teams, as well as on horse racing, car racing, tennis, and skiing. One even finds reports of dog and horse shows on the sports page, which suggests that activities other than team-related activities are a part of sports. A variety of magazines are devoted exclusively to a particular leisure activity such as collecting stamps, collecting coins, building model airplanes, collecting miniature trains. Special sections of magazines and newspapers are devoted to informing readers who seek relaxation or amusement about the "what," "where," and "when" of events in the fields of music, art, travel, and theater. Thus the mass media provide a large body of topical information about leisure and recreation in a literate society. Such information is also useful as an indication of the changes in cultural emphasis attached to activities. For example, a recent series of games in an international chess championship was reported during a radio sports program, although the commentator himself was perplexed as to why it should have come in on "his wire."

Books on almost every known leisure activity tell the neophyte how to do whatever leisure activity he or she wants to learn how to do. The number of books on sports, outdoor activities, hobbies, handicraft activities, and so forth are legion. The mere existence of the titles suggests the tremendous variety of such activities in an industrial society. They are useful as indications of the repertoire in a culture, but even sales figures are unreliable indicators of the number who participate in such activities.

Another source of information about leisure activities is the reports of attendance at motion picture theaters, football games, concerts, zoos, parks, amusement parks, and so on. While these reports may be useful for estimating the possible volume of sales for an activity at some future time, such information is publicly available for only a handful of all leisure activities. Moreover, there are no reports for leisure activities that occur where such enumeration is impossible—namely, in the private home.

While a great deal of information about leisure and recreational activities is available from popular sources, most of it is not accurate enough for systematic studies of the organization of leisure and recreation in a society. At best, even the most sensitive observer obtains only a partial answer from such sources. It is thus almost impossible to generalize reliably about patterns of leisure and recreational behavior in a society from such information.

However, in several societies, including the United States, Canada, and Great Britain, systematic studies have been undertaken on outdoor recreation. In the United States, these studies were made in the latter part of the 1950s and are known collectively as the ORRRC studies (Outdoor Recreation Research Review Committee). In Great Britain and Canada, such studies occurred during the 1960s. What ties these studies together is the observation that, in each society, a great deal of public money was being spent annually on providing facilities for selected outdoor recreation activities. These studies were attempts to justify continued public expenditures and to provide a basis for anticipated requirements for the future. In the United States, a number of other studies in several states were undertaken during the 1960s and into the 1970s as a part of the continuing involvement of governmental bodies in planning and providing public facilities and programs. Collectively these are called the SCORP (Statewide Comprehensive Outdoor Recreation Plan) studies. (Unfortunately as a source of data about recreational behavior there is tremendous variation in the soundness of these studies. All are essentially political documents and, hence, share the known strengths and weaknesses of such documents.) In this book we will examine some of these data as they reflect changes in the composition of a universe of leisure in a society. The importance of these data for an understanding of the organization of leisure and recreation in the contemporary industrial nations is difficult to ascertain since we have little knowledge about how outdoor recreation is related to other kinds of leisure. For example, do people who fish regularly for sport also go to motion pictures frequently? Do older adults continue going to museums while gardening intensively? Many similar questions cannot be answered from the outdoor recreation studies. Yet such knowledge is essential if our understanding of the organization of leisure and recreation is to advance.

During the late 1960s and into the early 1970s, several studies were made that began to provide data, obtained systematically, about the universe of leisure behavior in several societies. Under the auspices of the United Nations, the twelve-nation, time-budget studies have been developed. These studies make it possible to see how the segmented existences of adults in various industrial societies are organized. Thus one can note how much time is allotted to work and how much to leisure, how much to personal maintenance and how much to home maintenance, and so forth. These data provide a cross-cultural perspective not usually available from other sources. We shall examine this material at several points in the book. During this same time period, several studies were conducted, within the United States, that provide data allowing a broader examination of leisure than has been accomplished previously. We want to examine these data to ascertain the presence of empirical regularities about what leisure activities people engage in and where and when they engage in them.

PARTICIPATION IN SELECTED LEISURE ACTIVITIES

The number of different leisure activities available to people is a function of the culture. How particular people participate in specific activities and at what rates may be functions of other factors. It is possible, however, to establish empirically some knowledge about the frequency of participation in specific activities among the members of a society without necessarily positing in advance why the particular distributions that emerge exist as they do. In the beginning stages of investigation for a field of inquiry, the necessity for accurate descriptive materials of the phenomenon is of fundamental importance. Sampling theory provides guidelines so that the results can then be generalized to a known population. Yet the selection of a particular population for sampling makes certain implicit substantive assumptions that require acknowledgment. In the case of the studies about to be examined, two such substantive matters are involved. One is the selection of a limited number of leisure activities and the second is the selection of adult members of the population as the initial sample. (These matters are examined in a methodological footnote at the end of this chapter on page 36.)

The first study, unique in many ways, is the more recently completed. The study was carried out by the National Opinion Research Center (NORC) at the University of Chicago during 1973, under a grant from the Research Answering the Nation's Needs (RANN) program of the National Science Foundation (NSF). The grant was for the development of the Continuing National Survey (CNS), through which data could be obtained from an appropriate sample of adults on a weekly basis with respect to a broad array of topics of interest to policymakers both in the government and outside of it. The topics included housing, adequacy of employment, satisfaction with educational facilities, community characteristics, transportation needs, and so forth. Among these topics there was a group of questions about the respondent's participation in selected leisure activities, as well as related questions—such as satisfaction with present leisure opportunities and time usually available for participation in leisure activities. The data presented below were obtained in this series of studies from face-to-face interviews conducted in the respondent's home. Because of the design of the study, a particularly unique aspect of these data deserves mention.

Each battery of questions was asked of a weekly sample of adults. The same battery was asked of 4 independently chosen samples for 4 consecutive weeks. Each sample consisted of 173 adults, chosen through a sampling design constructed to provide a probability sample on a national basis. Because of the manner in which the design was constructed, it is possible to treat each weekly sample independently for analytical purposes or simultaneously as one 4-week sample of 692 respondents. A particular battery of questions might occur solely in one set of 4 weeks (called henceforth a cycle) or in more than one such cycle. Thus it became possible to analyze the cycles as replications using different samples from the same universe, making it possible to examine the stability of response patterns from one time to another and between samples.

Weekly Pattern

The data presented in Table 1 shows the percentage of the people sampled who indicated they had participated in the particular activity at least one time during the week immediately preceding the date of the interview. One should notice that several of the response categories contain multiple activities such as going to a "zoo, fair, or amusement park" or "swimming, boating, or waterskiing." These categories are reported as they were asked during the interviews. Thus while there are 30 different categories of leisure activities investigated, the actual number of different leisure activities represented is 45.

Only a comparatively small number of the activities are participated in on a weekly basis by a majority of the respondents—namely, reading for pleasure, driving for pleasure, watching television, visiting friends or relatives, listening to records or tapes, and reading a newspaper. The data in the table are grouped in descending order of the percentage of the sample indicating participation. Thus we can note that only 4 categories are quite widely participated in on a weekly basis—that is, those in which more than 70 percent of the

TABLE 1   ADULT PARTICIPATION IN SELECTED
LEISURE ACTIVITIES DURING ONE WEEK, PERCENT[a]

Activity Category	%	Activity Category	%
Reading a newspaper	87	Playing indoor sport	18
Watching television	84	Taking class for enjoyment	12
Visiting friends/relatives	75	Going to movies	12
Reading for pleasure	73	Bicycle riding	11
Listening to records/tapes	54	Watching sporting event	11
Driving for pleasure	53	Dancing	10
Walking for pleasure	48	Camping/hiking/climbing	8
Dining out	46	Hunting/fishing	8
Window-shopping	38	Maintaining collection	8
Playing table game	35	Picknicking	8
Attending club/religious/		Swimming/boating/waterskiing	8
civic meetings	34	Going to zoo/fair/amusement	
Going to nightclub/bar/lounge	33	park	8
Gardening	32	Going to museum/gallery	6
Making things (crafts,		Going to theater/concert	4
woodworking)		Horseback riding	2
Playing outdoor sport (team			
sports)	23		

[a]Unless specified otherwise, all tables in this chapter were derived from materials found in *Recreational Activities: Trends and Patterns of Participation Among Adults,* Technical Report, Texas Agricultural Experiment Station, n. d.

sample indicated participation. By way of contrast, there are 9 categories of leisure activities in which less than 10 percent of the sample indicated participation—namely, picknicking, hunting/fishing, horseback riding, attending the theater or concerts, maintaining collections (for example, stamps or coins), going to museums or galleries, going to a zoo/fair/amusement park, camping/hiking/climbing, and swimming/boating/waterskiing.

Another broad grouping of activities sharing similar participation percentages are the 6 categories in which between 10 percent and 19.9 percent of the sample engaged. These include: going to motion

TABLE 2   PERCENT OF SAMPLE PARTICIPATING BY
NUMBER OF LEISURE ACTIVITIES PARTICIPATED IN, PERCENT

% of sample participating	#	% of activities
Less than 10	9	30
10 to 19	6	20
20 to 39	7	23
40 and more	8	27
Total	30	100

TABLE 3 LEISURE ACTIVITIES GROUPED ACCORDING TO PERCENT OF ADULTS PARTICIPATING DURING ONE WEEK

Less than 10%	10% to 19%
Camping/hiking/climbing	Playing indoor sport
Hunting/fishing	Taking classes for enjoyment
Maintaining collection	Going to movies
Picnicking	Bicycle riding
Swimming/boating/waterskiing	Watching sporting event
Going to zoo/fair/amusement park	Dancing
Going to museum/gallery	
Going to theater/concert	
Horseback riding	

pictures, participating in an indoor sporting event, dancing, watching a sporting event where it occurred (hence not on television), bicycle riding, and attending educational classes for enjoyment (in subjects not related to occupational matters).

A fourth clustering of activities with similar participation percentages consists of those in which between 30 percent and 39 percent of the sample engaged. These include: window shopping, making things (that is, crafts, woodworking and metalworking, and so on), gardening, playing table games (for example, cards or pool), attending club/religious/civic meetings, and going to nightclubs/bars/lounges.

Examining the broad clustering or grouping of activities sharing similar percentages of participation by the sample, we notice that 15 categories or one-half of those in the study are ones in which less than 20 percent engaged. (See Table 2.) Thirty percent of the activity categories are ones in which less than 10 percent of the sample had participated during the previous week. Another 7 activities, about 23 percent of the categories, are those with between 20 and 30 percent participation taking place (most of these fall between 30 and 39 percent). The remaining 8 categories all share percentages of participation of 40 percent or more. There are among these 30 categories of leisure activities, 4 broad clusterings or groupings in terms of the percentage of participation by respondents in the sample.

1. Those in which less than 10 percent participate
2. Those in which less than 20 percent but 10 or more percent participate
3. Those in which 20 percent or more but less than 40 percent participate
4. Those in which more than 40 percent participate (See Table 3.)

20% to 39%	40% or more
Walking for pleasure	Reading newspaper
Dining out	Watching television
Window shopping	Visiting friends/relatives
Playing table game	Reading for pleasure
Attending club/religious/	Listening to records/tapes
civic meetings	Driving for pleasure
Going to nightclub/bar/lounge	
Gardening	
Making things	
Playing outdoor sport	

Assuming that the activity categories are representative of the cultural universe of such activities, we can note as an empirical summary statement the existence of these four broad clusterings, which we will examine in greater detail.

Exploring for the moment a previously mentioned limitation of the outdoor recreation literature, we note that the 30 categories of leisure activities used in this study are about evenly divided among several kinds considered on a continuum of outdoor/nonoutdoor locations. There are 11 categories of activities that usually require an outdoor setting, 10 categories that can occur either in outdoor or nonoutdoor settings (even though one or the other may be more usual for a particular category), and 9 categories that usually occur is nonoutdoor settings. (See Table 4.) Using these 3 classifications we can examine Table 1 to ascertain if any particular empirical regularities are noticeable.

We can observe that of the 9 categories in which less than 10 percent of the sample indicated participation, two-thirds (or 6) of them are activities that usually occur in an outdoor setting. (See Table 5). On the other hand, of the 8 categories in which 40 or more percent indicated participation, one-quarter (or 2) are those requiring an outdoor setting. In the middle categories (between 10 percent and 40 percent), which contain 13 different activity categories, a little over one-fifth (or 3) are located outdoors. Thus in terms of the reported participation, outdoor-based categories tend to be most prevalent among those categories with the smallest percentages. The 6 categories with reports of less than 10 percent participation comprise some 12 different leisure activities.

There are numerous reasons as to why the distributions we are observing occur as they do. Some may have to do with the representativeness of the thirty activity categories, some with the time frame employed in the questions (namely, weekly participation),

TABLE 4   LEISURE ACTIVITIES BY OUTDOOR/
NONOUTDOOR SETTING

Outdoor	Outdoor/Nonoutdoor	Nonoutdoor
Picnicking	Window shopping	Making things
Hunting/fishing	Watching sporting	Playing indoor sport
Driving for pleasure	event	Watching television
Gardening	Dancing	Attending club/
Horseback riding	Reading for pleasure	religious/civic
Going to zoo/fair/	Going to movies	meetings
amusement park	Going to theater/	Maintaining collection
Playing outdoor sport	concert	Going to museum/
Camping/hiking/	Dining out	gallery
climbing	Listening to records/	Playing table game
Walking for pleasure	tapes	Taking class for
Swimming/boating/	Visiting friends/	enjoyment
waterskiing	relatives	Going to nightclub/
Bicycle riding	Reading newspaper	bar/lounge

and some with the particular season during which the data were obtained. Although each of these sources of error must be acknowledged to exist, what is important to observe is the nature of the empirical regularities that are emerging from these data.

With respect to the pattern of participation common to the respondents during a weekly time period, we are able to identify 4 groupings of leisure activities. Each of these is characterized by similar percentages of the population reporting participation. Thus there is one grouping of a few activities that large numbers of people report engaging in. This constitutes about 25 percent of all the activities. Conversely there is a much larger number of activities, nearly 50 percent, in which comparatively few people report participation.

Although the proportion of outdoor, outdoor/nonoutdoor, and nonoutdoor activities included in the study are about the same, we noted that the largest number of outdoor activities participated in occurred in that grouping of activities in which fewer people engaged.

Monthly Pattern

We have already acknowledged that the daily rounds of individuals differ. Hence the leisure activity categories may or may not be distributed similarly in terms of participation if the time frame reference is changed. During several cycles of the CNS study, the questions about the frequency of participation were asked with reference to the preceding month in contrast to the preceding week. In Table 6 appears the distribution as averaged over the several cycles. As in Table 1, the leisure activity categories are listed in descending order

TABLE 5 OUTDOOR ACTIVITIES AS PERCENT OF NUMBER OF LEISURE
ACTIVITIES PARTICIPATED IN BY PERCENT OF SAMPLE PARTICIPATING

% of sample participating	#	% outdoor
Less than 10	9	66
10 to 19 ⎱ 20 to 39 ⎰	13	21
40 and more	8	25

of magnitude, by percentages. Several characteristics are noteworthy.

The overall effect of asking respondents about participation in the leisure activity categories during the month preceding the date of the study is to *increase percentages of the sample reporting such.* In contrast to the distribution in Table 1, the magnitudes of the percentages associated with most of the same activity categories in Table 6 are greater. The time frame being different appears to have an effect. But its precise nature is not simple and direct. Thus there appear to be some people who may participate in a leisure activity at one time but not at another. *One cannot assume that knowing the frequency of participation for one time frame enables a simple linear projection to participation for another time frame.* For example, in Table 1, 12 percent of the sample indicated participation during the preceding week in the category of movies. In Table 6 the same activity was reported as being participated in during the preceding month by 31 percent of the sample. Apparently a number of people go to motion pictures occasionally and these people were not necessarily included when the question was asked in the shorter time frame. This suggests that there may be overlapping participation by different persons although the same general frequency pattern may exist.

In other words, participation in a leisure activity may occur in differing intervals, although the frequency may be the same for the people engaging in it. Some may engage in an activity quite often during a short interval and then have longer intervals during which they do not participate in that activity. Others may participate in an activity regularly throughout a similar interval, but at no point is their engagement in that activity bunched together. Each may contain the same frequency of engaging in the activity.

As with weekly participation, there appears to be a broad clustering of activity categories by percentage of sample indicating participation. In Table 6 we can note the following groupings:

1. Those in which less than 10 percent indicate participation
2. Those in which less than 40 but more than 10 percent indicate participation

TABLE 6 ADULT PARTICIPATION IN SELECTED
LEISURE ACTIVITIES DURING ONE MONTH, PERCENT

Activity Category	%	Activity Category	%
Reading a newspaper	90	Playing outdoor sport	32
Watching television	88	Going to movies	31
Visiting friends/relatives	86	Swimming/boating/waterskiing	28
Reading for pleasure	75	Going to zoo/fair/amusement	
Driving for pleasure	66	park	25
Dining out	65	Watching sporting event	24
Listening to records/tapes	62	Hunting/fishing	20
Walking for pleasure	54	Playing indoor sport	20
Window-shopping	48	Camping/hiking/climbing	17
Playing table games	45	Going to theater/concert	15
Making things (crafts,		Bicycle riding	14
woodworking)	40	Going to museum/gallery	13
Gardening	38	Taking class for enjoyment	10
Picnicking	36	Maintaining collection	10
Attending club/religious/civic		Motorcycling/driving jeep/cross-	
meetings	35	country skiing	5
Going to nightclub/bar/lounge	34	Horseback riding	5

   3. Those in which less than 70 but more than 40 percent indicate
      participation
   4. Those in which more than 70 percent indicate participation

Within cluster 2 there are 3 almost equal subgroupings. The first is
less than 20 but more than 10 percent participation and includes:
camping/hiking/climbing, going to theater/concert, bicycle riding,
going to museum/gallery, taking class for enjoyment, and maintaining collection. (See Table 7.) The second subgrouping includes:
swimming/boating/waterskiing, going to zoo/fair/amusement park,
watching sporting events, hunting/fishing, and playing indoor sport.
All of these categories were participated in by less than 30 but more
than 20 percent of the respondents. The third subgrouping consists
of those categories in which less than 40 but more than 30 percent
of the sample reported participation. Included in the subgrouping
are the following: gardening, picnicking, attending club/religious/
civic meetings, going to nightclub/bar/lounge, playing outdoor
sport, and going to movies. The number of activity categories in the
clustering numbered (2) is 17, which is almost three-fifths of the
total number of activity categories in the study. This suggests that, as
before, the number of leisure activity categories in which a majority
of the adults in the society participate during a common time frame
is somewhat limited.

    In the cycles during which the leisure activity battery of ques-
tions were asked with reference to participation during a month,

there was an increase in the number of categories of outdoor recreation activities from 11 to 12 and a decrease in the middle out-
door/nonoutdoor grouping from 10 to 9. In the former the category
of motorcycle/jeep/cross-country was added, and in the latter the
category of dancing was deleted.

It is worth noting that of the 13 leisure activity categories with
less than 30 percent of the sample indicating participation, 7 of them
are outdoor recreation activity categories. These constitute more
than half of the outdoor recreation categories in the study. Unlike
the weekly distribution, there are no outdoor activities in the clustering of activities that are more widely participated in. Although
among those 8 activity categories in which a majority of the adults
indicate participation, 2 are outdoor activities: driving for pleasure
and walking for pleasure. These empirical observations once again
emphasize the caution with which the outdoor recreation literature
must be treated whenever the objective is to understand leisure behavior in a society.

Weekly-Monthly Pattern Comparison

By comparing the distributions of participation between the 2
time frames employed during the study (weekly and monthly), it
will be possible to assess the relative nature of the stability of the
pattern. In Table 8, the leisure activity categories are listed in descending rank order, with the category having the largest percentage
assigned the rank of 1, and the category with the smallest percentage assigned the rank of 30. To assist in the analysis, a column showing the differences in the magnitudes of the rank for an activity between the 2 time frames is provided. The direction of any change is
indicated as well. Thus the activity category "taking class for enjoyment" is assigned the rank of 17.5 for weekly participation and
27.5 for monthly participation. The difference is a magnitude of 10,
and, because it is a substantial decrease in the overall rank order
of all the activities, it is assigned a minus value. Thus the rank order
of the activity "taking class for enjoyment" varies greatly between
the 2 distributions.

To examine the relative stability of the distributions, we can look
at the overall pattern. First we notice that among the activities assigned the ranks from 1 through 10, no change occurs between the
2 distributions. That is, while there are some differences among the
rank order of individual leisure activity categories, there are no new
activities found. The same 10 activity categories occupy the top 10
ranks in both distributions. Continuing to examine the overall pattern, we note that the 2 distributions vary with reference to the rank
order of particular activities. Considering the second third of the
ranks (11 to 20), 3 changes in rank order position occur. The 3 activ-

TABLE 7 LEISURE ACTIVITIES GROUPED ACCORDING TO PERCENT OF
ADULTS PARTICIPATING DURING ONE MONTH

Less than 10%	Less than 40%, more than 10%
Motorcycling/cross-country skiing Horseback riding	Gardening Picnicking Attending club meetings Going to nightclub/bar/lounge Playing outdoor sport Going to movies Swimming/boating/waterskiing Going to zoo/fair/amusement park Watching sporting event Hunting/fishing Playing indoor sport Camping/hiking/climbing Going to theater/concert Bicycle riding Going to museum/gallery Taking class for enjoyment Maintaining collection

ity categories occurring among the second third in the monthly
distribution but not occurring in the weekly distribution are: picknicking, swimming/boating/waterskiing, and going to zoo/fair/
amusement park. Likewise in the last third of the distributions (ranks
21 to 30), the following three categories found in the monthly distribution are not found in the weekly distribution: playing indoor
sport, taking class for enjoyment, and bicycle riding. In terms of the
overall pattern between the 2 time frames, no change occurs among
the activities assigned the ranks of 1 through 10, 3 changes occur
among the activities assigned the ranks 11 through 20, and 3 changes
occur among those assigned the ranks of 21 through 30. (See Table
9.) The 6 activities that changed comprise 20 percent of all activities
in the study. Considering that these changes occurred in the lower
two-thirds of the rank orders, where comparatively smaller percentages of participation fall, the overall patterns appear to possess substantial stability. This suggests that uniformity of participation associated with each activity category may underlie the empirical pattern.
Further analysis is appropriate to try to identify such uniformities.

The 3 leisure activity categories that moved from the lower third
of the distribution of weekly participation to the middle third of the
monthly distribution were all outdoor activity categories. Of the 3
activities that moved from the middle to the lower third of the distributions, playing indoor sport and taking class for enjoyment

Less than 70%, more than 40%	More than 70%
Driving for pleasure	Reading newspaper
Dining out	Watching television
Listening to records/tapes	Visiting friends/relatives
Walking for pleasure	Reading for pleasure
Window-shopping	
Playing table games	
Making things	

were not outdoor related, but bicycle riding was. One reason for the shift into the middle third may be attributed to the influence of the season during which the data were obtained. In temperate climates, such as in the North American continent, certain outdoor, water-related leisure activities are subject to variations not common to other leisure activities. Yet the comparative location of a majority of the outdoor leisure categories in the lower-participation clusterings, for both distributions, suggests that variation is probably not solely attributable to seasonal factors.

To summarize, there appears to be an empirical pattern of participation in leisure activities among the adult population of the United States that remains comparatively stable in terms of rank ordering among the several activities. This pattern, though exhibiting variations, appears to remain stable for both time frames of weekly and monthly participation. Moreover, differences exist with reference to outdoor leisure activities from those not of this nature. These empirical differences appear to be similar between weekly and monthly participation distributions. Differences within each distribution for particular activities suggests that not all respondents participate in a similar manner. Some may perhaps participate with greater frequencies than others in the same activity. Yet the social organization of the leisure activity may be the same for all participants (this will be examined in Chapters 3 and 7). Nor do we know how

TABLE 8 COMPARISON OF RANK ORDER AMONG SELECTED LEISURE
ACTIVITIES PARTICIPATED IN BY ADULTS DURING DIFFERING TIME PERIODS

		Rank	
Activity Category	Weekly	Monthly	Diff.
Reading a newspaper	1.0	1.0	—
Watching television	2.0	2.0	—
Visiting friends/relatives	3.0	3.0	—
Reading for pleasure	4.0	4.0	—
Listening to records/tapes	5.0	7.0	− 2.0
Driving for pleasure	6.0	5.0	1.0
Walking for pleasure	7.0	8.0	− 1.0
Dining out	8.0	6.0	2.0
Window-shopping	9.0	9.0	—
Playing table games	10.0	10.0	—
Attending club/religious/civic meetings	11.0	14.0	− 3.0
Going to nightclub/bar/lounge	12.0	15.0	− 3.0
Gardening	13.5	12.0	1.5
Making things (crafts)	13.5	11.0	1.5
Playing outdoor sports	15.0	16.0	− 1.0
Playing indoor sports	16.0	21.5	− 5.5
Taking class for enjoyment	17.5	27.5	−10.0
Going to movies	17.5	17.0	.5
Bicycle riding	19.5	25.0	− 5.5
Watching sporting event	19.5	20.0	− .5
Dancing	21.0	—	—
Camping/hiking/climbing	24.5	23.0	1.5
Hunting/fishing	24.5	21.5	3.0
Maintaining collection	24.5	27.5	− 3.0
Picnicking	24.5	13.0	11.5
Swimming/boating/waterskiing	24.5	18.0	6.5
Going to zoo/fair/amusement park	24.5	19.0	5.5
Going to museum/gallery	28.0	26.0	2.0
Going to theater/concert	29.0	24.0	5.0
Horseback riding	30.0	29.5	.5
Motorcycling/driving jeep/cross-country skiing	—	29.5	—

TABLE 9 STABILITY OF RANK ORDER POSITION AMONG
SELECTED LEISURE ACTIVITIES DURING DIFFERENT TIME PERIODS

Rank order position	# of changes	% stable
Between 1 and 10	—	100.0
Between 11 and 20	3	66.6
Between 21 and 30	3	66.6

participation in one activity category is related to participation in
another or if there is any relationship at all.

Yearly Pattern

During 1970, another study of the leisure patterns of adults in the United States was conducted. While the activity categories were not precisely similar to those used in the 1973 CNS study, sufficient similarity exists for some comparisons to be worthwhile. Most importantly, the 1970 study used 12 calendar months as the time frame for the respondents to report upon their participation. The study sampled the adult population of the United States.[1] The sample was a national probability sample of 944 respondents. The data were obtained by face-to-face interviews, conducted in the abode of the respondent. Thus the population being studied was similar to that in the CNS study in 1973. Table 10 contains the information obtained regarding participation in leisure activities. The categories are ranked in descending order of magnitude of percentage of the sample indicating participation in the activity during the preceding 12 calendar months.

While this study obtained information on some activities not included in the 1973 study, the relative ordering of the activities between the studies can be observed by excluding those not common or combining categories as appropriate. Thus there are 12 comparable categories of activities common to the 2 studies upon which the examination of pattern may be made. Those excluded are religious-related activities (the 1970 study included actual church attendance), neighborhood park, fairs/exhibits (the 1970 study did not specify amusement parks), and parks outside of the city. The combined category of boating/swimming, picnicking/driving for pleasure in the 1970 study apparently derives its usually large total percentage because of the inclusion of the driving for pleasure component. The single category for participation in sports combines the 2 categories of the 1973. Hence when comparing rank order, a middle value can be constructed from the 2 categories in the 1973 study as they are adjacent ranks. (This is an imprecise measure, but our interest here is in the overall pattern of responses.) The fishing/hiking/camping/hunting category again combines 2 independent categories of the 1973 study. As was true for the category of sport participation, these categories appear adjacently, hence we can construct a relative ranking of the combined category.

Patterns Compared

By inspection between Tables 8 and 10, the comparative rank ordering of the several studies can be observed. Of the 12 common

[1]The study was sponsored jointly by the United States Department of the Interior and the New York Zoological Society. Persons interested in more details on the methodology of the study should contact the author.

28/THE SOCIAL ORGANIZATION OF LEISURE IN HUMAN SOCIETY

TABLE 10 ADULT PARTICIPATION IN SELECTED LEISURE
ACTIVITIES DURING ONE YEAR, PERCENT AND RANK ORDER

Activity Category	%	Rank
Visiting friends/relatives	93	1
Boating/swimming/picnicking/driving for pleasure	76	2
Going to religion-related activity	73	3
Going to movies	63	4
Going to neighborhood park	59	5
Going to fair/exhibit	54	6
Going to park outside city	52	7
Watching sporting event	49	8
Going to club meeting	47	9
Going to nightclub/bar	46	10
Playing active sport	40	11
Going to zoo	38	12
Going to class/lecture	36	13
Fishing/hiking/camping/hunting	34	14
Going to theater/concert	27	15
Going to museum	26	16

categories, the rank orders are essentially the same, with 3 exceptions. Thus there is about 75 percent agreement in terms of overall pattern. The exceptions are going to movies (annual rank higher than weekly/monthly), watching sporting event (annual rank order higher than weekly/monthly average), and fishing/hiking/camping/ hunting (annual rank order higher than weekly/monthly average). Although the differences between the 2 studies are of interest, the similarities are more striking, *suggesting the presence of a stable underlying pattern that emerges in the weekly, monthly, and annual frames.* (See Table 11.) While this general statement appears reasonable in the face of the data, we must inject a note of caution.

In all of these studies, the responses are not mutually exclusive— that is, the same respondent could indicate participation in as many activity categories as appropriate. Thus the percentages are larger than would be true if the respondent had been limited to a single category, for example, the leisure activity most frequently participated in by the respondent during some particular time frame or the respondent's single most preferred activity. This characteristic of these data does not undermine the observation of the pattern of participation as it might in other kinds of studies. Since the object here has been to discern the organization of leisure and recreation in a society, the participation of an individual in a number of different activities during the same time frame gives us more information about the manner in which leisure and recreation is organized.

To summarize, with reference to the frequency of participation

TABLE 11 AGREEMENT OF RANK ORDER AMONG LEISURE
ACTIVITIES PARTICIPATED IN DURING DIFFERING TIME PERIODS

Time Periods	% of agreement
Between weekly and monthly pattern	80
Between monthly and yearly pattern	75

in selected leisure activities among adults in the United States, several statements can be made based upon the data examined:

1. There appears to be an empirically identifiable pattern with reference to participation. This pattern can be described in terms of the relative rank ordering of percentages of participation found among a sample of adults.
2. The general pattern tends to be similar regardless of whether a weekly, monthly, or annual time frame is employed to elicit responses.
3. There are certain broad kinds of commonalities with respect to categories of activities that exist within distributions and also comparatively across the time frames.
4. Differences exist with respect to certain broad categories such as outdoor, mixed, and nonoutdoor leisure activities.

LOCATIONS OF PARTICIPATION

The segmentation of the day is symbolized for many people by the separation of various activities by location. In literate societies this is a pervasive characteristic encompassing nearly all members of the society, including children. Generally speaking people move away from a central common abode to a variety of other locations, reassemble at various moments for varying durations throughout the day, and finally come together for purposes of repose. Children go to places of education, return home briefly, depart again to places of play, and then return to abodes for food and rest. Many adults leave home for places of employment, go to eating places, return to employment places, return home, perhaps later sally forth to places of meetings, and then return home again for final rest. Other adults move in and out of their homes to various other places such as markets, then return for intermittent periods frequently connected with the arrivals and departures of others. There exists an almost infinite variety of patterns of movement common to members of the same society. The place from which departures and arrivals occur tend to become standardized in terms of the kinds of behavior usually transacted. Almost without being aware of it, people become accustomed to associating particular kinds of activities, presence or absence of kinds of persons, durations of transactions, and frequency of appearance with particular places. One becomes aware of such habits only when something unusual occurs. While it might at first appear unimportant to be concerned with the locations where people ordinarily participate in leisure activities, it is a significant component of the investigation of the organization of leisure in a society. It seems reasonable to expect that people might come to associate particular locations with leisure activities in the same way as they do with employment, education, medication, and so forth. Implicitly this is recognized in the distinction made between activities occurring outdoors or elsewhere.

In industrial societies, technology enables the creation of a variety of locations for leisure activities that could not occur without these locations. The establishment of reservoirs may create settings for different leisure activities from those otherwise available in an area. Similarly snow skiing occurs regularly in places where it is augmented through technological means. Ice-skating occurs in even subtropical climates nowadays. People swim in containers located next to their homes even though the area is a desert climatically. Bridge and card parties occur regularly in travel trailers in parklands.

These examples indicate that knowledge about participation in leisure activities is considerably augmented by information about the locations where people usually engage in the activities. There are two ways of obtaining such information. The means most frequently employed is studying people while they are at some particular location participating in leisure activities. The largest number of these studies are found in the outdoor recreation literature; and most of these are studies of persons in parklands or similar locations. Taken together, such studies are usually called "on-site studies." Although the purposes of these studies tend to be quite varied, one purpose is to ascertain the numbers of people present during a variety of time periods. Other information, such as attitudes, demographic characteristics, socioeconomic data, distances traveled from point of origin, is usually also sought. The single major difficulty of interpreting such findings is the matter of the sample. To what statistical universe may one generalize the findings? Yet these studies do provide information about people who are present at one kind of leisure location. (These comments are also germane to other locations where attendance figures are regularly acquired.)

A second means of obtaining information about locations associated with leisure activities is to sample some known population and inquire about such matters. As with other aspects of the literature, there are comparatively few such studies in existence. We will consider two and explore their findings.

TABLE 12ᵃ USUAL LOCATION FOR PARTICIPATION
IN FAVORITE OUTDOOR ACTIVITY BY ADULTS, PERCENT

Location of Activity	%
Home (own or relative's)	23
Park	18
Beach, river, lake, and so forth	33
Stadium and so forth	6
Other	20
Total	100

ᵃTable derived from data found in research report *North Pacific Border Study—Sociological Studies*, U.S. National Park Service, 1971.

In 1971, as part of a large study, a sample of 2000 adults residing along the coastal areas of Washington, Oregon, and parts of California extending inland to the western slopes on the mountains were asked to indicate where they usually engage in their favorite *outdoor* leisure activity. The response distribution was as shown in Table 12. In view of the restriction to outdoor activities, the preponderance of such locations reported in the study is to be expected. The category of water locations is mutually exclusive to others. Thus there were locations not within a parkland. In a second study conducted during 1972, a sample of 1500 adults residing in the Piedmont plateau region were asked to indicate where they usually participated in their favorite leisure activity. Both of these studies obtained the data through interviews conducted by telephone. The results from the second study are presented in Table 13.

With reference to the former study, the respondents named 43 different leisure activities of an outdoor nature in which they participated at the locations shown in Table 12. The respondents in the 1972 study named 76 leisure activities that were engaged in at locations in Table 13.

In Table 13 we can notice the importance of the home as the location where most people engaged in their favorite leisure activity. Considering the information from Table 12, we know that the home as a leisure location is not exclusively limited to nonoutdoor kinds of activities. The importance of water sites is shown by the 20 percent who indicated it was the usual location for their participation. Since many activities at such locations are outdoor recreation, we note the comparative importance of the category. If we reflect upon the rank ordering of some water-based leisure activities—as in Table 8—in light of the locations indicated in Table 12, we can begin to obtain additional understanding of the organization of leisure and recreation. For example, while a large percentage of adults choose

TABLE 13 USUAL LOCATION FOR PARTICIPATION
IN FAVORITE LEISURE ACTIVITY BY ADULTS, PERCENT[a]

Location of Activity	%
Home (own, friend's, relative's)	40
Park	5
Beach, river, lake, and so forth	20
Stadium and so forth	9
Other	26
Total	100

[a]Table derived from data found in research report *The Piedmont Study—Socio-logical Studies*, U.S. National Park Service, 1972.

water sites for their usual location, the rank ordering among leisure activity categories suggests comparatively low participation in specific activities. Of interest in Table 13 is the percentage of the respondents who usually choose locations other than those previously mentioned. This is a large percentage, almost one-quarter of the total. As a residual category it includes many locations such as night-clubs, club rooms, billiard parlors, bingo halls, motion picture theaters. The importance of examining locations will be seen later when we examine certain other characteristics of locations. (See Chapter 7 on parks and camping.) *The nature of recreation in industrial societies is symbolized by the prevalence and incidence of certain kinds of locations specialized for leisure activities.*

To summarize, we have observed empirically that adults tend to participate in leisure activities regularly in certain locations. The predominant location seems to be the home, although it is not the location for the majority of the sample. Moreover the definition of home varies. For some people the land around the house is considered a part of the home. Hence the entire range of outdoor to non-outdoor leisure activities may occur at such locations. The importance of water sites for many activities is suggested by its prevalence among the locations mentioned. Ordinarily one would think of activities directly involved with the water as those associated with such locations. However, there are a number of activities that can be carried out near water (for example picnicking, camping, card playing, games) without directly involving water. Water sites seem to be preferred by some for reasons other than an activity directly related to water (such as boating, fishing, swimming). A large percentage of the respondents indicated water sites as the usual location for a favorite leisure activity.

A similar note of caution must be sounded with respect to the home. A variety of leisure activities, including some that are water based, may occur adjacent to the abode. One should not presume that abodes located near lakes, streams, oceans, and rivers are populated by adults who prefer water-based leisure activities. These two studies taken together, one conducted near a major coastal area and the other not, suggest this note of caution.

We have observed some empirical regularities with respect to location of participation in leisure activities. These are very limited data, and much more remains to be investigated. In a later chapter we shall examine the interrelationships between location and leisure activity participation. We want to turn now to the third component of the preliminary examination of the organization of leisure and recreation.

TEMPORAL ASPECTS OF PARTICIPATION

The arbitrary manner in which men conceptualize temporal aspects of daily life varies from culture to culture. Whether there exists a natural unit of temporal order inherent in the makeup of the universe or not is difficult to establish. Yet every known culture seems to have developed some conceptions of temporal ordering. In industrial societies, the productive processes at the core of the dominant economic institutions have encouraged great cultural emphasis on temporal matters. The extent to which daily life for many persons is segmented with reference to time is greater in such societies than in others. (We treat time in an extensive manner in Chapter 4.) Because leisure activities are part of culture, it seems reasonable to expect that they might be ordered, as are other activities, in some temporal manner. As with many aspects of the literature, only a very few studies are available to help answer appropriate queries.

The time-budget studies, such as the twelve-nation study, help examine the query as to the amount of time individuals have for leisure activities during some standard time frame, often a day. These materials aid in assessing the time apportioned to different categories of activities. Hence they assist in answering empirically how certain categories vary in certain populations. One observation frequently made in the popular media is that more people in the United States have more free time now than ever before and that the amount of free time per person as well as the number of persons having this greater amount of free time is increasing. Yet it is not clear from time-budget studies whether this assertion is supported empirically. Even if this observation were true, it would be difficult to know how to interpret it for a greater understanding of the organization of leisure and recreation.

The availability of the amount of time seems not to be as important as the manner in which it is distributed in daily life. It seems

TABLE 14 COMPARISON OF WEEKDAY FREE TIME AVAILABLE TO ADULTS DURING DIFFERING TIME PERIODS OF REPORTING, PERCENT

Length of Available Time	Time Frame of Reporting Participation	
	Weekly	Monthly
Less than ½ hour	7.6	8.0
Less than 1 hour, more than ½	7.2	8.0
Less than 2 hours, more than 1	18.8	18.6
Less than 4 hours, more than 2	32.6	29.1
Less than 6 hours, more than 4	15.9	17.2
Less than 8 hours, more than 6	6.7	6.6
Less than 10 hours, more than 8	2.8	3.6
10 hours or more	8.1	8.9
Total	99.7	100.0

important to understand what factors influence such a distribution and how stable it might be for one individual as contrasted with another. Knowing how each day is like all others is also necessary. For example, while many adults in the United States engage in the forty-hour work week, the manner in which those 40 hours of toil are distributed varies substantially from occupation to occupation as well as within each occupation. Thus the amount of time per se has a somewhat limited value for understanding the organization of leisure in a society, unless a dominant cultural characteristic can be identified that cuts across the forces that segment life. One such characteristic found in the United States is the segmenting of 7 consecutive days into 2 additional divisions—weekdays and the weekend.

During the cycles of the 1973 CNS, the respondents were asked to estimate how much free time was usually available to them during a weekday and also on a weekend day. These data are displayed in Table 14 and Table 15. In Table 14 the data are for an average weekday and in Table 15 they are for an average weekend day. Each table distinguishes between the response pattern of persons who reported participation in leisure activity categories on a weekly basis from those reporting on a monthly basis.

While there appears to be some variation between persons reporting participation on a weekly as contrasted with a monthly basis, the differences are slight. Of importance is the similarity of the response distributions. Thus the *modal* category is the same for both participation groupings on weekdays and weekend days. Similarly the relative ordering of the response categories remains constant for each grouping. These regularities suggest that each participation grouping is similar, and discussion of the two distributions can be carried out simultaneously.

TABLE 15 COMPARISON OF WEEKEND DAY FREE TIME AVAILABLE TO ADULTS DURING DIFFERING TIME PERIODS OF REPORTING, PERCENT

Length of Available Time	Time Frame of Reporting Participation Weekly	Monthly
Less than ½ hour	2.9	3.3
Less than 1 hour, more than ½	2.4	2.7
Less than 2 hours, more than 1	5.6	5.4
Less than 4 hours, more than 2	14.5	13.1
Less than 6 hours, more than 4	18.5	18.7
Less than 8 hours, more than 6	15.1	16.1
Less than 10 hours, more than 8	14.1	11.8
10 or more hours	26.8	29.1
Total	99.9	100.2

Comparing the weekday and weekend data, it is clear that the respondents recognize the difference between weekend days and weekdays with reference to the number of hours of free time available. On weekdays the modal category is less than 4 hours and more than 2. It is also noticeable that the majority of the respondents report less than 4 hours per weekday as free time. On weekends the modal category is 10 or more hours, yet the majority of the respondents report less than 8 hours as free time. The availability of free time is more compact for the majority of respondents during the weekdays than on weekends. For example, the number of response categories required to include a majority of respondents is smaller in the weekday distribution than in the weekend distribution (4 contrasted to 6).

These data help establish empirically that people share at least two divergent kinds of temporal orderings with reference to availability of free time. Although we do not know how this is directly related to leisure activity participation, we would expect that such considerations are involved. We can assume that leisure activity categories vary in terms of temporal requirements—for example, some table games require more time to complete than others, outdoor recreation activities may require different temporal orderings from nonoutdoor activities, and perhaps home-based recreation differs from nonhome-based recreation in terms of temporal dimensions as well. It seems worthwhile to examine temporal dimensions of leisure activities closely with the availability of free time and also with the manner in which such free time is available—that is, in one period or more during the day. In order to extend our knowledge of the organization of leisure and recreation, we need to have more specific information about the amount of free time available for individuals.

To summarize, the data suggest the existence of an empirical regularity with respect to temporal orderings of availability of free time. Weekdays differ from weekend days in terms of the amount of free time available as well as in the distributions of such time. The weekday is more sharply constrained than is the weekend day.

SUMMARY

In this chapter we have examined several studies that provide data, in one industrialized society, about the participation of adults in leisure activities. It has been possible to identify several kinds of patterns underlying these data. Thus we have seen that not all activities are equally participated in by all adults; some activities tend to be participated in by more people than do other activities. The general rank ordering of the frequency of participation among the activities examined remained the same when we examined weekly, monthly, or annual data. Similarly we were able to identify common locations, such as the home and water sites, as particularly important to the social organization of leisure. We also observed the presence of a temporal order. The distinction between weekday and weekend day in terms of the reported free time suggests another dimension of engaging in leisure activities. The importance of these patterns for the study of leisure arises because they suggest the presence of underlying factors common to what on the surface may appear to be a vastly diverse area of human behavior. In short, we are challenged to understand the common properties of leisure and recreation, regardless of apparent differences. What is important is why people behave in certain ways, although the reasons for so doing may differ. In the next chapter we begin to examine some of these reasons. This chapter has suggested that if leisure is truly *free* time during which people do as they please, then remarkably many people appear to behave quite like their fellows.

Methodological Footnote to Chapter 2

In all studies in which the data are obtained through interviews there is the difficulty of assessing the validity of the respondent's reports. This has two aspects. One is the degree to which the reported participation is an accurate measure of true or real participation, lacking any other independent measure such as attendance figures to substantiate the former. These studies do not overcome this difficulty directly, but they do tend to do so collectively—that is, by comparing response patterns across studies one can obtain some suggestion of stability or lack thereof. A related aspect is the accuracy of the respondent in reporting frequency of an activity or behavior, retrospectively. This is an important concern that has received considerable attention from methodologists without a definitive resolution of the matter. In part this is because each case must be decided upon the theoretical consequences of the introduced error. In the case of these several studies, the assumption is that the respondent is at least minimally capable of recalling participation or lack of participation during a particular time frame. The presence of a degree of response pattern stability suggests that this assumption is viable. Hence the information reported is of the presence/absence variety not dependent upon actual reported frequency of participation.

Some questions may be raised about the appropriateness of the sample. All respondents in all studies were adults as conventionally defined—that is, eighteen years of age or older. (A theoretical argument with respect to this point is developed in Chapter 5.) This is not an arbitrary matter. Societies differ in the shared definitions of the attributes of social persons. Hence all cultures distinguish between categories of adults and nonadults, or children. Expectations for behavior differ on many matters for these broad categories. Chapter 2 is concerned with the identification of a limited number of aspects of the organization of leisure and recreation in industrial societies. Thus to study children, who are, sociologically speaking, raw materials being developed for the social statuses in the society, may or may not tell us about the configuration or presence of such. This is not to say that knowledge about leisure activity categories among children is of no importance. But it is necessary to know the behavior of adults in order to more fully understand the organization of leisure in the society.

Are the particular, leisure activity categories used to elicit the responses as an indication of the organization of leisure in a society adequate? How representative of the universe of leisure activities in the culture are the categories used in the study? Since there is no detailed catalog of categories existing, it is difficult to answer the questions precisely. To our knowledge no such catalog exists, hence other means must be employed. In the literature there are several studies with substantial listings of leisure activities (McKechnie, 1974), numbering as many as 120. But as mentioned, the literature for this kind of inquiry is sparse because of the place of the emerging field. Another aspect of this difficulty is how representative the listing in these studies is of those activities acquired in other studies of freely given responses. To our knowledge no single national study of this type exists. One systematic study of a region of the United States is known to us (USNPS, 1971). This study elicited some 74 different activities from a sample of 1500 adults in response to a question concerning the person's most frequently engaged in leisure activity. The list of leisure activities used in the 1973 and 1970 studies employed categories similar to those obtained spontaneously from respondents in the 1971 study by Field.

While these kinds of validity claims are important, they do not provide a basis for addressing the question about the adequacy of the list of activities used in any study of the organization of leisure in a society. Unless the list offered to the respondents is exhaustive (clearly beyond the scope of most studies), the choice of some particular activity is made upon an implicit metatheoretical construct of the phenomenon under inquiry or is based upon some common-sensical typology (such as examples of hobbies, team sports, crafts, amusements, entertainment, games) or upon the existing literature. Thus the answer to the concern is largely pragmatic. These data provide a systematic basis for identifying the existing social organization of leisure and recreation. It is not exhaustive but appears to be representative of what is known systematically about leisure behavior among adults based upon the current literature. As future studies of a similar type become available, these findings can be modified accordingly.

3

WORK
AND
NONWORK
IN
INDUSTRIAL
SOCIETY –
VARIATION
AND
ORDER

3

In the last chapter we discussed how nonwork is temporally ordered. There are some activities that have a weekly participation pattern, and others that have a consistent participation pattern over large blocks of time. Further, there are some activities that involve only a small proportion of the population, and still other activities that are nearly universally attractive to the population. In general, nonwork activities near the home seem to have the widest popularity and the most frequent and regular participation rates.

Yet our observation of certain regularities in nonwork activity patterns merely tells us "what is." Our larger interest remains in accounting for the observed regularities. And in this attempt at explaining the patterns of nonwork, work has most often been treated as *the* determinant. That is, once we know the nature of a society's economy or what a person's particular job is, we should be able to predict the likely leisure pattern. In this traditional view, nonwork activities are always seen as dependent upon variation in work. We suspect this explanation is too simple.

To be sure, even a windfall of nature, such as a beached cargo ship or plunder from a neighboring tribe, requires the expenditure of human energy in order to convert it into the material base of a society. The gathering, transporting, fabricating, and distributing of transformed natural resources will always be of central importance to individuals and their societies. We are not surprised that, though workers dislike their present jobs, they still wish to work (Morse and Weiss, 1955).[1] Nor are we surprised that workers will choose improved income over improved status (Weiss, Harwood, and Riesman, 1971). The survival of individuals, their dependents, and their society is uniquely bound into the prevailing division of labor, the expenditure of energy, and the technology for transforming natural resources. Work is a reality of survival.

[1]Studs Terkel (1974) records people talking about their work, which poignantly illustrates this mixed attitude of needing work yet disliking its constraints and emptiness.

As we indicate in Chapters 4 and 5, only certain individuals, occupations, and economies view work as a central life goal. Most often the time at work is seen as something to be passed through as quickly as possible or passed on to subordinate social strata. But there is a form of work—for example, that performed by the dictator of a nation or the president of Standard Oil—that is actively sought and assiduously performed in order to accomplish nonmaterial goals such as power and prestige. There are still other forms of work, such as artistic creation, that are sought as ends in themselves.

Work, then, has a variety of social meanings and influences upon life-style. But in spite of these important variations, work has certain natural and invariant properties. All persons clearly know when they are working and when they are off duty. Unlike social life with intimates—kin, friends, peers—or the large social spheres concerned with sustaining myth—such as religion, sports, and politics—work exhibits a fundamentally different pattern of organization. In work, participation is coerced by necessity, only a narrow segment of one's person is required, the selection of co-workers is made by necessity rather than choice, and the timing and sequence of action is usually external to the worker—that is, set by seasons, tools, machines, materials, or work organization—and finally there is usually a tangible outcome.[2]

In short, the significant difference between work and nonwork is not a conceptual one or one that inheres in a specific activity or specific person, rather the significant difference is in the kinds of social organization that are involved. Fishing practiced as an industry requires a different organizational pattern, system of normative constraints, and involvement pattern of the social individual than is found in fishing practiced as leisure. Thus fishing is work for a Maine guide and play for his New York City client because they are involved in different organizational networks.

The recent studies of hunter-gatherer economies (see Chapter 4) report that only a small portion of the day is required to provide the necessities of survival. Hunter-gatherer economies intermix work and nonwork; while in more elaborate economies the distinction between work and nonwork is much sharper. Yet the distinction occurs, not because work and nonwork have altered their balance, but because different organizational forms have emerged to manage them.

The organization of work and nonwork reflects the tendency of all social beings to observe some form of hierarchy (Lenski, 1966; Wilson, 1975). Indeed, hierarchical patterns are such a fundamental

---

[2]Obviously any attempt to clearly define the distinction between work and nonwork will satisfy few and offend most scholars. Kelly (1972) indicates something of the complexity involved in simplifying distinctions between work and nonwork.

feature that all discussion of social behavior must start by identifying the particular hierarchical form of a given larger society, its smaller subunits, and the existing interpersonal relations. As Melvin Kohn (1969:3) argues, class position within the larger society is crucial to the individual's behavior and well-being:

> Remarkable though it seems, one aspect of social structure, hierarchical position, is related to almost everything about men's lives—their political party preferences, their sexual behavior, their church membership, even their rates of ill health and death. Moreover, the correlations are not trivial; class is substantially related to all these phenomena.

It is obvious that the study of hierarchy could be as broad as it is significant. Studies could range from interpersonal strategies for advantage, such as name dropping, to the structuring of dominant and subordinate positions within intimate associations, to the various symbols, coalitions, and deceptions that emerge from the dynamics of hierarchy and shape the rise and fall of civilizations. Through all these topics, and more, may be significant dimensions of work-nonwork patterns, we shall only touch upon such issues, instead giving most attention to how the struggle itself is a regularity that sustains the remarkable stability of life-styles and nonwork behavior.

There is fair agreement and understanding of the consequences, shape, and function of the various hierarchical patterns observed in social species. There has been less success in identifying or gaining agreement concerning the identification of the mechanisms that make for the observed regularities.

One of the consistent patterns observed in hierarchical systems is the better ability of business and elite groups to maintain class solidarity than that maintained by the lower strata. Elites, as Simmel (1955) and Schumpeter (1960) infer, because they consist of limited numbers and have differential access to a community's prestige and material resources, are better able to maintain cohesiveness and class consciousness while dividing the lower groups. This seems clearest in numerous voting behavior studies. Anderson and Davidson (1943) seem representative in that they found there were great numbers of poor in both political camps, battling each other not for class but for party supremacy. Their study is of particular interest because even deep in the Depression, in 1934, they found that 39 percent of the unskilled workers were still registered Republicans. As found in other studies, Anderson and Davidson (1943) report that business group solidarity is increased by the fact that the business group has a greater rate of political activity and influence. Also, the business group tends to better reflect and determine the prevailing dominant community ideology, whereas the "working class . . . is loyal to the dominant middle class ideology. . . ." The poor believe that their children will advance to higher status and that there are many opportunities awaiting, if not for them, certainly for their off-spring. This pattern was also found by Lipset and Bendix (1959), who report that upward social mobility in the United States was no greater than in Europe, but that in the United States people believe it is possible, while in Europe people do not believe that it is possible.

The community ideology exerts an influence on those who do not have a direct role in constructing these values. For example, Katherine Archibald's (1953) study of shipyard workers found that, while there was great resentment among workers toward the possessors of privilege, it never developed into resentment against the privilege itself. This philosophy discouraged any criticism of the hierarchical system itself because each worker hoped to be lucky so that he could be part of the dominant group.

Thus even in what would seem the most crucial of nonwork arenas—political action—there are confused regularities. There are behavioral tendencies associated with certain positions in the social hierarchy; however, the upper strata are more consistent in their behavior, while the lower strata do not always follow their own "best" interest. Hopefully, by examining a variety of studies on nonwork behavior, we can sort out the sociological processes that regularize the confounding of expected class treatment.

In the following discussion, we will restrict ourselves to societies with industrialized production. We will first look at the effects on life-style of the differential distribution of material rewards (class) and prestige rewards (status) of work. Important as they are, we will suggest that such factors provide only a rough explanation of variations in life-style. Therefore, we will direct more attention to findings on the influence on life-style of specific occupational role structures. Hopefully we shall uncover some of the ways in which social integration is maintained when work-nonwork cycles vary in timing, organization, and cultural meaning.

Even the most casual observer of any society will note the important consequence of differential distribution of wealth. And in industrial societies such differences are largely a consequence of one's work role. Although in social surveys, "class" position is most often a statistical aggregate—persons are grouped together on the basis of some shared trait, such as money income, rather than some regularized pattern of interaction—it is associated with many social outcomes.

TABLE 16 PERCENT OF PERSONS 12 AND OLDER
PARTICIPATING IN VARIOUS OUTDOOR ACTIVITIES, BY INCOME, BY YEAR

Activity	Year	Income (in Thousands)ᵃ							Totalᵇ
		<3	3–6	6–8	8–10	10–15	15–25	>25	
Bicycling	1960	4	—ᶜ	12ᵈ	11	9	12	—	9
	1965	10	15	19	22	21	21	—	16
	1970	9	13	18	20	23	28	26	22
Playing Outdoor Games or Sports	1960	13	—	38	37	43	44	—	30
	1965	17	35	43	52	51	55	59	38
	1970	13	23	33	37	43	45	48	36
Walking for Pleasure	1960	25	—	37	37	38	46	—	33
	1965	36	45	51	58	58	63	55	48
	1970	20	26	28	31	34	40	36	30
Picnicking	1960	35	—	63	59	57	53	—	53
	1965	38	58	64	68	65	61	50	57
	1970	23	38	50	54	60	55	47	49
Canoeing	1960	NAᵉ	NA	NA	NA	NA	NA	NA	NA
	1965	—	3	4	4	5	—	—	3
	1970	NA	NA	NA	NA	NA	NA	NA	NA
Hiking	1960	2	—	8	10	9	9	—	6
	1965	3	7	7	10	9	11	—	7
	1970	NA	NA	NA	NA	NA	NA	NA	NA
Bird Watching	1960	NA	NA	NA	NA	NA	NA	NA	NA
	1965	3	5	5	8	6	11	—	5
	1970	3	3	3	3	5	7	7	4
Photographing Wildlife and Birds	1960	NA	NA	NA	NA	NA	NA	NA	NA
	1965	—	2	2	4	4	—	—	2
	1970	2	2	2	2	4	5	5	3
Taking Nature Walks	1960	7	—	20	23	16	19	—	14
	1965	5	12	15	21	18	25	—	14
	1970	9	13	16	18	22	25	20	18
Camping	1960	3	—	10	13	18	10	—	8
	1965	3	9	12	13	12	13	—	10
	1970	8	14	21	24	26	26	19	21

ᵃBecause the 1970 data format included more income categories, these categories were aggregated and weighted means were computed.

ᵇThe Total column indicates the mean percent participation in the given activity for the entire sample.

ᶜDashes indicate insufficient sample size for computation of percentages.

ᵈNA indicates data not available.

ᵉThe underlined numbers indicate the modal class.

Source: Ferris (1962), Bureau of Ourdoor Recreation (1967), Bureau of Outdoor Recreation (1972).

CLASS GROUPINGS

In general, income level is assumed to have a significant influence upon life-style. However, studies on outdoor recreation indicate a

Activity	Year	Income (in Thousands)[a]							Total[b]
		<3	3–6	6–8	8–10	10–15	15–25	>25	
Hunting	1960	12	—	14	14	10	11	—	13
	1965	9	15	14	13	13	11	—	12
	1970	7	12	16	14	14	12	9	12
Fishing	1960	22	—	32	31	39	27	—	29
	1965	21	30	32	36	35	31	33	30
	1970	16	25	32	31	33	32	29	29
Swimming	1960	23	—	56	58	63	57	—	45
	1965	21	45	55	63	64	77	68	48
	1970	16	30	43	47	56	65	67	46
Waterskiing	1960	2	—	7	9	14	12	—	6
	1965	—	5	6	10	10	12	—	6
	1970	NA	NA	NA	NA	NA	NA	NA	NA
Skiing	1960	NA	NA	NA	NA	NA	NA	NA	2
	1965	—	2	4	4	7	12	—	4
	1970	NA	NA	NA	NA	NA	NA	NA	NA
Sledding	1960	3	—	12	11	14	11	—	9
	1965	4	11	16	20	20	21	—	13
	1970	NA	NA	NA	NA	NA	NA	NA	NA
Ice-skating	1960	2	—	10	10	9	9	—	7
	1965	4	7	11	14	15	16	—	9
	1970	NA	NA	NA	NA	NA	NA	NA	NA
Sailing	1960	NA	NA	NA	NA	NA	NA	NA	NA
	1965	—	—	2	4	5	—	—	3
	1970	NA	NA	NA	NA	NA	NA	NA	NA
Other Boating	1960	7	—	28	33	41	36	—	22
	1965	9	22	26	34	36	38	30	24
	1970	NA	NA	NA	NA	NA	NA	NA	NA
Driving for Pleasure	1960	35	—	62	60	64	55	—	52
	1965	38	55	59	66	64	59	54	55
	1970	NA	NA	NA	NA	NA	NA	NA	NA
Sightseeing	1960	25	—	50	52	60	50	—	42
	1965	26	47	55	62	62	65	50	49
	1970	NA	NA	NA	NA	NA	NA	NA	NA

curious pattern of participation rates associated with income level. The patterns Abbott L. Ferriss (1962) found in a U.S. national survey seem typical. Participation rates for activities such as pleasure driving, attending sports events, picnicking, and camping increase with increases in income at the lower levels, but then flatten out or decline for higher than average incomes. Some activities, such as walking for pleasure, fishing, and hunting, have a neutral relationship to income. While activities such as playing games, swimming, sightseeing, and motorboating have a curvilinear relationship between participation rates and increasing income levels. If we remain with income alone, there seems little explanation of such variation.

In Table 16 we attempt a time perspective on the relation between participation rate and income level. In this table we have remained with these data, which are consistent for the three U.S. national surveys. If we consider the modal proportion for each year (indicated by underscoring in the table), we find no real evidence of trends. Indeed, some proportion of all income classes participates in all the activities. And yet, except for picnics, the modal participation rate is found at the higher levels; even though activities such as hiking, taking nature walks, and bird watching, could hardly be considered activities requiring high income. But high participation rates for persons in the higher social strata seems to be characteristic. Reissman's (1954:82) observation is a useful summary. He notes:

> . . . it was found that regardless of the variable used to measure class position—occupation, income, or education—the higher class shows a higher degree of participation and involvement in the community. That is, individuals in this class read more books and magazines, attend church more frequently, belong to more organizations, and more often hold office in those organizations. The present study thereby lends further support to previous studies on that relationship. Phrased in more general terms, it can be said that the middle class, on the whole, tends to dominate the organizational activity, the intellectual life, and the leadership of the community.

Thus income seems to operate more as a constraint. It appears to also affect distance traveled, the length of stay, trip expenditures per day, and expenditures per trip (see Tables 17 and 18). A variety of other studies from the 1930s to the mid-1960s seem to validate these findings. Whether it is parks (U.S. Park Service, 1938; Hutchins and Trecker, 1961); Illinois grammar school children (Stendler, 1949); older persons (White, 1955); campers (Gray, 1962; Merriam, 1963; Shafer, 1965); canoeists (Taves, Hathaway, and Bultena, 1960); or rural Iowa residents (Yoesting and Burkhead, 1971), there is some association between class position and pattern of nonwork behavior.

Yet, as Lundberg, Komarovsky, and McInerny (1934) found in the 1930s, the actual quantity of time devoted to various activities, such as listening to the radio or reading, is very similar among the social strata. What is different is the quality of the activity. Interestingly, they found that both high-income and low-income women felt they had no leisure. For the upper class, social obligations fill free time, while sheer survival fills the time of the lower class. It seems equally important to note that a two-week vacation in Vermont, as opposed

TABLE 17 DISTANCE TRAVELED PER PERSON 12 YEARS AND OVER
ON ALL VACATIONS AND OUTDOOR RECREATION TRIPS AND OUTINGS,
JUNE 1960–MAY 1961, BY SELECTED SOCIOECONOMIC CHARACTERISTICS

Socioeconomic Characteristics	Distance Traveled (in round-trip miles per person)
All Classes	1288
Male (age in years)	1338
12–17	1210
18–24	1451
25–44	1499
45–64	1382
65 and over	774
Female (age in years)	1242
12–17	1195
18–24	1354
25–44	1159
45–64	1553
65 and over	723
Family Income	
Less than $1,500	375
1,500–2,999	526
3,000–4,499	936
4,500–5,999	1214
6,000–7,999	1610
8,000–9,999	1937
10,000–14,999	2069
15,000 and over	3192
Residence	
In SMA	
Urban—over 1 million	1501
—under 1 million	1371
Rural	1498
Not in SMA	
Urban	1197
Rural, farm	727
nonfarm	1072

Source: Ferriss (1962): 368.

to two weeks in the game parks of Kenya, reflect meanings deeper than cost. Thus specific patterns of nonwork may be influenced more by occupational patterns and levels of educational attainment than by income. As Robert Lucas (1964:46) reports:

Income seems to be more necessary than sufficient as an explanation of recreation choices. Money does not form tastes, it

TABLE 18 EXPENDITURES AWAY FROM HOME PER
PERSON 12 YEARS AND OVER ON ALL VACATIONS,
OUTDOOR RECREATION TRIPS, AND OUTINGS FROM JUNE
1960–MAY 1961, BY SELECTED SOCIOECONOMIC CHARACTERISTICS

Socioeconomic Characteristics	Expenditures (in dollars per person)
All Classes	74.9
Male (age in years)	78.8
12–17	48.9
18–24	77.5
25–44	84.0
45–64	—
65 and over	59.7
Female (age in years)	71.1
12–17	43.9
18–24	64.2
25–44	62.6
45–64	107.4
65 and over	51.5
Family Income	
Less than $1,500	13.6
1,500–2,999	28.3
3,000–4,499	42.1
4,500–5,999	63.3
6,000–7,999	88.9
8,000–9,999	108.1
10,000–14,999	136.4
15,000 and over	324.1
Residence	
In SMA	
Urban—over 1 million	119.6
—under 1 million	77.8
Rural	69.2
Not in SMA	
Urban	61.5
Rural, farm	27.2
nonfarm	45.8

Source: Ferriss (1962): 367.

limits their expression, but few people would be priced out of the market here [Boundary Water Canoe Area in Minnesota and Ontario, Canada] for any type of recreation, with the possible exception of the American plan resorts and private cabins.

STATUS GROUPINGS

A variety of other studies (Anderson, 1961; Hollingshead, 1949; Kaplan, 1960; Komarovsky, 1946; Palmer, 1960; Thomas, 1956) suggest the importance of social status as an influence on nonwork behavior and challenge Robert Havighurst's (1957) contention that leisure style is simply a matter of personal predilection. Saxon Graham's (1959:350–351) survey findings are typical:

> . . . the upper classes were more active in most of the forms of recreation studied here than were the lower classes. There were fairly large differences in the proportions of upper and lower classes participating in mild and strenuous exercise activities, in home activities, and in visiting.

It would seem that position within the larger social structure has a continuing pervasive influence upon the life chances and opportunities of those in a particular stratum. And, further, social status is part of a self-perpetuating system. As Lipset and Bendix (1959:197–198) noted in their detailed cross-cultural study:

> Occupational and social status are to an important extent self-perpetuating. They are associated with many factors which make it difficult for individuals to modify their status. Position in the social structure is usually associated with a certain level of income, education, family structure, community reputation, and so forth. These become a part of a vicious circle in which each factor acts on the other in such a way as to preserve the social structure in its present form, as well as the individual family's position in that structure.

Our argument in this chapter assumes that both economic and honorific rewards of a society are scarce social resources. Meaningful class and status rewards are dependent on this scarcity, for they are differentially distributed among a group's population. Yet, access to the one does not always ensure access to the other. One may acquire a considerable amount of wealth. However, if, in the course of acquisition, socially "unclean" work was required, one would be unable to cash in this wealth at the prestige bank. High economic (class) position reflects an opportunity to command material factors, while high honorific (status) position reflects an opportunity to command a style of life. The parvenu is seldom successful in commanding the subtleties of a style of life for it must be learned rather than bought.

Certainly occupational variations are associated with fine grada-

TABLE 19 SOCIAL CLASS OF VISITORS TO RECREATION AREAS

Social Class	G.B. Population	G.B. Car Owners	Ragley Hall	Tatton Park	Slimbridge Wildfowl Trust	Forest of Dean
AB	13	19	30	20	36	24
C1	22	28	34	34	29	36
C2	31	35	27	36	27	28
DE	33	18	9	10	9	11
Total	100	100	100	100	100	100

Note 1. Definition of social class

Social Status	Occupation
AB Upper middle class	Managerial and Professional
C1 Lower middle class	Supervisory and Clerical
C2 Skilled working class	Skilled manual
DE Working class	Semi- and unskilled manual, casual workers and pensioners

Note 2. Sources of information
Columns 2 and 3. Abrams, M. (1970), *Trends in Car Ownership and Leisure*, a paper given at Roads and Leisure, a conference organized by BRF and BTA in association with MOT and MHLG at Keele University, July 1970.
Columns 4 and 5. British Tourist Authority and Countryside Commission (1970), *Historic Houses Survey*.
Column 6. Countryside Commission, British Travel Authority, Wildfowl Trust (1971) *Slimbridge Visitor Survey*.
Column 7. Colenutt, R. H., and Sidaway, R. M., Forest of Dean Day Visitor Survey to be published by the Forestry Commission.

Source: Sidaway (1971: 101).

tions of difference within recreational activities. A study by G. D. Taylor and R. Y. Edwards (1960) is representative. They divided their sample of auto campers into two styles of camping—accessible and remote. Their data indicate that sales people and clerical workers are the most predominant type of campers in remote areas, while workers in the skilled crafts are the predominant type of campers in the accessible areas. When placed with the U.S. studies, which include backpack campers, their data illustrates that, within middle-income groupings who participate in forest recreation, there is a tendency for each step away from civilization to be a step up in the predominant status (prestige) level of the participants.

Sidaway (1971) reports similar patterns for forest areas in the United Kingdom. His data indicate (see Table 19) that those having certain kinds of jobs and owning cars are overrepresented in the countryside areas. The working class, which is 33 percent of Great Britain's population, has only a 9 to 11 percent representation in all countryside settings; while the upper middle class, which is 13 percent of the population, has 20 to 36 percent representation in countryside areas. The contrast between skilled manual workers and unskilled manual workers seems much sharper than between the

managerial and professional groups and their counterparts in super-
visory and clerical occupations. Given Britain's excellent public
transportation system and the relatively easy access to the countryside for urban areas it would seem that taste rather than income is
the primary constraint upon use of the countryside.

Alfred Clarke (1956) also found significant differences in the life-
styles of the various social strata. Clarke used the North-Hatt scale
to place his respondents (randomly sampled, adult males in Columbus, Ohio) into five prestige levels and identified frequency of participation rates for various activities by the prestige levels. Clarke
found that cultural and self-improvement activities were more characteristic of high-prestige respondents, while activities such as working on an automobile, playing poker, and spending time in a tavern,
were, significantly, associated with respondents in the lower-prestige
levels.

Rabel Burdge (1969) used an approach similar to Clarke's for a
random, stratified sample study in Allegheny County, Pennsylvania.
He found that persons in the highest occupational level were the
most active in all types of leisure. Of greatest interest is his finding
on hobbies. High-prestige levels were associated with cultural hobbies, middle-prestige levels were associated with property maintenance and improvement activities, and the lowest-prestige level preferred basic activities like sewing and cooking.

As Mueller and Gurin (1962) found, different rates of outdoor
recreation participation by different occupational groups become
minor when education is held constant. Their findings are similar to
Dave King's (1965) market study of Michigan campers. King found
that median incomes of campers tended to be above their "submar-
ket" populations, yet the more important association was the higher
proportion of household heads with college education, or more, and
professional occupations.

The series of studies by John Hendee and his associates (Hendee,
Catton, Marlow and Brockman, 1968; Harry, Gale, and Hendee, 1969;
Hendee, Gale, and Catton, 1971) consistently confirm the importance of educational attainment for nature "appreciative-symbolic
activities" (that is, the enjoyment of wild nature for itself rather than
for some utilitarian gain, such as fish or game). Hendee and his associates report that 60 percent of wilderness campers in the Pacific
Northwest are from the upper 10 percent of the population in terms
of educational attainment.

Table 20 provides summary data from three U.S. national surveys.
The underlined numbers indicate the modal class. The overrepre-
sentation of persons with college education is consistent for nearly
all activities.

Reinhard Wippler's (1968:10) analysis of sociological predictors

TABLE 20 PERCENT OF PERSONS 25 AND OVER PARTICIPATING IN VARIOUS OUTDOOR ACTIVITIES, BY EDUCATION, BY YEAR

Activity	Year	Education[a]			Total[b]
		< 8 Years	High School	College	
Bicycling	1960	—[c]	4	4	9
	1965	3	9	11	16
	1970	3	11	16[d]	22
Playing Outdoor	1960	—	25	36	30
Games or Sports	1965	10	33	43	38
	1970	7	24	40	36
Walking for	1960	—	32	39	33
Pleasure	1965	29	48	56	48
	1970	16	27	42	30
Picnicking	1960	—	60	56	53
	1965	37	61	62	57
	1970	25	49	56	49
Canoeing	1960	NA[e]	NA	NA	NA
	1965	—	2	—	3
	1970	NA	NA	NA	NA
Hiking	1960	—	5	8	6
	1965	—	4	7	7
	1970	NA	NA	NA	NA
Bird Watching	1960	NA	NA	NA	NA
	1965	3	6	8	5
	1970	2	4	8	4
Photographing	1960	NA	NA	NA	NA
Wildlife	1965	—	3	—	2
and Birds	1970	1	3	5	3
Taking	1960	—	15	16	14
Nature Walks	1965	6	14	24	14
	1970	7	13	27	18
Camping	1960	—	10	7	8
	1965	4	9	10	10
	1970	7	17	21	21

[a]Because the 1970 data format included more education categories, these categories were aggregated and weighted means were computed.

[b]The "total" column indicates the mean percent participation in the given activity for the entire sample, ages 12 and over.

[c]Dashes indicate insufficient sample size for computation of percentages.

[d]NA indicates data not available.

[e]The underlined numbers indicate the modal class.

Source: Ferriss (1962), Bureau of Outdoor Recreation (1967), Bureau of Outdoor Recreation (1972).

of leisure behavior in the Netherlands also found level of educational most important. He reports:

Activity	Year	< 8 Years	Education[a] High School	College	Total[b]
Hunting	1960	—	12	9	13
	1965	10	11	9	12
	1970	9	12	12	12
Fishing	1960	—	26	27	29
	1965	21	29	26	30
	1970	20	27	30	30
Swimming	1960	—	49	56	45
	1965	15	44	60	48
	1970	10	34	54	46
Waterskiing	1960	—	6	4	6
	1965	—	4	6	6
	1970	NA	NA	NA	NA
Skiing	1960	NA	NA	NA	2
	1965	—	2	—	4
	1970	NA	NA	NA	NA
Sledding	1960	—	6	6	9
	1965	2	9	13	13
	1970	NA	NA	NA	NA
Ice-skating	1960	—	5	7	7
	1965	1	6	8	9
	1970	NA	NA	NA	NA
Sailing	1960	NA	NA	NA	NA
	1965	—	—	7	3
	1970	NA	NA	NA	NA
Other Boating	1960	—	26	25	22
	1965	10	25	30	24
	1970	NA	NA	NA	NA
Driving for Pleasure	1960	—	58	56	52
	1965	38	59	61	55
	1970	NA	NA	NA	NA
Sightseeing	1960	—	51	57	42
	1965	29	54	66	49
	1970	NA	NA	NA	NA

Of the three measures of social stratification (educational level, income level, level of occupational prestige) the educational level is the most important predictor, although the level of occupational prestige plays an independent part; the income level, on the contrary, makes no independent contribution toward explanation of variance when the influence of the other two measures of social stratification is kept constant.

Thus our problem remains one of sorting out relative influences of formal training and occupational milieu and then accounting for the particular regularities we find.

OCCUPATIONAL PARTICULARITIES

Our discussion of social class and status has remained at the level of statistical aggregates. That is, persons sharing a particular attribute are aggregated for certain statistical manipulations. In our case, prestige and income aggregates certainly reflect life chances and establish "at risk populations" for certain nonwork activities; however, they fail to account for important within group variations. We are still at the point where Lundberg and his associates found themselves in 1934; that is, we can account for frequency of certain participation rates, but we know nothing about the more socially significant qualitative differences.

Kohn (1969) would argue that qualitative differences in life styles are occupationally derived. His (1969:190) interpretation is

> ... that the conformist values and orientation held by people in the lower segments of the class hierarchy are a product of the limited education and constricting job conditions to which they are subject. Education is important because self-direction requires more intellectual flexibility and breadth of perspective than does conformity; tolerance of nonconformity, in particular, requires a degree of analytic ability that is difficult to achieve without formal education. But education is not all that is involved. The conformity of people at lower social class levels is in large measure a carryover from the limitations of their occupational experiences. Men of higher class position, who have the opportunity to be self-directed in their work, want to be self-directed off the job, too, and come to think self-direction possible. Men of lower class position, who do not have the opportunity for self-direction in work, come to regard it a matter of necessity to conform to authority, both on and off the job. The job does mold the man—it can either enlarge his horizons or narrow them. The conformity of the lower social classes is only partly a result of their lack of education; it results also from the restrictive conditions of their jobs.

Kohn's study provides a careful empirical elaboration of the "spillover" hypothesis, in which nonwork behavior is found to be similar, or "congruent," to occupational style. The alternative is the "compensatory" hypothesis, which argues that leisure is the direct opposite of work and, therefore, "compensates" for its limitations. Harold Wilensky (1960) has provided the best theoretical discussion of these two hypotheses in that he attempts to go from ideological soundings to an analysis as to how studies of occupations, labor markets, stratifications, and family life can be combined with leisure. Certainly Wilensky's discussion suggests that life-style patterns are determined in a more complex manner than that suggested by Kohn's interpretation.

Some of this complexity is illustrated by Kohnhauser's (1965) study of industrial workers, which found a high degree of similarity in the nonwork activities of blue-collar and white-collar employees. His data strongly support the spillover (congruence) hypothesis as opposed to the compensatory hypothesis; that is, dissatisfaction in one sphere of life—home, work, leisure—did not seem to compensate in one of the other spheres. However, it is important to note "that different circumstances produce different feelings, that to an important degree satisfactions are *situationally* determined rather than depending solely on individual differences of personality."

Wippler's (1970:60) Netherland study also found that "the variables representing aspects of the work situation . . . explain only a small part of the variance in leisure behavior when compared with other predictors." This is especially so for the compensatory hypothesis, which has hardly any support from his empirical data. He did find support for the congreunce hypothesis and suggested that cognitive dissonance theory[3] may account for similarities between work and leisure.

Harry (1971) found similar patterns of little transfer in the social content of work and leisure, but some transfer of cultural content. That is, the way in which social relations are organized was different between work and nonwork, but the value, or technical orientation, was similar. Dowell (1969), also, found that the typical (largest percent of) participation of each occupational group was: professionals —reading, businessmen—entertainment media, city workers—fishing, rural workers—fishing and hunting.

Parker (1971) provides one of the best attempts at sorting out the spillover ("extension") and compensatory ("opposition") relationship between work and nonwork. He lines up factors such as the nature of the work task, work-related friendships, and level of education required for the work with the nonwork meanings and functions. Thus, professionals and others in high-status occupations tend to extend work rewards into nonwork, clerical and other middle-status workers are neutral, and the working class requires nonwork as compensation. Table 21 provides a summary of his discussion.

---

[3]In general this theory suggests that people manage dissonance between their existing state and some other, possibly preferred but unattainable, state by cognitively emphasizing the desirable attributes of the present position. See Festinger (1957) for details on the logic of the theory.

TABLE 21 TYPES OF WORK-LEISURE RELATIONSHIP AND ASSOCIATED VARIABLES (INDIVIDUAL LEVEL)

Work-Leisure Relationship Variables	Extension
Content of work and leisure	similar
Demarcation of spheres	weak
Central life interest	work
Imprint left by work on leisure	marked
Work variables	
Autonomy in work situation	high
Use of abilities (how far extended)	("stretched")
Involvement	moral
Work colleagues	include some close friends
Work encroachment on leisure	high
Typical occupations	Social workers (esp. residential)
Nonwork variables	
Educational level	high
Duration of leisure	short
Main function of leisure	continuation of personal development

Source: Parker (1971: 103).

Unhappily, the nature of Parker's variables remain at a fairly gross level; and when we begin to sort specific nonwork activities, much of the variation slips through. Indeed, most of the studies in this area seem to support Alfred McClung Lee's (1966) argument that life is multivalent. Just as we think we have found the uniting variable that accounts for complex behavior, the subjects under observation slip into another level of their personal and social dimension.

The spillover hypothesis seems to have a certain ready logic and empirical support. Still, it is difficult to see how wilderness camping, bicycling, and walking for pleasure are continuations of the work of professionals. Yet our U.S. national survey data from 1960 to 1970 force us in such directions. Table 22 combines comparable national survey data and has the modal percent by activity year underlined. Except for hunting and boating other than sailing, participants most often come from white-collar occupations rather than blue-collar occupations.

These data and those cited previously suggest that nonwork activity is associated with status position in general and life situation in particular. For example, on the basis of a national sample, Morse and Weiss (1965) report that work is more than simply a means of

Opposition	Neutrality
deliberately different	usually different
strong	average
—	nonwork
marked	not marked
—	low
("damaged")	("bored")
alienative	calculative
—	include no close friends
low	low
"extreme"	routine clerical
(mining, fishing)	and manual
low	medium
irregular	long
recuperation	entertainment

survival. Indeed, 80 percent of their sample would continue working even if they no longer needed to financially. Most of the sample saw work as providing them a purpose and a means for being tied into the larger society. Interestingly, 86 percent of the middle class would continue to work, and 61 percent would continue in the same type of work; while 76 percent of the working class would continue to work, but only 34 percent would continue in the same type of work. The variation within each group of these two class groupings is even more revealing for the middle class—among professionals there are a higher proportion who would continue in the same line of work and a higher proportion who are very satisfied, when compared to managerial and sales people. In the working class, this same pattern exists only among tradespeople; and, on the satisfaction scale, 32 percent of tradespeople are very satisfied, while only 23 percent of the managerial group are very satisfied.

This would seem to be in line with Dubin's (1963) finding that there is little exchange between the industrial workers' work world and their world of leisure and with Orzack's (1963) finding of opposite-trends for nurses. Yet the main issue seems to be the contrast between industrial workers who want to work and those who find little central interest in work. Perhaps the seemingly contradic-

TABLE 22 PERCENT OF PERSONS 12 YEARS AND OVER PARTICIPATING OUTDOOR ACTIVITIES DURING JUNE-AUGUST 1960 AND 1970, BY OCCUPATION

Activity	Year	Professional Technical & Kindred Workers	Managers, Officials & Prop. Excluding Farm	Clerical & Sales Workers
Bicycling	1960	5	2	9
	1970	23[b]	15	17
Playing Outdoor Games or Sports	1960	34	25	36
	1970	47	39	36
Walking for Pleasure	1960	35	26	37
	1970	46	32	33
Picnicking	1960	58	40	59
	1970	61	51	53
Hiking	1960	8	3	7
	1970	NA[c]	NA	NA
Taking Nature Walks	1960	17	10	14
	1970	30	20	19
Camping	1960	14	4	8
	1970	26	18	20
Hunting[d]	1960	11	14	9
	1970	13	19	13
Fishing	1960	30	31	28
	1970	32	38	26
Swimming	1960	53	38	57
	1970	62	49	51
Waterskiing	1960	4	5	8
	1970	NA	NA	NA
Sledding[e]	1960	7	4	7
	1970	NA	NA	NA
Ice-skating[e]	1960	7	3	9
	1970	NA	NA	NA
Other Boating	1960	25	25	30
	1970	NA	NA	NA
Driving for Pleasure	1960	61	56	64
	1970	NA	NA	NA
Sightseeing	1960	57	46	49
	1970	NA	NA	NA

[a]This column indicates the mean percent participation in the given activity by all employed persons, 14 and older. Becatuse the 1970 data format included more occupation categories, the categories were aggregated and weighted means were computed.
[b]The modal percent by activity year is underlined.
[c]NA indicates data not available.
[d]Data for hunting was collected during September–November, 1960.
[e]Data for these two winter sports was collected for the period December, 1960, to February, 1961.

Source: Ferriss (1962), Bureau of Recreation (1972).

Craftsmen, Foremen, & Kindred Workers	Operatives & Laborers	Service Workers	Farm Workers	All Employed (14 and over)[a]
4	4	8	5	5
10	10	17	7	16
30	28	22	18	29
32	30	28	17	31
25	26	32	19	29
24	23	28	12	30
53	48	48	49	51
50	47	45	38	47
4	3	6	1	5
NA	NA	NA	NA	NA
14	10	11	8	12
16	13	15	10	17
11	7	7	9	8
<u>26</u>	20	18	12	19
22	22	9	<u>41</u>	17
30	22	8	<u>31</u>	13
45	33	23	<u>39</u>	33
47	34	23	32	27
48	42	34	27	44
41	38	39	19	42
6	8	6	5	6
NA	NA	NA	NA	NA
10	7	2	3	6
NA	NA	NA	NA	NA
4	6	2	2	5
NA	NA	NA	NA	NA
<u>32</u>	21	17	19	24
NA	NA	NA	NA	NA
57	50	49	38	54
NA	NA	NA	NA	NA
47	34	44	29	43
NA	NA	NA	NA	NA

tory trends in the data mean that we are looking in the wrong direction. The circles of tastes may *contain* occupational factors but are seldom determined by such factors.

For example, Rottenberg's (1952) study of West Indian workers dealt with the notion that such workers have small fixed wants, are "voluntarily underemployed" and, therefore, do not respond to income incentives. He found that, far from a strong desire for leisure and a weak desire for income, there are certain jobs that are deemed socially inferior or are regarded as unfit for a male; while many persons considered themselves artisans and would refuse other forms of employment.

Liebow's (1967) study of streetcorner men in Washington, D.C. offers similar findings. For the streetcorner men the value placed on the jobs offered them was simply a larger statement of their social inferiority. They existed in a culture of failure rather than a culture of poverty, with each social circle—transient friendship, serial marriage, thin ties of kinship—seeming to confirm the dead-end characteristics of the "jobs" offered to them. Thus, work as such was not a useful concept, given the realities of their existence. This pattern of ever-enclosing circles of failure seldom appears in the standard survey research.

A large proportion of the streetcorner men and women, whether blacks studied in the 1960s or white ethnics studied by Whyte (1943) in the 1930s, are likely to remain outside the main social system. Others who will also be out of the mainstream are persons who are socially disabled, functionally illiterate, unemployable due to various addictions, too old, or too highly migratory. They, along with the institutionalized physically and mentally disabled and the incarcerated, are likely to remain between 10 to 25 percent of the industrial populations. Though these dependent populations provide work for a growing professional cadre (Romano-V, 1974), to suggest that such populations share a rich and distinctive culture seems the cruelest joke of intellectual romanticism.

Important though such enforced leisure may be, it is not a central focus of this volume.[4] The consistent patterns of traditional working-class culture provide a longer history and a more steady and a more hopeful expression of work-nonwork cycles.

Consistency of cultural order seems to have been true of the industrial working class regardless of increased income or nationality. Richard Hoggart's (1963:33) study of the British working class suggests that

> ... the more we look at working-class life, the more we try to reach the core of working-class attitudes, the more surely does it appear that the core is a sense of the personal, the concrete, the local: it is embodied in the idea of, first, the family and, second, the neighbourhood.

S. M. Miller and Frank Riessman (1961) have summarized a variety of studies on the working-class subculture that seem to substantiate

---

[4]See Georges Friedmann's (1961) discussion for some of the implications of enforced leisure.

Hoggart. They suggest that the working class has manufactured from their conditions of existence a successfully adaptive pattern of life. The working-class life-style reflects values that are traditional, old-fashioned, religious, and patriarchal. The working-class person likes structure and order, is family centered, has a negative attitude toward leaders, and is often stubborn when confronting change. The working-class person is concerned with stability and security, believes strongly in an eye-for-an-eye psychology, shows considerable interest in new possessions, is person centered—that is, relates to people rather than roles—and has a strong touch of pragmatism and antiintellectualism—although an exaggerated and vague respect for the learned.

However, new levels of living may somewhat modify traditional life-style. Young and Willmott (1957) report that in working-class districts an individual is viewed as a whole person with a multiplicity of statuses. Yet, when he moves to lower middle-class housing, possessions become significant forms of status placement. And though this change may somewhat modify nonwork behavior it is in a value consistent pattern—that is, an increase in artifacts does not mean a change in values.

Small-town, lower middle-class culture also seems to have a high degree of persistence. A 1935 study (Anderson, 1936, 1937) of married young men and women, 15 to 29 years of age, living in Tompkins County, New York, found that the leisure-time activities most frequently engaged in were of the "indoor passive type," such as reading and listening to the radio. "Outing activities" and "household activities" were next in importance. The home was the center for leisure activity. A later study of unmarried youth in the same area found they had leisure activities similar to the young marrieds. Though both groups of these rural, small-town people said reading was their most important leisure activity, this reading was primarily of newspapers and magazines. In a burst of what now seems quaint, small-town morality, W. A. Anderson (193:26) says that "a chief problem with regard to magazines is the character of those read; many are trashy." And of the few who read books, they "read fiction almost exclusively." These people now comfortably settled before the television set in their suburban homes may have simply substituted video entertainment for their past forms of literary entertainment.

Thirty-two years seem to have made little impact upon this culture. Gans (1967:418) in his study of Levittowners reports:

> If left to themselves, lower middle-class people do what they
> have always done: put their energies into home and family,
> seeking to make life as comfortable as possible, and supporting,

> broadening, and varying it with friends, neighbors, church, and a
> voluntary association. Because this way of life is much like that
> of the small-town society or the urban neighborhood in which
> they grew up, they are able to maintain their optimistic belief that
> Judeo-Christian morality is a reliable guide to behavior. . . . If
> "blandness" is the word for this quality, it stems from the transi-
> tion in which the lower middle class finds itself between the
> familial life of the working class and the cosmopolitanism of the
> upper middle class. In viewing their homes as the center of life,
> Levittowners are still using a societal model that fit the rural
> America of self-sufficient farmers and the feudal Europe of
> self-isolating extended families.

Gans (1967) reports that though there were changes in leisure
time and activity in the move to the suburbs, the changes in leisure
style were minimal. Of those changes, there was a tendency towards
more sociability, more work around the house, and more organizational participation. Such changes suggest that the pleasure seeking
of the new middle class will continue to emphasize fixing the home,
gardening, and family pleasures such as boating and camping.

Kohnhauser (1965) did find considerable similarity between blue-
collar and white-collar nonwork activities. There seemed to be an
emphasis upon kin-centered social relations, interest in mass entertainment, such as television, and interest in home improvement activities. However, he also found that white-collar employees mention
reading more frequently, give far greater attention to artistic and intellectual activities, and participate more, both formally and informally. That is, the only real difference is the interest on the part of
the higher-status white-collar group in activities that contribute to
social mobility. The blue-collar workers seem, in their hobbies and
other nonwork activities, to take more pride in surviving than in preparing for social advance.

In a study of workers in a new California autoworkers suburb,
Bennet Berger (1960) reports similar findings. There was little participation in formal associations by the newly suburban working
class, and this included participation in community improvement
groups, churches, and the union. There was little increase in the
small amount of home entertaining when these workers moved to
the suburb. Indeed, Berger found—as have most other students—
consistent patterns of frequent visiting between kin. The workers
seldom went out on the weekends or to parties; and when they did
go out, the party usually involved kin groups. Their favorite television shows were "those shows without middle-class content"—that
is, Westerns and sports events. Berger (1960:79) suggests that much
of the taste of these new suburbanites was largely a reflection of
strong pressure from magazines and other salesmen. He argues:

*It is possible that the vast improvements in material standard of
living for workers represented by their trek to suburbia (without,
it should be emphasized, the social mobility represented by white
collar status and a college degree) may provide the conditions
for the development of a cultural style which, though not that of
the suburban middle class, is not that of the urban working class
of the past either.*

Berger (1960) goes on to suggest that the values of the shop-
keeper and of others in the middle stratum of American life are being maintained by the well-paid industrial working class. This trickle-
down life-style theory is similar to that proposed by the Lynds
(1956:281) in their 1929 Middletown study. They suggest that "it
must be borne in mind that in leisure-time pursuits as in so many
other activities, the workers of Middletown still do many of the
things the business group did a generation ago." The main points
that emerge from the studies of Gans, Berger, and the Lynds—all
done in very different places and at different times—seem to be that
in working-class life the value of stability, sought in family centered-
ness, is the constant, while for the more mobile middle strata—business groups and the new, educated bureaucratic elite—search for
change is the constant.

Thus social strata (an aggregate) develop different adaptive strategies (life-styles) because their life conditions are different. It is wise
for the working class to place emphasis upon extended-kin social
relations, for the mobile middle-class to place emphasis upon circles
of friends (surrogate kin), and the upperclass to emphasize kin and
the interlocking contacts these require in maintaining elite status. In
this sense the social structure maintains itself through providing
quite different social contexts in which the strata act.

As Kohn (1969:76) reports on class differences in work orientation:
*Essentially, men of higher class position judge jobs more by
intrinsic qualities, men of lower class position more by extrinsic
characteristics. That is, the higher men's social class, the more
importance they attach to how interesting the work is, the amount
of freedom you have, the chance to help people, and the chance
to use your abilities. The lower their class position, the more
importance they attach to pay, fringe benefits, the supervisor,
co-workers, the hours of work, how tiring the work is, job
security, and not being under too much pressure.*

Nonwork becomes a central mechanism for maintaining behavioral regularities associated with particular social strata. Thus Kohn's
finding of working class conformity seems reflected in why so few
blue-collar people are in a wilderness area; or if they are in such an

area, why they are seeking tangible trophies such as fish or game. The logical survival strategy is to avoid complicated, intellectualized, intangible pay-offs. Riding motor bikes, waterskiing, bait fishing (rather than fly fishing), hunting, snowmobiling conform to clear-cut norms; the roles are predetermined, the routine is externally set and is familiar, and there are traditions of sex segregation. The latter is especially important in the converging forces that bind young factory workers into a frustrating grind. Stan Udy[5] recently stated that early marriage and start of family, the purchase of leisure equipment and/or a second home, the presence of "buddies" to recreate with, and the tight regulation of the job locked the worker into a program from which he could never escape. Indeed, Udy suggested that the family and leisure demands might be so great that the grind of the assembly line was seen as a routine, welcome relief.

Some laborers in the industrial system of stratification, are not so much alienated or dissatisfied with their work but rather with the life condition in which each crucial element binds the individual ever tighter and tighter into a routine beyond his or her control. And all the while the media keeps promising a much more exciting, sexy, active male life, indeed, one which is being had by "guys just like him." Thus the regularities become ever more constant, while the hopes of mobility continue to escalate. In short, nonwork strategies are logical adaptations to given sets of conditions, which in turn reinforce existence within those conditions.

The stages of individual and family life-cycles influence nonwork activity patterns within working-class culture, while occupational community provides a further variation. Though Weiss, Harwood, and Riesman (1971) document how career lines and motivations are significantly different among blue-collar, white-collar, professional, and managerial groups (and almost too insistently remind us that workers like money and want to work), they also illustrate that within these broad status groups, there are equally significant variations in career lines and motivations—that is, there are characteristic cycles that greatly influence the ways in which occupational patterns cojoin with nonwork activity.

For the masses of workers, the rhythms of industrial time are their unavoidable personal rhythms. Yet some modern occupations have managed to transcend this limited frame. Curiously, those persons who have the most enriched and perhaps dignified leisure, voluntarily have the least off-work time. Wilensky (1963:109) has presented national sample data that indicates that men who control their own time work longer hours:

[5]Personal conversation.

. . . with economic growth the upper strata have probably lost leisure. Professionals, executives, officials and proprietors have long workweeks, year-round employment. Their longer vacations and shorter worklives (delayed entry and often earlier retirement) do not offset this edge in working hours. Although lifetime leisure decreases with increased status, the picture is one of bunched, predictable leisure for elites whose worklives are shorter; and intermittent, unpredictable, unstable leisure for the masses, whose worklives are longer.

As Chapter 4 indicates, housewives are another group who do not have much leisure. Though the wife without another job has the frame of her time scheduled by children's school hours, husband's work hours, the time shops open, and so forth, yet within that frame the disposal of time and tasks are at her discretion. Thus the housewife's occupation is peculiar because of time inconsistencies. Like many professions it seems freed from routinized time demands, yet its flow of work-nonwork is routinized by the routines of significant others. So what seems open is very much closed.

Gerstl (1963), in a study of admen, dentists, and professors found that they all work long hours. However, the professors have the most difficulty in telling when their work ends and leisure begins, and even their small bits of leisure are spent on activities similar to work (see Table 23).

As Gerstl (1961:48) in another article suggests:

For many of the professors of Sauk College, the separation of work from the rest of their lives is virtually impossible even if it is thought desirable. Their work is their life; their vocation is their avocation.

TABLE 23 HYPOTHETICAL USE OF TWO EXTRA HOURS BY OCCUPATION

Activity	Admen	Dentists	Professors
Relaxation	12.1%	29.4%	0.0%
Family-Home	24.3	14.7	9.4
Recreational Reading	12.1	14.7	28.1
Hobby or Recreation	33.3	32.4	12.5
Work or Work-Connected Reading	18.2	8.8	50.0
Total	100.0	100.0	100.0
Number of Responses[a]	(33)	(34)	(34)

[a]Multiple responses were given.
Source: Gerstl (1963: 149).

Why do these occupational groups work so hard? Cynically we could say because they are preserving their image or, having limited the market of practitioners, they are compelled to work twice as hard to keep even with the demand for their services. Perhaps there is a less cynical and more realistic explanation. Many professionals have large rather than minute rhythms of work; they have seasons and duties, not rational time measurements. Most have a high degree of control over the flow of their work and the opportunity to determine the nature of the task and how it will be met. The professional's work is more than a simple means to an end; work is a central life purpose. Like Gerstl's professors, many other professionals have a hard time determining what is work and what is leisure.

Those in the industrial order who come closest to the preindustrial concept of time are those of this new leisure class—the artist, scholar, philosopher, professional athlete, timber faller. These persons have a rhythm of seasons: the theatre season, the symphony season, the baseball season, the logging season. For the teacher, the cyclical movement of students entering and leaving allows some mediation between the world of rationality and the world of leisure productivity. Perhaps this explains some of the conflict between these occupational groups and the larger society. Administrators and their publics hold to the myth that work occurs only when time is spent rushing about within the occupational time-space locale, all other time is play, nonproductive, and therefore useless. Reflect upon the late-arriving or failing-to-arrive professor as he battles the rational and appointment-minded administrator who seeks to keep detailed working records so that he can allow the professor to accumulate annual leaves, sick leaves, and other timed benefits, and who is miffed when the professor rejects the benefits and mutters about bureaucrats and time clocks.

As Galbraith (1958:267) suggests:

> Some of the attractiveness of membership in the New Class, to be sure, derives from a vicarious feeling of superiority—another manifestation of class attitudes. However, membership in the class unquestionably has other and more important rewards. Exemption from manual toil; escape from boredom and confining and severe routine; the chance to spend one's life in clean and physically comfortable surroundings; and some opportunity for applying one's thoughts to the day's work, are regarded as unimportant only by those who take them completely for granted. For these reasons it has been possible to expand the New Class greatly without visibly reducing its attractiveness.

As we argued earlier, the status of an occupation and its associated ability to control work flow are important factors producing within class level variations. However, as Galbraith suggests the structure of timing (when work "must" occur) is as crucial as the prestige of the occupation in influencing the nature of social circles and their corresponding life-styles. In this matter not all professions look alike, indeed not all manual occupations look alike.[6]

In their classic study of printers, Lipset, Trow, and Coleman (1956: 158) suggest four reasons why there is a high sense of occupational community and frequency of interaction with fellow craftsmen. Printers have a unique status, being marginally between manual and nonmanual occupations. The craft aspect gives a common ground of interest. The printers have a substitute system where chances for employment are directly related to the number of friends among the regulars. And the night work

> . . . reduces printers' opportunities to associate with nonprinters or to take part in neighborhood activities and mass entertainment; early in a man's career, it habituates him to occupation-linked leisure activities and releases him from the pressure of regular family life.

Parker (1964:216) found similar patterns in his study of business and service groups in the United Kingdom. He found that service professionals were more likely to have close friends in the same or related work than were business people. Because of the nature of the problems faced by service workers, friends in other jobs might be discouraged because "this job makes outside contacts difficult to keep up because you can't rely on being able to keep evening appointments." Also, "contact with customers of clients gives more material for 'talking shop' in non-working hours, and co-workers are usually better for this purpose." And like the printers, the friendship network was important in "exchanging information about job opportunities." Finally, he found that where the nature of the professional work encroached upon free time, there was more likely to be a circle of close friends in the same occupation.

Kaufman's (1960) study of foresters found a similar pattern. Foresters usually exist as a salaried group of two or more professionals (as opposed to independent-fee, solo professionals) in the relative isolation of small, remote towns, where they often have a higher level of education than prevails in the host town. The Forest Service

[6]The importance of occupational timing was dramatized in an experimental program of a California aircraft-parts manufacturing company, which altered the work schedules so that once a month workers had a three-day weekend. At first the employees accepted the new calendar, until they found they were "off-phase" with the larger social routines of family, media, and friends. The "discipline" of traditional work routines was soon desired by the majority of workers (Meyersohn, 1963).

has a policy of rotation to build loyalty to the organization rather than the locality. Then the similar socialization at forestry schools provides a unique condition where one's set of friends, training, and organizational position combine to fashion work, values, and life-style into a similar mold.

However, professionals exhibit considerable variation. Gerstl (1961) found that 84 percent of the college professors he interviewed, 48 percent of the admen, and only 16 percent of the dentists had at least two of their three best friends as occupational colleagues. He notes that opportunities for association—such as working alone or doing group work—and timing—such as night work or day work—as well as different values placed upon the three types of work influenced the variations in friendship choice.

Heckscher and deGrazia's (1959) study of a large sample of American executives suggests slightly different patterns than those found among the middle-level business people sampled by Parker. They found that over 62 percent of the executives under 40 years shared friendship on the job, while 52 percent of the executives between 40 and 50 years had such a pattern, nearly as high a proportion had periods of working alone. Thus those with higher executive positions had less friendship on the job and more periods alone. Heckscher and deGrazia's (1959:12) study also noted that, for the executives, work and leisure are hard to distinguish. They suggest that the executive may picture himself as constantly at work because "so much of what he does is not capable of being readily evaluated. . . . Hours of work thus become one vivid sign—an outward and discernible mark—of the extent of his labors." Many long-hours occupations probably reflect a similar motive, but of importance to our argument is the influence of such timing upon the components of one's social circle.

Occupational variation in terms of its sense of community, its timing, its danger, and so forth is a strong influence upon variations in nonwork activity. As noted earlier, Parker (1971) reports that miners and distant-water fishermen see their work as a means of survival, while leisure serves as compensation for dangerous and damaging work. He finds that professions such as youth employment and child care have nonwork activities similar in content to their work activities, while bank employees use leisure neither as an extension of nor in opposition to their work. However, of greatest interest is his data comparing the three middle-strata occupations in amount of nonwork hours spent alone. We find rather startling numbers of nonwork hours spent alone by the youth employment and child care professionals when contrasted with the white-collar workers in banking (see Table 24). Indeed, professional training and activity that so greatly involves the person may require such intensive indi-

TABLE 24 LEISURE HOURS SPENT WITH OTHER PERSONS, BY OCCUPATION

Leisure hours per week spent:	Banking		Youth Employment		Child Care	
	Single	Married	Single	Married	Single	Married
	hrs.	hrs.	hrs.	hrs.	hrs.	hrs.
with family	20	34	12	26	10	23
with work colleagues	3	2	1	1	3	3
with other friends	15	2	11	3	12	4
by oneself	5	2	10	3	10	4
Total	43	41	34	33	35	34
(N)	(58)	(44)	(48)	(64)	(44)	(36)

Source: S. R. Parker (1965: 69).

viduation that it must certainly contribute to the individual's greater adaptability to spatial and social mobility. Rather than being bound into the ethnic, religious, and familial life of the upper and working classes, the new bureaucratic professionals seem self-prepared for their social destiny. The career lines of salaried professionals require transient ties to localities, and thus there is little opportunity to build up the traditional culture of the more stable blue-collar workers.

If specific patterns of friendship cluster around specific occupations, it seems likely that patterns of nonwork participation would vary in the same way. Unhappily, data for speculation about specific occupations is scanty. Millard Jordan (1956) found, in his sample of sociologists and attorneys, patterns similar to those of other relatively high-prestige occupations: neither profession showed much activity in sports such as baseball and volleyball, but did show high activity rates for cardplaying and attendance at cultural events and committee functions. Yet within the prestige class there were variations.

A much higher proportion of attorneys played golf, tennis, and fished than was the case for sociologists; while sociologists showed almost double the time spent hiking than did attorneys. Apparently in this time-sampling period Jordan asked similar questions of physicists and a general Cleveland sample, and he found similar occupational variations.

Following Gerstl, Burch (1969) attempted to examine whether specific occupations within the professional group differed in terms of primitiveness of camping style. He found that a large proportion of the primitive campers were technical persons, such as engineers, rather than intellectuals, such as authors or artists. It should be noted that his sample failed to uncover representatives of a variety of professions; no actors, airplane pilots, architects, athletes, chiropractors, designers, entertainers, pharmacists, public relations people, or veterinarians were found to do any type of camping.

It would seem that the organizational milieu of some occupations predispose one to participate with a particular social circle and to share its particular life-style variation. Gerstl's (1961) study clearly indicated that there are considerable life-style variations among occupations that are usually lumped together in a high-prestige category. Bishop and Ikeda's (1970) study followed a more quantitative approach in expanding upon Gerstl's ideas. They found that high-prestige occupations are associated with highbrow activities. However, their multivariate analysis uncovered other associations. Occupations that have a masculine or feminine cultural image are associated with nonwork activities having a similar image. Occupations involving high sociability tend to have high sociability in leisure, while those who have occupations requiring high energy expenditure tend to seek leisure activities requiring low energy expenditure. Their data suggest mixed exchange between work and nonwork—with some occasions of congruence and some occasions of compensation.

The findings of Bishop and Ikeda (1970), as those of Gerstl (1961), suggest a pervasive organizational pattern in which vocation and avocation reflect a mutual blending rather than a one-directional causality. Nonwork does not neatly reflect a pattern of spillover, or compensation, with work, but is tied to matters of timing, circles of friends and kin, the structure of sanction mechanisms, and the relative permeability of certain life-styles. As we suggested at the beginning of this chapter, these variations in organization may be more crucial than any particular relationship between work and nonwork.

The character of nonwork is closely intertwined with the other dimensions of life. Where time is seen as a highly quantifiable capital good, nonwork is construed as having a tangible payoff as in rising production or consumption indexes. It becomes recreation. (This is discussed extensively in Chapter 10.) Where time is viewed as being seasonally marked, the aesthetic of nonwork may become an end in itself. It becomes leisure in the classical sense. Further, though nonwork may have certain therapeutic qualities, it is no substitute for a meaningful occupational life. Those who direct the behavior of machines and those who avoid machines in their work will seek much different forms of nonwork than those who have their work behavior determined by machines.

All cultures contain social and personal variants that challenge the "trained incapacities" that each culture seeks to impose. There may be a blue-collar culture, but printers and steelworkers residing in the same city will exhibit quite different interpretations of blue-collar life-style. In the industrial order, the new class of professionals and technical workers represent one subculture that not only has different time conceptions but different nonwork values.

Occupational cultures offer considerable variations from the main trends of national culture. For example, we strongly suspect that humanities professors from the multiversity are more likely to emphasize the aesthetic and abstract qualities in a nonwork activity; while technicians are more likely to emphasize the practical and concrete aspects, such as the challenges met, the number of miles traveled, and the number of trophies collected. Persons whose occupations require, instill, and reward self-mastery will very likely be persons who minimize television, put emphasis on the higher arts, walk for pleasure, hike, cross-country ski, and sail. In contrast, those persons whose occupations require, instill, and reward conformity to routines established by others, may very likely be persons who put emphasis on television, minimize the higher arts, avoid walking, dress for downhill skiing, undress for water-skiing, and drive powerboats for pleasure. These patterns are likely to occur because there is organizational congruence in terms of group size, sanctions, and reward structure between vocation and avocation. Such patterns do not necessarily inhere in the nature of the activity—whether it is passive or active. Nor do these patterns reflect a consistent exchange of congruence or compensation between work and nonwork. Rather, they reflect our species' propensity to create organizational patterns and to then live within the strictures that such organization imposes.

SUMMARY

Work has a variety of meanings and influences upon life-style. The wealth it provides sets the necessary conditions of nonwork enactment, but wealth alone does not determine the shape and type of that action. Other hierarchical patterns such as differential prestige, access to power, and levels of educational attainment seem better determinants of nonwork. However, even here there are confused regularities—with a high proportion of the poor voting for the wealthy, who are likely to see that such inequalities of wealth remain.

Persons in higher class (income) and status (prestige) groupings have higher participation rates in nearly all nonwork activities. Educational attainment seems the best predictor of nonwork behavior.

There seems most support for the spillover, or congruence, hypothesis that nonwork activities are similar to work activities. However, when we look at specific occupational milieu, we begin to note significant variation. For example, the trades of printing and university professorship have relatively high prestige among their respective types, require friendships within the occupation to maintain and improve employment, have involving tasks, and have a high degree of job satisfaction. On the other hand, industrial workers and dentists have relatively low prestige among their respective types, seldom have frienships within the occupation, have routine tasks, and have a low degree of job satisfaction. And a crucial factor is the difference in the timing of work-nonwork cycles. For dentists and industrial workers, the timing is highly regular, routinized, and abstract; while for printers and professors, it is a flow determined by the task at hand and is usually off-phase with the timing of the larger society.

Thus one set of timing serves to bind occupation into the social circles that create and sustain a unique life-style, while another timing leaves one open for the life-styles of other existing traditions. In such a way are person and work role bound into the larger social world.

Again the reader should be reminded that we have not intended to "prove" any particular proposition. Rather our intent has been to suggest that there are some likely regularities that emerge from existing studies. Some of these regularities may confound the conventional wisdom of the field. There is available a large number of studies that can be ordered and integrated in such a manner that they set the base for an emergent theory.

This chapter has suggested that work is not the central life goal for all who work, nor is it the prime determinant of nonwork behavior patterns. Rather the crucial factor is the variation in the social organization associated with a particular activity. Printers and professors exist in different organizational settings from their counterparts in the blue-collar and professional worlds, just as the commercial fisherman exists in a different organizational pattern from the person who fishes primarily for pleasure.

In the next chapter we will continue this exploration by considering ethnographic studies of societies at different levels of complexity and with different economies. In this way we will explore how variation in societal organization influences the nature and timing of work-nonwork patterns.

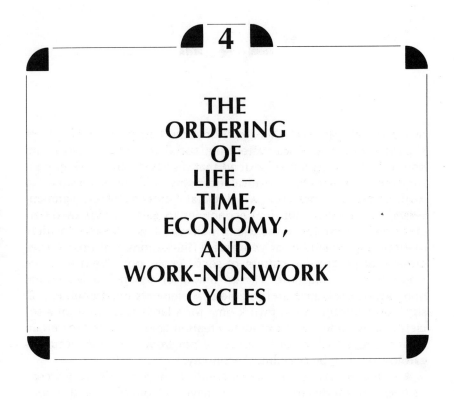

4

THE
ORDERING
OF
LIFE –
TIME,
ECONOMY,
AND
WORK-NONWORK
CYCLES

4

In the last chapter we considered how the timing of a job, an occupation, or a career can affect the social meaning of work and nonwork. This chapter will extend that discussion by considering if variation in a society's political economy influences variation in work-nonwork cycles. We will look at hunter-gatherer, agrarian-village, and market-industrial economies to gain an idea of differences and similarities in the use of nonwork time. We use a variety of ethnographic studies as convenient illustrations, but posit no regressive or progressive pattern of social evolution.[1] We have three major points to illustrate: (1) the timing of action is a behavioral node where biological and sociological elements interpenetrate, (2) significant amounts of nonwork time for a large proportion of a society's population is not a modern creation, and (3) there are certain invariant uses and social functions of nonwork time that occur regardless of the type of political economy.

A system of norms, or rules of conduct, mirrors a desire for consistency and predictability in the behavior of ourselves and others. Yet the concern over consistency implies that deviant behavior is also part of the social order. Indeed, as Kai Erikson (1966) has argued, there is the need for a certain level of deviation to maintain the functioning of the normative system. While students such as Howard Becker (1963), Alfred Lindesmith (1947), and others argue that social deviants are really persons who are well-integrated into alternative sets of norms.

These students of deviation suggest that we become most aware of behavioral consistency only when we experience inconsistency. Further, our perception of behavioral consistency is often confounded by the great diversity of cultures other than our own. For any given culture is a unique, adaptive strategy that recalls the his-

[1]It should be noted that few of these societies are "earlier" in time; indeed, most, from hunter-gatherer to postindustrial, are contemporaries of one another. This fact alone should inhibit any grand evolutionary visions.

tory of survival pressures faced by a persisting social group. These strategies come not in genetic codes but in words, sentences, and packages of grammar that shape our perceptions of time and our meanings of work and nonwork.

Aldous Huxley (1939:309–310) stated it very elegantly when he said:

Our souls are so little "us" that we cannot even form the remotest conception how "we" should react to the universe, if we were ignorant of language in general, or even of our own particular language. The nature of our souls and of the world they inhabit would be entirely different from what it is, if we had learnt to talk Eskimo instead of English. Madness consists, among other things, in imagining that our soul exists apart from the language our nurses happen to have taught us.

Benjamin Lee Whorf (1947:214) stated it more technically when he said:

We dissect nature along lines laid down by our native languages. The categories and types that we isolate from the world of phenomena we do not find there because they stare every observer in the face. . . . We cut nature up, organize it into concepts, and ascribe significancies as we do, largely because we are parties to an agreement to organize it this way.

Huxley and Whorf represent challenges to the conventional wisdom of an earlier time, which, in turn, have become part of the conventional wisdom of our time—namely, cultural relativism. That is, the notion that cultural items are so unique that comparative appraisals cannot be made, that the human being is infinitely malleable, that the only behavioral properties that are universal to the species are likely to be trivial, and that social processes in animals other than man have nothing to tell us about human society. As the earlier chapters indicate, we believe there may be some virtue in seeking to account for those elemental, universal behavioral characteristics that are shared by all members of the species. Once we can roughly identify these forces and estimate the conditions and magnitudes of their influence, then we may better understand the conditions under which cultural relativism operates. In short, ours is a zoological approach, which sees culture as the unique adaptive strategy of the species, but which does not deny those characteristics we share with all other social species. In this sense, *time* seems a fortuitous node at which biological and social elements interpenetrate.

In a highly perceptive essay of a few years ago, Wilbert Moore (1963) built a strong case that time served as a boundary condition and as a measure of social persistence and change. That is, time has in addition to biological constraints, the constraints of social meaning. In our terms, these latter constraints are part of a shared vocabulary, for, as Moore (1963) notes, part of the social ingenuity in molding the biological entity is the temporal location of activities such as that recurrence permits order and predictability. In this sense the distribution and allocation of time should reflect both the invariant properties and the highly variant properties of our species.[2]

When we examine the realm of time it quickly becomes clear that the industrial order, in its short span of existence for but a fraction of the total human population, reflects a most curious adaptation. Its conversion of all the world into a commodity that could be handled by its market system is reflected in the peculiar centering of all attention upon work as the central life goal of human beings. The market society ignored all the contrary evidence from many generations of human experience.

HUNTER-GATHERER PATTERNS OF TIMING

Lee and DeVore (1968) give us some idea of the magnitude of deception involved in assuming that industrial meanings of work and nonwork can be projected on the human race. They (1968:3) note:

> Cultural Man has been on earth for some 2,000,000 years; for over 99 percent of this period he has lived as a hunter-gatherer. Only in the last 10,000 years has man begun to domesticate plants and animals, to use metals, and to harness energy sources other than the human body. Homo sapiens assumed an essentially modern form at least 50,000 years before he managed to do anything about improving his means of production. Of the estimated 50,000,000,000 men who have ever lived out a life span on earth, over 90 percent have lived as hunters and gatherers; about 6 percent have lived by agriculture and the remaining few percent have lived in industrial societies.

Since hunter-gatherer organizational forms—the clan, the band, the tribe—have been the major adaptive pattern for our species, their treatment of work and nonwork time could be expected to tell us more about regularities of our species than the very brief moment

---

[2]Barry Schwartz (1974) has an original analysis of the implications of time distribution for the ways in which social power is established and maintained.

of the industrial order. It should be noted that until recently hunter-gatherer groups have tended to be either fit subjects for romanticizing the noble savage or for excusing the ills of the industrial order by depicting tribal life as short, nasty, and brutish with the search for food a constant necessity. Happily, recent empirical research has satisfied neither polar view, though major theories, such as that of Coon (1962) and Lenski (1966) will need substantial revision, for the data indicate that longevity and leisure are essential characteristics of most hunter-gatherer groups.

The scholarly deception in assuming a dismal life-style for hunter-gatherers is partially due to a theoretical stance that uses linearity and "progress" as explanations of cultural variation. Thus, if we—Victorian England or postindustrial United States—who are at the "apex of human development" struggle so hard and remain so unfulfilled, then certainly those at lower levels must be even worse off. If work is our unending burden, it must be even more so for hunter-gatherers. As Sahlins (1968:86) notes:

> *Scarcity is not an intrinsic property of technical means. It is a relation between means and ends. We might entertain the empirical possibility that hunters are in business for their health, a finite objective, and bow and arrow are adequate to that end. A fair case can be made that hunters often work much less than we do, and rather than a grind the quest is intermittent, leisure is abundant, and there is more sleep in the daytime per capita than in any other conditions of society. (Perhaps certain traditional formulae are better inverted, the amount of work per capita increases with the evolution of culture and the amount of leisure per capita decreases.) Moreover, hunters seem neither harassed nor anxious. A certain confidence, at least in many cases, extends their economic attitudes and directions. The way they dispose of food on hand, for example—as if they had it made.*

The "affluence" of tribal society seems borne out by Raymond Firth's (1929; 1936) classic studies of the New Zealand Maori and an isolated Pacific Island tribal society, the Tikopia. Firth reports that the Tikopia were engaged in productive work around six to eight hours a day, and that this work time had many elements of play. As he indicates, subsistence is the goal, but it is approached somewhat casually. The number of holidays based on seasonal changes, weddings, puberty, and other celebrations, indicates that the amount of leisure time is considerably greater than in the present United States. The Maori had around an eight-hour day with two months set aside for rest, and many holidays to celebrate accomplishments and special events.

Other studies of tribal societies in varied parts of the world indicate similar patterns of work and play. A. I. Richards (1939:392–394) in her study of the Bemba of Northern Rhodesia, found that:

> The whole bodily rhythm of the Bemba differs completely from that of a peasant in Western Europe, let alone an industrial worker. For instance, at Kasaka, in a slack season, the old men worked 14 days out of 20 and the young men, 7; while at Kamamba, in a busier season, the men of all ages worked on an average 8 out of 9 working days. The average working day in the first instance was 2¾ hours for men and 2 hours gardening, plus 4 hours domestic work for the women, but the figure varied from 0 to 6 hours a day. In the second case the average was 4 hours for the men and 6 for the women, and the figures showed the same daily variation.

J. H. Provinse's (1939) study of the Siang Dyak of Borneo indicates that though there was considerable individual variation, approximately one-third of the time was spent on nonproductive activities. Hogbin's (1937–1938) study of the people of Wogeo Island indicates a workload similar to that of the Tikopia.

It is important to note that the division of labor in these societies is based upon gender, with gathering, in general, being the responsibility of females, and hunting, the responsibility of males. Within these gender divisions, the tasks are age graded (see Table 25).

It should be noted that the gathering activities of the women provide the bulk of the sustenance. As Richard Gould (1970:64) notes:

> What impressed me most, however, was the ease and relative speed with which the women found enough food for the whole group, even under what seemed superficially, to be adverse conditions. It was neither gourmet eating nor a balanced diet, but it was enough; and it took only a few man-hours to collect. So much for the commonly held view of hunter-gatherers as people without any leisure time because of their constant need to search for food. Under the conditions at Pulykara, the women spent most of their day in camp sleeping or talking among themselves. Their foraging was so efficient that it gave them abundant time to relax, while at the same time it freed the men for hunting and other activities. It also became obvious that the group could never have survived on the fruits of hunting alone, although no opportunities for getting game were overlooked.

Since most of the ethnographic studies referred to above deal with groups in tropical or semitropical ecosystems, it could be ar-

TABLE 25 ALLOCATION OF HUNTING TASKS BY AGE

Tribe	Age Division	
Ainu (Watanabe 1964a)	Younger men: Bear hunting in areas distant from the settlement Younger men: Spearing fish (cold season)	Older men: Deer hunting in areas nearer to the settlement Older men: Peep-hut fishing (cold season)
Chukchee (Bogoras, 1904–09)	Son: Long expeditions for sea mammals	Elderly father: Shorter trips for sea mammals
	Communal reindeer hunting	
	Younger men: Stabbing the animals in canoes	Older men (with women and children): Interception of the wounded animals carried away by the stream
Tikerarmiut (Larsen and Rainey, 1948)	Able-bodied men: Winter seal hunting	Old people (and children): Fishing crabs through ice holes
Nunatarmiut (Larsen and Rainey, 1948)	Younger people: Winter hunting in the mountains	Aged (and some women and children): Left in semi-permanent villages in winter
Iglulimiut (Damas, 1963)	Younger men: Roaming inland after caribou (August–September)	Older men: Hunting sea mammals (August–September)
Dogrib and Yellowknife (Spencer, 1965)	*Located by the Hunt Leader*	
	Younger men: Far afield for trapping	Older people (and children): Berry picking or at a fish camp
Paiute (Steward, 1938)	*Communal Deer Hunts*	
	Young men: Driving of deer	Older men: Hiding by game trails to shoot deer
	Communal Buffalo Hunts	
	Young men: Sent out to find the game	Older men: Butchering of the kill

Source: Lee and DeVore (1968: 76).

gued that favorable conditions for maximum biomass productivity lure tribal groups into a life of ease. And since such conditions affect only a narrow band of human communities, our argument is a variant of climatic determinism. Yet examination of groups under the harshest of conditions—the Kahlahari desert, the Australian desert, or the Shoshone of the American desert—indicates a similar pattern of nonwork. Lee's (1966:67) study of !Kung Bushmen seems typical:

> The work week varied from 1.2 to 3.2 work days per adult. In other words, each productive individual supports herself or himself and dependents and still has $3\frac{1}{2}$ to $5\frac{1}{2}$ days available for other activities. The Index of Subsistence Effort varies from .11 to .31. For instance, during Week I (July 6–12), thirty-seven man-days of work were expended to provide 179 man-days of consumption. The value $S = .21$ indicates twenty-one days of work per hundred man-days of consumption; or each days's work provided food for the worker and four other people. During Week IV (July 27–August 2), seventy-seven man-days of work provided 249 man-days of consumption for an "S" value of .31 (31 work days per 100 consumption days). The work input during Week IV is 50 percent higher than Week I. This rise reflects an increased difficulty in reaching food, although, in terms of actual time devoted to the food quest, the average rises from two days per week to three per week per individual producer.

AGRARIAN-VILLAGE PATTERNS OF TIMING

If we look at more complex organizational forms such as agrarian villages, whether partly or fully within the industrial orbit, we find an increasingly complex division of labor, a higher loading of symbolic burdens due to greater scale, more elaborate hierarchies of caste and class, and much less nonwork time. Oscar Lewis's (1958) study of Rampur, a village in northern India, indicates a fairly low number of workless days even though the festival cycle is quite extensive. The data from Lewis's study indicate, however, that the festival cycle is the essential means for maintaining solidarity at the family and caste level. That is, the more complex social system, like other forms of machinery, requires a great deal of time and energy in simply maintaining the existence of the system.

Salz's (1955:101) detailed study of Ecuadorian Indians offers further evidence that self-employed agrarians are constantly employed. They have no concept of leisure and no adult games for passing time. "Apart from fiestas, celebrations of personal life events, mass, and market, there are few discernible occasions of such importance as to distract from working time." Even the nonwork time of the festival requires a tremendous input of highly structured time.

It would seem that one of the fruits of the higher material standards of agrarian society is the greater amount of time that must be spent on simply keeping the system in the same place. There must be the saving of seeds for planting next season, the storing of surplus for off-seasons, the saving for festivals and religious assurance, the preparation for droughts and pestilence, the savings for ultimate replacement of draft animals, the saving to support rulers, scholars, and noblemen, who produce symbols of unity rather than bushels of grain. These and all the myriad other maintenance tasks of a more complex social order leave little room for leisure by the masses of agrarians.

This seems the case in John Embree's (1939) prewar study of Suye Mura, a Japanese village surrounded by a society determined to move toward industrialism. It is a mixed barter and moneyed economy, with production shifting from the family as the major productive unit to other broader associations. William's (1956) study of Gosforth, an English village, represents an agrarian society that is a step closer to accepting not only the artifacts of industrialization but many of the thought patterns. It is a moneyed economy with mechanized agriculture.

Both Suye Mura and Gosforth show a marked decline in leisure time, and, more importantly, a changed orientation to the social meaning of time. Though both societies have more leisure than did nineteenth-century industrial society, they have considerably less leisure than the Tikopia or the proletariat of urban Rome.

As Harold Wilensky (1963:109) reminds us:

> . . . among the citizens of antiquity, as well as among primitive agriculturalists, the number of days of leisure often approached half of every year. The transformation of tabooed or unlucky days into holy days, and the latter into holidays . . . occurred long before the Middle Ages. . . . In the old Roman Calendar, out of 355 days, nearly one-third (109) were marked as . . . unlawful for judicial and political business. In the last two centuries of the republic, festival days were stretched to accommodate more spectacles and public games. The Roman passion for holidays reached its climax in the middle of the fourth century when days off numbered 175. If we assume a 12-hour day, which is probably on the high side, total working time would be only about 2,160 hours a year. Whatever the work schedules of slaves and women, leisure for the ruling classes, for administrative and professional men, was never again so abundant. Hours of work for comparable

populations in subsequent centuries seem to have increased sharply.

In Moore's (1963) terms, the temporal ordering of synchroniza-tion, sequence, and timing takes on a more specialized and meas-ured quality as we move from hunter-gatherer economies to indus-trial economies. Thus, the precise coordination of timing, which the hunter observed for relatively brief moments of the hunt, becomes diffused throughout the more complex social order, drought cycles, seasonal cycles, tax cycles, and all the other evolving time overlays lead to valuing milliseconds, atomic clocks, and light years. Timed anticipations, therefore, become more and more standardized, with quantitative priorities that must be adapted to with an even greater precision.

For hunter-gatherers the timing of most leisure activities is less formalized and, of course, takes place with small numbers of inti-mates. Lee (Lee and DeVore, 1968:37) reports that leisure time is re-lated to work rhythms:

> *A woman gathers on one day enough food to feed her family for three days, and spends the rest of her time resting in camp, doing embroidery, visiting other camps, or entertaining visitors from other camps. For each day at home, kitchen routines, such as cooking, nut cracking, collecting firewood, and fetching water, occupy one to three hours of her time. This rhythm of steady work and steady leisure is maintained throughout the year.*
>
> *The hunters tend to work more frequently than the women, but their schedule is uneven. It is not unusual for a man to hunt avidly for a week and then do no hunting at all for two or three weeks. Since hunting is an unpredictable business and subject to magical control, hunters sometimes experience a run of bad luck and stop hunting for a month or longer. During these periods, visiting, entertaining, and especially dancing are the primary activities of men. (Unlike the Hadza, gambling is only a minor leisure activity.)*

Firth (1929:68) suggests that, for the Maori, time measurement is correlated with economic activity. He tells us that the Maori "fol-lowed a closely determined sequence of operations in accordance with seasonal change and the movements of the animal and plant life around him." The Maori observed a twelve-month lunar calen-dar containing ten of work and two for resting. And "from this cal-endar one can easily see how each task has its place in a definite scheme of work; how the coming of each season, and indeed of each month, brought forward its fresh need of work to be done."

(Firth, 1929:64) However, he finds that the calendar varied under different environmental and economic conditions. Thus, "Agriculture gave one calendar of work to the Northern Tribes, seafishing another to the people of the coast, reliance on birds, rats and forest food a third to the dwellers of the bush-clad ranges of the Urewera, eels and freshwater fish yet another. . . ." (Firth, 1929:55).

The Tikopia have no calendar, no measure of time, and no divisions of time; their activity is governed by their intrinsic requirements. In fact, "The whole atmosphere is one of labor diversified by recreation at will, and exhibits what even the cold-blooded objective scientist may be allowed to call touches of essential humanity." (Firth, 1936:97) However, the Maori with his lunar calendar has a schedule of work and leisure more closely assigned than the Tikopia. As Firth (1929:190) notes. "It must be remembered that in former times feasts, games, carnivals and even war expeditions were not indiscriminately arranged affairs, but were planned to fit in with the gaps in the working seasons of the year."

The Tikopian attitude toward time seems characteristic of most tribal societies. In his study of the Nuer, Evans-Pritchard says (1940: 103):

> *Though I have spoken of time and units of time the Nuer have no expression equivalent to "time" in our language, and they cannot, therefore, as we can, speak of time as though it were something actual, which passes, can be wasted, can be saved, and so forth. I do not think that they ever experienced the same feeling of fighting against time or of having to coordinate activities with an abstract passage of time, because their points of reference are mainly the activities themselves, which are generally of a leisurely character. Events follow a logical order, but they are not controlled by an abstract system, there being no autonomous points of reference to which activities have to conform with precision. . . .*

Dorothy Lee (1959:151) notes that present-day rural "Greeks 'pass' the time: they do not save or accumulate or use it. And they are intent on passing the time, not on budgeting it. Although city people say that this picture is changing, that they are now made aware of the need to use time, the attitude is still widely prevalent, even in the area of private life among the urban groups."

Much as the Greek villagers, the life rhythm for residents of Suye Mura (Embree, 1939) was tied to the seasons, despite the fact that the national government was imposing the rationality of the Gregorian calendar. As Embree indicates, a large share of the older residents continued to operate by the lunar calendar. However, under the impact of modern methods of agriculture and new conceptions of time, there is gradual attrition occurring and many of the festivals centering on the seasons have been dropped. As Embree (1939:266) notes: "The yearly festivals were more generally observed in the old days than they are today. Increased work demanded by the money wheat crop and other side work encouraged by the prefectural government have tended to reduce these celebrations and encourage people to do work and more work."

Thus, in Suye Mura, with time assigned a rational money value, there is constriction in both the amount of leisure and its social value as celebration of communal accomplishment. Work, not leisure, is beginning to take on positive values in a non-Western culture. Nonwork becomes only a means of refreshment or re-creation to aid production.

In Gosforth (Williams, 1956) the seasons, though playing an important role in rural life, are seen as facts of life, much as the machinist sees an imperfect piece of metal. The work continues on a rational basis, and the seasons are only slightly more important events than are heavier clothing and snow tires to the urban dweller. The pubs are empty as the farmer no longer acts upon the occasional whim to spend a day drinking beer with his friends. Farmer and his friends have an investment in their equipment and a mortgage on their farms. Time is money. Gosforth's dominant religion is Catholic, though its values are those that have been ascribed to Protestants.

INDUSTRIAL-MARKET PATTERNS OF TIMING

In Gosforth, time has almost reached the exaggerated meaning described by Georg Simmel (1950:413):

If all clocks and watches in Berlin would suddenly go wrong in different ways, even if only by one hour, all economic life and communication of the city would be disrupted for a long time. . . . Thus, the technique of metropolitan life is unimaginable without the most punctual integration of all activities and mutual relations into a stable and impersonal time schedule. Punctuality, calculability, exactness are forced upon life by the complexity and extension of metropolitan existence and are most intimately connected with its money, economy and intellectualistic character. These traits must also color the contents of life and favor the exclusion of those irrational, instinctive, sovereign traits and impulses which aim at determining the mode of life from within, instead of receiving the general and precisely schematized form of life from without.

Thus far our discussion has indicated how time is both a physical and a symbolic constraint. Time is not simply a function of planetary movement but of social meaning, so that variation in political-economy alters the nature of time and work-nonwork cycles. As we move from hunter-gatherer societies to industrial societies, per capita nonwork time declines, and work is no longer embedded in social relations but is given moral force and a dominant role in shaping social approval.

In the early and middle forms of industrialization, the factory whistle became as eloquent a voice as the peal of medieval church bells had once been. To social scientists attempting to understand this period of great change, a work ethic with a theological underpinning seemed a possible explanation of man's behavior. Though there is no need to go into detailed discussion of Max Weber's analysis of the Protestant ethic, we are dependent upon those ideas of his that deal with nonwork behavior.

In discussing the struggle between the king and the Puritans over the *Book of Sports*, Weber (1958a:167) links the ethic to the new middle classes:

The feudal and monarchial forces protested the pleasure seekers against the rising middle class morality and the anti-authoritarian ascetic conventicles, just as today capitalistic society tends to protect those willing to work against the class morality of the proletariat and the anti-authoritarian trade union.

Weber (1958a:167–169) says that for the Puritans:

Sport was accepted if it served a rational purpose, that of recreation necessary for physical efficiency. But as a means for spontaneous expression of undisciplined impulses, it was under suspicion; and insofar as it became purely a means of enjoyment; or awakened pride, raw instincts or the irrational gambling instinct, it was of course strictly condemned. Impulsive enjoyment of life, which leads away both from work in a calling and from religion, was such the enemy of rational asceticism, in the form of seigneurial sports, or the enjoyment of the dance-hall or the public-house of the common man.

Weber, though believing that Puritan values may have been instrumental in forming the spirit of capitalism, suggests that such ethical rewards are no longer available. The modern industrial order has secularized such values so that now they are part of existence for all persons, regardless of their religious affiliation.

Weber (1958a:181) argues:

The Puritan wanted to work in a calling; we are forced to do so. For when asceticism was carried out of monastic cells into every-

*day life, and began to dominate worldly morality, it did its part
in building the tremendous cosmos of the modern economic
order. This order is now bound to the technical and economic
conditions of machine production which today determine the
lives of all individuals who are born into this mechanism, not
only those directly concerned with economic acquisition.*

Though many theorists have seen a sensate, postindustrial consumption society as banishing scarcity, we should be aware that
tightly structured time will continue to organize industrial societies.
This is so even if a significant proportion of the labor force is idle
due to recession, depression, or energy shortages. The rationalized
market orientation toward time is different from that of the work-
centered agrarians, for the machine rhythms permeate all aspects of
life, even those where such precise coordination is not essential.
Interesting data on the consequences of this transfer comes from
studies of assembly line workers by Chinoy (1955), Walker and Guest
(1952), Swados (1967), Blakelock (1960) and others. Patricia Cayo
Sexton (1962:56) seems to summarize the findings when she says:
". . . the Fisher worker is paced by Chaplin's 'modern times' metro-
nome; he can't unwind or slow down and his leisure is as taxing as
his work day." Thus, normative requirements for one context become a trained incapacity when transferred to other contexts.

Though Salz (1955:98–100) reminds us that work time is an all
pervading, ever-pressing demand upon agrarian society, it is quite
different from timing by the machine. Festivals and personal events
such as weddings occupy over a third of the year and are bunched
in large blocks of time. Further, work has a diverse set of cycles,
which is shaped by seasons and by the materials of the craft and
agricultural practice. In short, work is embedded in the social life of
the community, rather than being the routine of individual members.

James West's (1945:100) 1939 study of "Plainville," a small town in
the midwestern United States, provides a representative description:

*Hence his [merchant's] long hours (often from 7 A.M. to 10 P.M.)
are more pleasurable than tiresome. In fact, the great distinctive
characteristics of rural work, contrasted with most urban work,
are these: (1) the great variety in rural tasks; (2) the individual
control of speed with which they are performed; (3) the freedom
of the worker's mind from "racket" (noise), overseers, and the
tedium of strict, enforced, unsociable cooperation with other
workers. Rural group work is, of course, highly social, but most
rural work is done alone, or with a child "follering" (looking on).
The solitary worker's mind is free to roam, dream, scheme. (4)
The immediate, personally understood, and simple relationships
between work and livelihood.*

*These characteristics of rural work apply particularly to farmers,
but they also apply to small-town businessmen. It is perhaps
significant that while many Plainvillers were heard to complain
of distasteful individual tasks, of having to work "too hard," and
of poor rewards for their work, no adult was heard to express
general distaste for his work.*

Studies of agrarian communities, then, suggest that work-nonwork
cycles are more a means of enhancing social relations than being a
result of "economic" people driven by pure gain.

It is equally important to note that scarcity in the usual economic
sense is *not* a grinding reality that all humans are born with. Indeed,
peoples sharing the fruits of Western culture seem to be those most
blessed by the rewards of scarcity. As Alfred McClung Lee (1966:75)
notes: "One of the most striking cross-cultural regularities yet dis-
covered is the almost universal practice of voluntary food sharing
among small-scale hunter-gatherers." He argues that such a norm
maintains the subsistence organizational pattern by tending to keep
food inventories at a minimum and maintaining minimal differences
in wealth between persons.

Karl Polanyi (1947:112) notes:

*Aristotle was right: man is not an economic, but a social being.
He does not aim at safeguarding his individual interest in the
acquisition of material possessions, but rather at ensuring social
good-will, social status, social assets. He values possessions
primarily as a means to that end. His incentives are of that
"mixed" character which we associate with the endeavor to gain
social approval—productive efforts are no more than incidental
to this. Man's economy is, as a rule, submerged in his social
relations. The change from this to a society which was, on the
contrary, submerged in the economic system was an entirely
novel development.*

Polanyi also cites a variety of ethnographic studies to indicate
that sharing was a norm in nonindustrial societies, and that, unlike
in industrial societies, the love for gain has never been the "impulse
to work." Polanyi (1947:113) argues that no social order other than
our own has made such an "unnatural" claim upon man.

*Incentives spring from a large variety of sources, such as custom
and tradition, public duty and private commitment, religious
observance and political allegiance, judicial obligation and
administrative regulation as established by prince, municipality,
or guild. Rank and status, compulsion of law and threat of*

punishment, public praise and private reputation, insure that the individual contributes his share to production.

There is face validity in Polanyi's argument concerning the much wider range of motivational symbols and social mechanisms available for administering sanctions than the starvation hypothesis offered by those who celebrate the market society. But we would argue that those other motives *are still* operative in industrial society. However, the sheer amount of time devoted to work and the celebration of its fruits tend to obscure these other motivational systems. Thus in considering our polar opposites of hunter-gatherer and industrial (market) economies, it seemed clear that the social organization of work and nonwork did not change. According to Salz (1955:96) "work is intentionally sober and unadorned activity related to the execution of a task or project." That is, work is universally a necessary task that engages social persons; there are sets of socially approved means for accomplishing the task, the rewards of accomplishment are clear, and "women's work" remains closer to home than does that of males (indeed the "commuting times of hunter-gatherers are probably greater than those of suburbanites carrying out their predation in urban centers).

Nonwork is the primary focus where social relations are created and maintained. It engages social groups; there are distinctive sets of rules, roles, and rituals that direct behavior; and the rewards are expressive rather than material and, therefore, richer in meaning though less tangible of use. As in work, males are likely to be more free ranging than are females. The emphasis, in hunter-gatherer societies, on sharing is not unlike the rights and obligations prevailing among kinship units in modern society. Certainly the need for sharing, appreciative gestures, and communion in nonwork situations remains.

The multinational time-budget survey (Szalai, 1966; 1972), for all its methodological limitations, provides our one best look at the uniformity of certain uses of time, despite great differences in level of industrial development and cultural patterning. Thus, the working time of whole populations (employed-unemployed, married-unmarried, male-female) from the 13 surveys ranges from a high of 5.8 hours in Bulgaria to a low of 3.7 hours nationwide in the West German Federal Republic. The trend in these data suggests that nations in the early stages of industrialization have more of the population working longer.

Yet the differences are not all that great; the similarities are far more striking. Time spent on the journey to work ranges from a low of 0.3 hours in Germany and the U.S.A. to a high of 0.7 hours in Bulgaria and Hungary. While housework obligations range from 2.6

hours in Bulgaria to 4.8 hours in Yugoslavia. Attention to physiological needs ranges from 9.2 hours in the USSR to 10.8 in France. The general uses of leisure time also seem remarkably similar, with Russians devoting slightly more time to educational pursuits, Americans to organizational activities and nonwork trips, Bulgarians to spectacles, and Germans to sports. But overall, when viewing these data as indices of a nation's value preference or necessity constraint, what is remarkable is the close uniformity in time budgets.

In terms of specific activities, the magnitude of difference is much greater; but even here this largely reflects access rather than strong cultural differences. Thus, far higher proportions of Americans watch television and spend more time viewing than people in other nations. A higher proportion of Russian males have reading as a primary activity than is the case for other nations. Interestingly, the proportion of males who read is greater than of females in all nations except the United States. This apparent cultural difference is balanced by the fact that employed, married Americans and Bulgarian males spend over one-half of their time alone, which is considerably more time than their counterparts in other nations spend alone; and further, American and Bulgarian males spend the least amount of their time with spouse and family.

While in all societies women, whether employed or not, married or not, with or without children, have more time alone than do men. And unmarried, unemployed women without children have the most time alone, ranging from 12.8 hours in Czechoslovakia to 16.8 hours in Bulgaria. Although all employed, married males spend a considerable and similar amount of time at or around home, they are not nearly as locale bound as employed, married women and are home far less than the 20 or better hours logged at home by nonemployed married women.

Indeed such patterns are not unlike those found in Murdock's (1949) detailed cross-cultural study, in which he reports:

> *A study of the distribution of economic activities between the sexes in 224 tribes scattered throughout the world has revealed that the tasks assigned to women in more than 75 percent of the societies with relevant information are grain grinding, water carrying, cooking, the gathering of fuel and vegetable products, the manufacture and repair of clothing, the preservation of meat and fish, pottery making, weaving, and the manufacture of mats and baskets. It will be noted that most of these tasks can be carried on in the house or its immediate vicinity, and that none of them requires an intimate knowledge of the tribal terrain. The tasks assigned to men in more than 75 percent of the sample societies, however, include the following: herding (84%), fishing*

*(86%), lumbering (92%), trapping (95%), mining and quarrying
(95%), hunting (98%), and the catching of sea mammals (99%).
All of these activities, as well as the characteristically masculine
pursuits of war, carry the men far from the dwelling and demand
a thorough knowledge of the environs of the community and of
the location of all its usable resources.*

Thus there is a seeming universality of locales where time is
spent; men, whether in tribal or modern society, are more free ranging than women. Yet the multinational time-budget study (Szalai,
1966) indicates that even males spend the bulk of their 24 hours
either at home or at their place of work. The American city sample
for employed, married males is representative—13.7 hours are spent
around the home, 6.5 are spent at the work place, 1.7 in streets and
parks, 0.8 at business places, 0.6 in restaurant and indoor leisure
places, and 0.5 in another's home.

The multinational study provides useful support for our contention that gender is an important determinant of leisure behavior.
Women—whether in hunter-gatherer or industrial societies, com-
munist or capitalist societies, rich or poor societies—consistently
have different work-nonwork patterns and different locales and patterns of work-nonwork cycles. But when viewed with the ethnographic studies, the multinational data clearly suggest that the nonwork realm is most significant in maintaining the intragroup bond.
And regardless of the complexity, size, or density of a society, this
pattern remains consistent. Indeed, these sets of data give us more
confidence in our inference that the intragroup bond formed in nonwork activities is essential for maintaining the larger intergroup
solidarity.

SUMMARY

We began this chapter with the notion that time was a node
where biological and social elements interpenetrate. As such the distribution and allocation of time was seen to reflect both the variant
and invariant properties of our species. To follow out our ideas we
looked at a variety of cultures and economies. We gave most attention to hunter-gatherer societies, for they represent the predominant
organizational form for the largest share of *Homo sapiens'* history.
The adaptive success of hunter-gatherer groups, the shape of their
work-nonwork cycles, and their ability to respond to transactions
between trophic levels are patterns often overlooked or obscured
by those building a rationale for high-energy market societies.

Because their wants are low and relatively easily met, hunter-
gatherer societies have large amounts of nonwork time, they have a

universal tradition of sharing, which minimizes hierarchical differences, the rhythms of work-nonwork are tightly bound to the given ecosystem that is being exploited, and gender and age are the major discriminants as to the work-nonwork cycles and behaviors. We argued that the higher material standards of agrarian and industrial societies mean more complex systems, which requires that much of nonwork time be devoted to maintaining the system.[3] But we also suggested that the fundamental patterns found in hunter-gatherer groups continue to exist in the more complex social orders, and that nonwork is consistently the arena where the intimate bonds are established and maintained.

The next chapter will deal with the behavioral continuities of nonwork associated with elemental variables—such as age, gender, and number—and primary associations—such as kin and friends.

---

[3]Alfred McClung Lee (1967) has a convincing argument that workers in the 1960s have no more free time than did workers in the 1850s. Modern workers have less on-the-job time but more work at home, more moonlighting work, and spend more time in work-related travel.

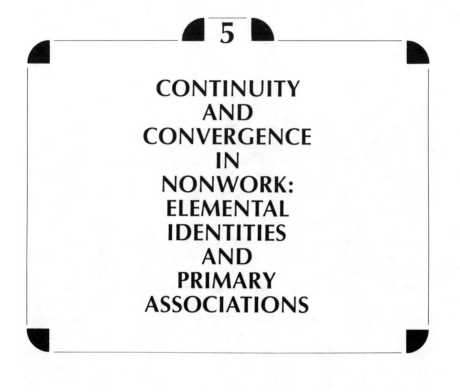

5

CONTINUITY AND CONVERGENCE IN NONWORK: ELEMENTAL IDENTITIES AND PRIMARY ASSOCIATIONS

The first four chapters have dealt with fairly large-scale aspects of social life—nonwork regularities in industrial society; class, status, and occupational groupings; variations in political economy. In this chapter we want to remain at the elemental and intimate level, where most of us conduct our daily lives. We will do this in two parts. The first part will be primarily conceptual and will examine how biological factors such as age, gender, and number serve as both elemental and symbolic elements in social life. We argue that these elemental factors are essential to understanding the emergence and continuation of certain group forms. We suggest there are certain important continuities between nonhuman and human primate groups. There are, also, certain important differences when we reexamine the meaning of social age in human life and the unique influence played by nonwork in sustaining human social unity. The second part of this chapter draws upon the perspective of the first point to analyze the relation among nonwork behavior, the elemental identities of age, gender, and number, and the primary associations of peers, friends, and kinship.

AN OUTLINE OF SOME CONCEPTUAL ISSUES

Among all living things certain, apparently universal phases of change can be recognized. Scientists, as well as poets and ordinary folk, note that a cycle of birth, development, maturity, senescence, and death is common to all living matter. Within human cultures elaborate symbolization develops to both demarcate and make sacred certain stages of the process. No human society is devoid of rituals associated with this universal process (see Chapter 8). These rituals are cultural mechanisms that teach individuals the appropriate behavior for dealing with the biological events of birth, maturity, and death. Therefore, the study of this training, or socialization— that is, the social processes by which an individual becomes a social person—is essential for understanding how human societies persist. As mentioned earlier there is considerable evidence that nonwork activities constitute important aspects of this process.

Grammarians employ the terms of person, number, and gender as analytical tools for formulating certain aspects of the structure of a language. Irrespective of the particular language being analyzed, these elements are examined. Not all languages share the same characteristic form or structural relations among these elements, but usually the grammarian is able to identify some of these expected relationships. The importance of these and other aspects of languages have been the object of recent attention among linguists, although earlier efforts (Whorf, 1956) are of considerable and enduring interest.

Every body of knowledge develops a concern for certain basic or fundamental aspects of the relevant phenomenon under study. Sometimes these are the basic conceptual terms appropriate to an inquiry. For example, Parsons (1951) suggests that the basic structural unit for social action theory is the social role. We have suggested that for the sociological study of human leisure it is imperative to recognize the differences among an individual, a social person, and a social group; while age, gender, and number are our elemental equivalents of the grammarian's analytic tools.

Age

The process through which living matter proceeds is similarly elemental, or basic, to both biological and sociological concerns. As singular organisms, each moves through the basic process characteristic of all living matter. Each of these stages of the process is mirrored physiologically in such a manner that conspecifics can recognize at which stage an individual is. Their basic observation is recognized as the elemental social fact of age. Thus each individual in a social group is of a particular age, in whatever way this may be symbolized in a particular culture. But age is not a finite concept, anymore than time is. It can be symbolized in numerous ways, some of which we will consider below. The main point is that while age has a biological component its meaning is an inherently sociological construct.

Gender

Every species that reproduces sexually has evolved two basic sexual types. Genetically each is necessary for the reproduction of new individuals of the species. Although we ordinarily expect such differences to be manifest in the physiological characteristics of individuals, this is not always apparent throughout the phylogenetic scale. For example, while secondary sexual characteristics usually make such identifications possible, plumage and pelage are not sure indices. Thus sexual identity in its biological aspects is usually recognizable among individuals. One is either physiologically equipped as a female or as a male. The presence of culture as a primary mode of species adaptation to its environment tends however to complicate the matter. Sexual identity becomes no longer a matter of anatomical configuration, but a matter of cultural definition. The matter of sexual identity is quite complex, as demonstrated by Garfinkel (1967) and others who have studied sex changes among *Homo sapiens*. However, regardless of these important nuances, as far as is known no human culture systematically defines all biologically constituted male individuals as social females or vice versa. Thus in most human societies, biological and cultural sexual identities are covariant elemental properties. The difference is that biological capacities are insufficient among many primates for complete social recognition of a particular gender. In other words, while sexual identity, like age, has a biological component, its reality in human societies emerges only through its social component. Like age, every individual member of a social group is also the possessor of a sexual identity.

Number

Social groups, as collectives of individuals, possess a characteristic that can best be described as number. It is an elemental factor that has clear implications for the mathematical opportunities of the formation of social bonds among individual members, other things being equal. However since, empirically, other things are not usually equal, the mathematically ideal configuration will be modified, either to a greater or lesser number (Cohen, 1971). The recognition of the importance of number has a long history in social science. Within industrial sociology, the concept of span of control is based upon the elemental variable, number. This conception presumes, quite incorrectly as later research has shown, that there is only a very small and limited number of other individuals with whom an individual can continually interact and maintain a desired level of efficiency. In short, the implication is that, as a biological entity, an individual *Homo sapiens* possesses a limited capacity for sustained interactions. If this were accurate, then social groups would be rather limited in terms of numbers. Among primates, there appears to be an approximate limitation of 40 to 50 individuals. Once a group reaches this number, it bifurcates. However, with culture as the *primary* adaptive mechanism, humans relate through symbols, and, therefore, collective unity is freed from the need for continual face-to-face contact. This considerably expands the potential group size. Thus, as Tiger and Fox (1971:34) report, numerous tribes numbered between one and five thousand individuals, who recognized each other as conspecifics in both the biological and cultural sense of the term.

In general, we are proposing that for the study of social groups, as defined herein, we begin by examining the form of such groups as defined through the elemental variables of age, sex, and number. We require some further specification of these variables, which will be considered below. Prior to that we need to consider some of the general aspects of the analysis we are proposing.

ELEMENTAL IDENTITIES AND SOCIAL GROUPS

Within sociological thought, there are perhaps few terms that evoke as much discussion and confusion as some of the ideas of Georg Simmel. Yet Simmel's analysis of the dyad and triad, his principle of *tertius gaudens*, and his eloquent analysis of secrecy provide the theoretical basis for much contemporary work on social groups. Perhaps his most difficult concept to grasp is his distinction between formal sociology and historical sociology. The confusion arises, in part, because Simmel fails to define "form" in any specific sense. Thus to understand a societal form as Simmel intended it, one must examine his illustrations. For example, sociation, or the interaction occurring between two individuals, was a pure form in Simmel's terms. One special case of sociation was superordination-subordination (Simmel, 1950). Within this form, its content may vary. Although Simmel was perhaps not as concise as those who followed him would have liked, he was, in our opinion, directing attention to what now appears to be a rather fundamental matter—that is, culture varies considerably over time. Its content may undergo substantial change within a generation. Ogburn's (1922) "cultural lag" hypothesis illustrates this nicely as have the studies of innovation (Katz, 1961). Although content may vary, the essential societal forms within which individuals interact tend to remain constant or, comparatively speaking, vary over much longer time cycles. While Simmel pointed the way, his insights seem to have fallen upon infertile ground. Yet with the recent emergence of appreciation among some sociologists of the ethological perspective, Simmel's perspectives may enjoy new significance. For example, Goffman (1971) has recently proposed that there are certain regularities of behavior that always occur between "participating units," regardless of other conditions. Goffman (1971:21) notes:

It should be borne in mind that—at one level at least—social settings and social occasions are not organized in terms of individuals but in terms of participating units.

True to the intent of Simmel, Goffman (1971:22) continues:

> . . . however, since it is often the case that an individual is qualified to participate in either unit . . . we often neglect to appreciate that rules at two different levels are involved, one regarding allowable units and a second regarding who is allowed in the unit. (emphasis added)

Our suggestions regarding the social organization of work and non-work attempt to acknowledge this important distinction.

Although Simmel does not refer directly to the biologically based characteristics of much social behavior, his considerable attention to such topics as domination and sociability are quite germane to any current concerns. In short, we are suggesting that additional insights into the study of social groups may be obtained by a closer examination of patterns of social behavior that are characteristic of the species per se.

PRIMATE SOCIAL SYSTEMS—AN ILLUSTRATION

As the number of studies of free-ranging primates have increased, particularly during the past fifteen years, previously accepted theories of primate social organization have been substantially revised (DeVore, 1965; Jay, 1968). Perhaps the most important contribution such studies have made is the opportunity for comparisons of social organizations across several species. From such comparisons it is possible to isolate characteristic features common to all. Since *Homo sapiens* is also a primate, it is unlikely that it does not also share, in some way, many of these features. Several aspects are worth noting. First, for primates the social group becomes a major building block of social organization (Tiger and Fox, 1971:31). The ability to form social bonds among individuals that persist over a lifetime is a basic mechanism for species survival. As Tiger and Fox suggest, unlike ungulates, which depend upon speed for escaping danger in whatever form, primates seem to have evolved into group-forming animals, using numbers and social bonds among individuals and groups to accomplish similar objectives. Second, the "attention" structure among primates, as demonstrated by Crook (1970), seems to also be quite important for people. Finally, it is worth observing as a general point that there exists in all primate social systems certain forms based upon the elemental variables we have previously discussed. How these variables are interrelated will be seen to be particularly important for the study of human leisure. The appearance of culture as an adaptive mechanism for the species, when combined with the basic common social organizational properties shared among all primates, helps explain the apparent rapid rise of Homo sapiens.

Unlike many species, the primates tend to associate year around in relatively closed groups. What appears unique is that these groups include both sexes. Although Solly Zuckerman's (1932) notorious observations regarding baboon behavior in the London zoo were interpreted to mean that it was continual sexual availability that accounted for grouping in primates, it now appears males and females are intrigued by one another only at certain times. This suggests that the social bonds that develop among males and females in primate groups do so only partially on erotic grounds. A final common characteristic of primate groups is that protection of mother-child units is a full-time function of males. In short, we can observe specialization of function among primates to a degree not noticed elsewhere in the phylogenetic scale.

To summarize, there are an increasing number of studies of primate social behavior that make it possible to compare various social forms common to all. The particular advantage of this comparison for the understanding of human social orders is an increased ability to more accurately differentiate aspects of social organization that are particularly bound up with culture from those bound to biosocial factors. While Homo sapiens share many common social forms with other primates, it is clear that a culture comprised of symbols has enabled the emergence of an important variation of social interaction. The basis for this, as will be detailed in the following chapter, is that primates relate to one another as individuals, whereas human beings relate to each other as members of symbolic classes of social beings. In short, as far as we can now tell, there are no social persons among other primate species. With this in mind, we want to reexamine the elemental variable of social age.

SOCIAL AGE REEXAMINED

There is a large amount of social science literature regarding aspects of human social development. In particular the literature in developmental psychology complemented by work in psychoanalysis and orthopsychiatry has stressed the importance of stages of social development. Piaget has produced a substantial contribution to our understanding of the social development of early childhood. There is however another aspect of age that we wish to emphasize. We call it social age.

Cheek (1972:4) discusses social age in the following manner:

Among many species recognition of a particular social status within a social grouping is necessary for certain behavior to occur

> among conspecifics. Thus, among many primate species, clear
> social distinctions exist among infants, juveniles, subadults, and
> adults with respect to the individual's appropriateness as a play-
> mate, hunting partner, warrior, copulatory partner, parent, and
> so on. This general pattern also appears to be characteristic of
> Homo sapiens. Thus, while most individuals are capable of
> reproduction from puberty onward, they are not defined as
> potential marriage partners until some years later. In short, human
> aging, while continuous as with most other forms of life, is
> experienced by many individuals as discontinuous. Particular
> segments of the continuous process tend to take on differential
> social meanings, symbols, and significance for both the individual
> and the larger group.

For the present discussion of social age it is useful to add an additional category—mature adult. A characterization of each of these
categories will follow shortly.

As is apparent from earlier discussion, social age is essentially an
imputation of meaning to a chronological age of a particular individual. Recognition of the appropriate chronological age is based
upon characteristic biological and physiological transformations experienced during life. There are changes in the appearance of secondary sexual characteristics, variations in muscle tonus, changes in
overall stature, variations in dentition, changes in pelage—both
quantitatively and in the coloration. These variations are often the
features that enable a conspecific to quickly structure cultural expectations of the way in which social interactions will proceed. Indeed, within a given culture, knowledge of others' social age and
sex enable ego to most accurately predict how a transaction may
proceed without any other information being initially available. Of
course, the manner in which symbolization of age occurs varies
among life-styles, and this information is also available to participants, which enables even more accurate expectations to be formu-
lated.

The social age categories suggested below tend to follow those
utilized among ethologists and some wildlife management specialists. Thus an *infant* is any human individual from birth to about 6
years of age. This is the period of great physiological dependency
upon conspecifics when much of basic character structure is being
laid down. A *juvenile* is between 7 and 17 years of age. Great physiological changes occur in both sexes during this period, but of most
importance is the long period of social dependency during which
individuals learn how to perform social roles and begin the formation of social personages that will endure for the remainder of their
lives. *Subadults* are individuals between 18 and 24 years of age. They

are capable of leaving their families of orientation and establishing families of procreation. Many individuals are completing education, beginning work careers, and selecting marriage partners during this segment of their lives. In the segment of 25 to 49 years of age, most individuals are recognized as *adults*. Most individuals (about 73 percent of both males and females) have begun a marriage or other relatively enduring association by the age of 25. Many have commenced child-rearing. Employment opportunities and patterns begin to stabilize for heads of households. Throughout this period, the social structural forces of work histories and child-rearing are the dominant determinants for most individuals. Around the age of 50 years, another segment begins. This is the social age category of *mature adult*. It is characterized by the termination of direct child-rearing responsibilities (for many individuals) except as grandparents, the culmination of work histories, and the establishment of new behavior patterns based upon differing social structural forces. Taken together these five categories describe the elemental social ages of human social orders. Within various cultures, the related symbols attached to particular chronological ages will vary. But in most societies we can recognize these overall sociological distinctions in the life process of the species.

ELEMENTAL VARIABLES RECONSIDERED

Thus far we have detailed several aspects of the human social order that are particularly important for the analysis of the social organization of work and nonwork. In particular, we have clarified the importance of social age as a necessary characteristic for a participant in a particular social form—that is, "work" or "nonwork." We have also considered the importance of sex and number as related to the formation of human social groups. It remains to consider why nonwork settings may be particularly conducive to such investigations.

Talcott Parsons (1942) described in detail how age and sex acted as conditions within the social structure of an industrialized society. Although his essay was written three decades ago, it retains valuable insights into how these elemental variables become transformed in the formation of social persons. Parsons (1942:613) cogent depiction of the masculine role is instructive:

The masculine role at the same time is itself by no means devoid of corresponding elements of strain. It carries with it to be sure the primary prestige of achievement, responsibility and authority. By comparison with the role of youth culture, however, there are at least two important types of limitations. In the first place, the modern occupational system has led to increasing specialization of role. The job absorbs an extraordinarily large proportion of the individual's energy and emotional interests in a role the content of which is often relatively narrow. This in particular restricts the area within which he can share common interests and experiences with others not in the same occupational specialty. *It is perhaps of considerable significance that so many of the highest prestige statuses of our society are of this specialized character. There is in the definition of roles* little to bind the individual to others in his community on a comparable status level. *By contrast with this situation, it is notable that in the youth culture* common human elements are far more strongly emphasized. *(emphasis added)*

No more cogent portrayal of the differences between social persons and individuals exists in the sociological literature. But of even greater significance is the implication that the worlds of work and nonwork may indeed be at least coequal for the understanding of human societies. For, as suggested above, it is communion not power that binds the social fabric of nonwork. It is to a further examination of the nature of social bonding that we now turn.

NONWORK AND THE
BONDING OF PRIMARY ASSOCIATIONS

We have outlined a perspective for considering age, gender, and number as elemental factors in shaping social life and corresponding nonwork activity. We have argued that communion not power is crucial in nonwork spheres of action. In the remaining pages we will examine the blending between nonwork, the elemental identities, and those fundamental social units that manage the elemental identities and that are the primary vehicles of communion.

Our concern with communion differs from the traditional analytic distinction between work and nonwork. As we outlined in Chapter 3, the traditional perspective views the nature of work, its rewards in wealth and prestige, and its social structure as the antecedents of a life-style. And yet we found that many of the traditional variables did not really account for much of the observed variance. Indeed it was not until we looked at level of educational attainment—a factor which is antecedent to type of work—that we found regular predictive capability.

We also explored in Chapter 3 how certain universal characteristics of blue-collar culture *shape* the meaning of work; and we found that certain occupational groups, such as academics and printers, had a life-style that spilled over into their work. Indeed we began to see what elites and many subordinate groups—women, blacks, and hippies—have known all along; that often style of life determines occupation. Our membership in human groups[1]—extended kin, peers, and social circles—largely set the occupational pattern we follow.

That is, we see the findings reported in most of the sociology of work literature as demonstrating a reciprocal process between work and nonwork. And this process suggests a much more complex and much different causal connection than the usual interpretation that the nature of nonwork is totally dependent upon the nature of work. We suspect that the reciprocal connections are passed over in most academic analyses because, as we noted in Chapter 3, work and nonwork for professors are so intertwined, it is difficult for the academic not to think that work is very important. This faith in the importance of work seems to hold even when the social scientist investigates developing societies that do not have a middle class or upward mobility aspirations, or deferred gratification patterns. In short, the constituent elements of an academic work ethic are missing. However, the consultant, with little hesitation, often ends by prescribing a set of educational programs and economic motivations most familiar to the consultant's own biography of social climbing.

As Lipset and Bendix (1959:197–198) note:

Much of the data presented in this and other studies of social mobility has dealt with the effect of family background on the occupational and social placement of individuals. The evidence indicates that educational attainment is a major determinant of career patterns, a fact which provides the strongest and most direct statistical link between family background and the assets and liabilities with which individuals enter the labor market. . . . If an individual comes from a working class family, he will typically receive little education or vocational advice; while he attends school his job plans for the future will be vague and when he leaves school he is likely to take the first available job which he can find. Thus, the poverty, lack of education, absence of personal "contacts," lack of planning, and failure to explore fully the available job opportunities that characterize the working-class family are handed down from generation to generation. The same cumulation of factors, which in the working class creates a series of mounting disadvantages works to the advantage of a child coming from a well-to-do family.

---

[1] The ensuing analysis is an extension and continuation of the primary group idea raised by Cooley (1909) and systematically analyzed by Homans (1950). We refer the reader to these original sources for the necessary grounding in assumptions and approach.

On the other hand, Kohn (1969:201) notes:

> The influences of the family have temporal priority and have commonly been viewed as predominant in importance. Our data argue otherwise, suggesting that where there is conflict between early family experience and later occupational conditions, the latter are likely to prevail. The more important point, though, is that early family and later occupational experiences seldom conflict. No matter how dramatic the exceptions, it is usual that that families prepare their offspring for the world as they know it and that the conditions of life eventually faced by the offspring are not very different from those for which they have been prepared.

It is clear that in spite of their difference of interpretation, these students, though giving primacy to work, emphasize that it is a reciprocal part of a person's entire social network. As we noted in Chapter 3, working-class culture quite logically views work more as a means for conducting a particular life-style. One's esteem among age-mates, friends, and family is far more important than the status issues of the upper crust. Thus family socialization, education, and so forth are not in preparation for a job and social mobility, but for the rights and obligations involved in the maintenance of primary associations. Work is a necessary means for furthering these more important issues. Such a perspective seems essential if we are to account for the consistently inconsistent associations between occupation, socioeconomic status, social class, and nonwork activity. The associations are weak or nonexistent because they occur in quite distinct social spheres and perform quite distinctly different social functions (we will discuss this in more detail in Chapter 8).

Let us emphasize that we are *not* treating work as unimportant in human affairs. We are fully aware that issues of utility start and stop the entire society; and in industrial societies, the scheduling of work is even more tightly routinized and throws a wider net over the timing of all activities. However, in nonindustrial societies, the rising and setting of the sun and the phases of the moon, rather than corporate clocks, start and stop the social routines; yet seldom do social scientists treat such celestial events as meaningful social causes.

SOCIAL AGE AND NONWORK PATTERNS

The play of infants and children seems the purest form of an activity entire of itself. Yet from the Schiller-Spencer surplus energy theory of the nineteenth century to the latest ethological report on the adaptive value of play forms, theorists have been reluctant to leave play as an autistic, self-contained activity. Play must be assigned its utilitarian function and not left in the hands of the players. And in this we are no different from the rest; we believe that play offers important clues about social life. Harlow and his associates in a long series of significant studies have found important links between play and adaptive socialization for primates:

> *Merely noting the manner in which a monkey plays in a social situation can tell us the approximate age, sex, social position on the dominance scale, and rearing history of the animal, as well as permit us to make a fair prediction of a young monkey's future social capability and status, adequacy as a mother or father, and the likelihood of developing abnormal behavior patterns. (Suomi and Harlow, 1971:72)*

Dolhinow (1971:70) reports that play is essential in training for survival, for learning from the environment, and as a way of maintaining long-term social relations:

> *Play is one of the most important factors in the establishment of social relationships that last a life time. The nonhuman primate is born into the highly structured social context of the group and the specific relationships its mother has with the group.*

Yet of most significance is her finding that for adult monkeys, and especially adult males, playful behavior drops out of the repertoire. She speculates that physical damage from the rough-and-tumble of play, the general sensitivity to violation of personal space, and the difficulty of discriminating playful from aggressive cues account for the disappearance of playful behavior.

Of most interest to us is Dolhinow's (1971:71) more basic explanation:

> *The learning activities of play, so important for the infant and juvenile, are no longer necessary for the adult. Presumably, by the time the individual has matured, it has mastered the skills it will need, learned the land it occupies, established its social relationships, and become coordinated motorically. Major forms of adult behavior are established and relatively immutable.*

Thus combining these ideas with those of Roberts (1962), and Avedon and Sutton-Smith (1971), we begin to see why *Homo sapiens* continue to play for a longer period of time and why there are variations between cultural groups.[2] Man has a longer period of existence and has a more dense cluster of meanings because there are a greater range of social roles at each of these important turning points in the life-style.

Of course, this relative density varies from culture to culture, one with a division of labor largely based upon age grade and gender will have a more fixed range than a highly complex urban-agrarian culture. Thus problems of career change, occupational alteration, the last child leaving home, retirement, and so forth require an extended attitude of playfulness throughout the life-cycle. For play is not unlike the role Kenneth Burke (1937) attributes to the comic stance where we use humor and laughter to test the prevailing institutional structure and the performance of incumbents in positions of authority.

It is interesting that scholars such as Loizos (1966), who emphasize the instinctivist position, should first ponder that animals do not need play for "practice" to fulfill adult roles. As she (1966:518) notes, "there is no reason why the animal should not just practice." Yet Loizos (1966:522) then identifies the strong element of ritualization in play and ends by noting: "It is suggested that the most likely area in which the precise differences between play and other forms of ritualized behavior will be isolated is that of relative rigidity in the ordering of the sequence." Thus it would seem that the author provides her own reason as to why animals do not simply practice and why some adult mammals continue to play.

Nonwork seems to involve a set-apart time-space arena of action, where failure in role performance is expected and where the rigidities of sequence can be played with as the individual organism attempts to fit its uniqueness to the social and physical constraints associated with its future role. The value of play is precisely this freedom to explore, to "play" with the anticipated gestures and rules of conduct. Such adaptive flux may permit exploring alternative ways of dealing with the social and ecological environment that ultimately becomes an essential strategy in the survival of a social species, and especially the higher mammals. For if the environment exerts a dynamic force of relatively constant change, then species whose responses are ritualized, but without social mechanisms for safely exploring alternative patterns of adaptation, will fail to survive.

Indeed play may be a partial explanation of the diversity of primate social structures observed by Aldrich-Blake (1970), Crook (1970), and others. Since these variations are not accounted for by physiological, genetic, or environmental variations, it may be that

---

[2]We will have a more detailed discussion of play, games and sport in Chapter Nine.

there is a broad range of possible social structures that are equally adaptable, and the lottery of playfulness decides which will become the normative direction. The research on the higher nonhuman primates, which suggests that play with peers and with older or younger conspecifics is essential for later successful adult performance, also illustrates the open-ended characteristic of play. That is, the utility function of play seems to be at its maximum when it is most afunctional. It would seem that "a continuous process of social learning arising from the pattern of interaction within groups" (Crook, 1970: 154), is an adaptive order where neophytes are required to accept a time-space realm of playful error which cannot be functionally evaluated if the program is to "take."[3]

In sum, the inevitable dynamics of society intersect with life cycle events such that the social being is temporarily released from the fixed social and environmental constraints that it will deal with when it actually assumes those future roles. Thus play permits exploration and may induce innovation into the wider collective response. As such, play can share both the fluctuations of fashion and the rigidity of concern over ensuing the permanence of its attendant rules and rituals.

LIFE CYCLE AND
CONSISTENCY IN NONWORK PATTERNS

However, we should not be led into the delusion that play is the work of children, and, thereby, force it into a familiar instrumental perspective. Play is a certain set of bounded social relations. The impetus may or may not spring from within the individual organism, due to instincts of play, creative impulses, or the need to discharge energy. What should be of interest are not matters of organic whimsy but the consistency of certain social patterns.

We are not surprised that Wylie (1953:233) found that "the great majority of the families have few interests in common with other families." Or that Schmitz-Scherzer (1972) found little variance explained by age, sex, education, and family status. Or that MacDonald, McGuire, and Havighurst (1949:519) found "systematic class differences in participation." Or that Noe's (1970) analysis of 78 nonindustrial cultures found little age and gender differences for the participation types of leisure he identified.

What does interest us is that some of the MacDonald, McGuire, and Havighurst (1949) sample do learn middle-class patterns from their peers. And that MacDonald and Havighurst (1959) find that

---

[3]See Schmitz-Scherzer and Bierhoff (1974) and others on intentional playgrounds and why adult conceptions often fail to be realized in children's play.

quite different nonwork activities provide identical meanings and these meanings remain stable regardless of variation in class, gender, and so forth. Also, Wylie (1953) did find *some* activities of high interfamily consistency; over 75 percent of his sample of families went for automobile rides, picnicked, and attended motion pictures. While Schmitz-Scherzer (1972) found that reading had a high loading on the educational factor (17.03) and moviegoing had a high loading on the age factor (41.99). That is, much of the reading is by the older and better educated, while much of the moviegoing is by the younger and therefore less educated. And finally Noe (1970) finds that adult and adolescent females have a much more work-dominated aspect than do their male counterparts.

Each of these studies suggests that there are some things one does with age peers or that are shared by all in an age aggregate (Shanas, et al. 1968; Drake, 1958; Polsky, 1967; Harris, 1943; Fox, 1934), there are some things done in single-sex associations (Leevy, 1950; Roth and Newark, 1958; Moore, 1961; Booth, 1972), and finally there are some things that one does with one's parents, spouse, children, and other kin (Litwak and Szelenyi, 1969; Booth, 1972; Cunningham and Johannis, 1960). And these patterns are further crosscut by the biological and cultural intersection that shapes the life cycle.

For example, Cressman (1937) used a detailed checklist of activities and diaries kept by children in the 7th, 8th, and 9th grades. After a variety of analyses, he found relatively little difference in terms of SES and IQ measures and the frequency and type of nonwork activity. Robinson (1936) eagerly tried to find support for the reformist sociological theories of his day. Yet regardless of his wishes to improve the leisure standards of his sample of second-generation, lower social-status children, their behavior reflects a consistency of nonwork activity not unlike their age-mates in higher social strata. Cramer (1950), for example, studied a group of economically privileged children, 6 to 14 years of age. Compared to studies of less privileged children, he found some higher participation in cultural activities and participation in organized activities such as Boy Scouts. Still, for these privileged children, the amount of time spent with parents, reading comics, listening to the radio, and so forth was very similar to that of their less privileged age-mates. Apparently there are some things one does with certain persons at certain times, regardless of class variation.

In their youth, the present 1970s middle management, middle-aged persons may have read the "better" passages of *Tobacco Road* by flashlight in bed or Captain Vengeance comics in the attic; and although these were important personal events and were likely done alone, they were always suggested by and shared with one's peers and always kept as a secret from adults. While today, significant increases in exotic drug use among secondary school youths seem most often to occur after the friendly policeman's helpful, illustrated lecture on the evils of drugs. Indeed, there seem to be certain nonwork activities whose element of deviation is fondly held by particular age peers, with parental influence having reinforcing but little inhibiting, influence upon the activity (Hollingshead, 1949; Coleman, 1961; Slocum, 1963; Kandel, 1973). As Simmel (1957) noted, fashion is the attempt to conform to the visible norms of our peers through slight individual differentiation.

There are life cycle moments, turning points as Anselm Strauss (1959) calls them, when it is appropriate, even pleasant, to take a family drive in the country; and yet these same pleasurable activities suddenly become totally inappropriate when one turns 16. James and Moore's (1940) study of a British working-class district found that by age 14 there is a shift from school to work, and the attendant release from domestic duties and the rejection of children's play; while at 16 there is the dramatic shift from most leisure involving single-sex groups to most leisure involving mixed-sex groups. It seems significant that a similar study 20 years later finds similar patterns (Crichton, James, and Wakeford, 1962). The prospect of marriage still dominates the girls' use of leisure. With increase in age there is a shift from sex homogeneity of nonwork groups to sex heterogeneity. At 15 to 16 years of age, the family is the most common holiday group; at age 17, friendship groups rival the family; and by age 18, they supplant the family.

GENDER AND NONWORK PATTERNS

Such turning points are even more clearly illustrated in Angrist's (1967) study of college alumnae. She argues that single-criterion categories, such as age, work status, and occupation, provide only gross distinctions. She examines the "natural history of the individual's roles in the social structure" as they are altered by stages in the life cycle. She uses a cross-sectional sample to identify how longitudinal patterns might vary with changes in marital status, age of person, ages and number of children. Thus her analysis links life cycle events, social structure, social relations, and patterns of nonwork. She finds that the *amount* of leisure participation is similar for all of her respondents; however, the nature of that participation has considerable variation.

As women move through the life cycle with the attendant role constellations of each stage, there are associated nonwork cycles. Television viewing tends to have low participation rates among young single women, moves to its highest rates for young married women with preschool children, and then declines as the children become older. Cultural and spectator sports activities have an opposite pattern, with the low point occurring with preschool children and the high points at the single stage and when the children are older. Organizational participation has a marked increase as the women move through the life cycle, and college courses tend to decline in their proportion of nonwork time, until the later stages when there is a slight increase in participation.

Angrist's (1967) data approximates the real complexity that prevails in work-nonwork associations. Her well-educated, female respondents clearly indicate that for a significant segment of industrial populations the nature of work (in terms of monied employment) is *dependent* upon nonwork social relations—marital status, ages of children, and access to domestic help. Further variations in the nature of nonwork activities are not matters of personal whim but are rather clearly determined by the role networks associated with given stages of the life cycle. We are tempted to suggest that most social science investigations of work-nonwork patterns are elaborate celebrations of adult, male, industrial work modes, and only marginally are they explanations of social life as it exists in the daily lives of persons.

Of course, gender is an important element in the complex of factors Angrist combines for her analysis. For, as Sheila Johnson (1971: 133–161) argues, women have had more experience in organizing their leisure time than men, and further, women retain their "jobs as housewives into old age, so that they are never entirely without chores around which to structure their leisure." Though she is straining for the "causality" of work, we find further evidence that the continuity of nonwork is overcoming the timed breaks imposed by industrial work life.

For example, she (1971) reports that research by others and her own study of a working-class, retirement, trailer community indicate a decrease in sexual role differentiation with aging. She observed little sex segregation in most household chores and leisure activities.[4] Yet her observations suggest considerable difference in terms of utilitarian activities—women are more active in community associations, men are more active in certain worklike activities (moving trailers, delivering newspapers). Further, in domestic crafts only women were involved in sewing and ceramics, while only men were involved in fishing, hunting, carpentering, rug weaving and painting pictures. Reading was predominantly a woman's activity, *but* was shared with men. There are several activities which were predomi-

---

[4]Marwell (1975) has an interesting discussion as to why urban-industrial social orders should exhibit *less* role ascription based upon gender. It does not take much imagination to recognize that, unlike a farming milieu, a milieu devoted to intellectual trades has little rationale for roles based upon gender.

nantly male—bowling, golf, going to ballgames—*but* shared with women. And there were several activities shared in equal or nearly equal parts—camping, driving, dancing, listening to music, gardening. Thus males at retirement regain many of the domestic chores they had as boys before they began work, retain many of the nonwork activities they have had throughout life, and gain some new ones (rug weaving) and, with peers, make them male activities.

AGE AND CONTINUITY IN NONWORK PATTERNS

Similar patterns of continuity seem to occur in voluntary associations as noted by Babchuk and Edwards (1965:153):

Babchuk and Gordon (1962) indicate that as age increases affiliation and participation change from one type of association to another. Specifically, they state that children tend to affiliate and participate in expressive organizations, while the mature adult, particularly the male, is more likely to affiliate with instrumental and instrumental-expressive associations. When an individual reaches old age his participation in instrumental activities declines and his involvement in expressive groups and activities increases. Hence there appears a cycle of associationally-typed participation that parallels the life cycle and points to variations in the obtained integration for the individual at different stages.

Continuity seems to be a pattern found among a lower middle-class sample of persons 28 to 60 years of age in Bonn, Germany (Schmitz-Scherzer and Strödel, 1971). Though the investigators emphasize the lack of association between age and nonwork activities, their data provide strong evidence of continuity of taste. Men intensify 3 out of 5 activities (reading, working in the garden, television viewing) and 2 of the 5 activities they practice less often (moviegoing and visiting). That is, there are some activities that one does throughout one's entire life, and there are others that are confined to young adulthood.

The common embarrassment many young adults experience when confronting aging seems clearest in S. J. Miller's (1965) argument that the aged (unspecified) should seek a career in leisure. He assumes that embarrassment regarding possible failure in role performance has people confining their social interaction more and more to those of the same age-group. Thus the aged develop a subculture to protect themselves. Miller's argument seems to assume that the aged, like children, will get in the way of young adults unless they are kept occupied with harmless and somewhat useful activities. Because the young adult professional is imbedded in work relations, there seems to be the assumption that all things are measured by work; and when you do not work, you have no identity. There is the man stripped of his job and the woman of her mothering, and their now-empty and meaningless time must be filled with activities programmed by the young adults.

What seems to be overlooked in such assumptions is that age grade is *one* of the natural bases of interaction for *all* ages. Secondary schools are age ghettos of the adolescent, and swinging singles bars for young adults are as age segregated as the retired people's trailer community. Yet seldom do we say that adolescents or young adults are "embarrassed" about their immature approaches to love and social relations, and therefore keep to themselves. What should be clear is the importance that nonwork has in maintaining continuity, and because one's friends and kin and associates are aging at the same rate, there is a certain age segregation.

Though Christ's (1965) study of "retired" stamp collectors seems another attempt to find something useful for the aged in its emphasis upon worklike leisure, it is a useful illustration of nonwork continuity. He noted with approval that in stamp collecting there are tight-knit trade associations, there is a substantial economic market, and there are media of communications, such as newspapers and journals. In short, stamp collecting is a "complete social system."

Yet all the persons in Christ's (1965:102) sample were stamp collectors 10 or more years (the median is 26.6 years) *prior* to retirement. That is, stamp collecting is a continuation of a particular social life. Indeed wives become involved in stamp collecting in self-defense. Christ (1965:103) reports on one wife who continued collecting after her husband had died. "She's not interested in stamps as stamps; she's just interested in the *group*" (emphasis added). One would hope that a sociologist might not find such data so surprising. Indeed, of his 53 interviewees, only 7 made statements that indicated they had identified themselves with the subculture of the aged. The other 46 identified themselves as part of a philatelic subculture. Because it is a complete social system, there is an intensity, a structure, and most importantly a continuity to stamp collecting that binds the individual into a social group that has a set-apart subculture (Christ, 1965:104). The use of markets and money is not unlike the interest middle-class, middle-aged, women potters studied by Wallace (1974) have in "sales." In these cases, money is important more as a standard social yardstick for keeping score on one's progress. Its value is more like the goal scored in the closing seconds of the game—a standard metric of social value far more important than money as capital or consumption opportunity (Duncan, 1962).

In a detailed analysis and synthesis of nearly 200 studies on children, nature education, and camping, Burch, Shelstad and Wallace

(1974) found that all of the studies were in one way or another concerned to see if nonwork activities would lead to better observance
of the work norms of school, shop, and home. It is important to note
that children's camp situations are usually entered by separate individuals rather than some kind of intimate kin or friendship group.
Further, this collection of age peers is set apart from home and
neighborhood and placed in the atypical, naturalistic camp setting.
Interestingly, the empirical studies have fairly mixed findings as to
the gains in school skills, home behavior, and "cure" of delinquency.
In other words, there is little evidence of transferability between
nonwork and work activities. However, the studies did seem to report consistent gains in self-esteem and understanding, improved
facility in social relations, and more extensive sets of social relations.
Thus, even a worklike structure of nonwork ends in improved sociability rather than improved productivity.

PRIMARY ASSOCIATIONS
AND NONWORK PATTERNS

We feel reasonably confident that work-related variables (such as
social class) cannot account for or be causally connected with nonwork patterns because they represent quite different social spheres
of life. Work represents the individual's segmented participation in
the larger societal system. Nonwork represents the multidimensional
life of intimate primary associations, which cushion and give meaning to the filtered messages of the encompassing social and ecological environments. And within this intimate, sociable realm, nonwork
provides the essential materials for cementing the social bond, for
building biographical continuity, and for creating and sustaining individual identity. It is in this latter realm where the individual plays
with future roles and may discover adaptive innovations.

Contrary to much speculative concern, primary associations have
not become weakened or made vestigial in industrial societies. Studies by Gans (1962), Axelrod (1956), Caplow and Forman (1950), Dotson (1951), and others suggest that neighborhoods have retained
many adaptive functions. Litwak and Szelenyi (1969), drawing upon
the long series of studies by Litwak (1960a, 1960b, 1960c, 1961, 1968)
and others, give a useful summary of the recent empirical rediscov-
ery of primary associations. They argue that friendship associations
are based upon similarities in sex, age, and stage of family life cycle
as well as income and educational factors. Friendship associations
deal "with edges of change and fluctuation," and such ties rest upon
"free choice and affectivity." Neighborhoods, on the other hand, provide short-time aid and are the context for access to immediate actions. There is high membership turnover, and institutions such as

TABLE 26 PROPORTION OF FAMILIES PARTICIPATING IN VARIOUS OUTDOOR RECREATION ACTIVITIES WITHIN AGE, CHILDREN, AND EDUCATION GROUPS (PERCENTAGE DISTRIBUTION OF FAMILIES)

	Golf	Outdoor Winter Sports	Other Outdoor Sports & Games
Age of Head			
Under 25	12	21	28
25–34	21	24	29
35–44	21	35	34
45–54	21	29	21
55–64	10	11	08
65 or older	02	02	03
Children in Family			
Yes	21	33	33
No	10	11	09

Source: Mandell and Marans (1972)

the parent-teacher association serve to maintain normative stability in spite of transient members. Neighborhoods are sustained through face-to-face contact, while kin associations are maintained in spite of social and spatial mobility factors, for they are permanent relations that aid in providing long-term solutions. Modern means of communication permit kin associations to be sustained. It is crucial to note that Litwak and Szelenyi (1969) argue that given the nature of technological society, these groupings of friends, neighbors, and kin provide unique supportive services that cannot be substituted one for the other.

Obviously the persistence of these three types of primary association is maintained by each group's unique cluster of nonwork activity. Thus as persons become involved in nuclear family maintenance, rather than friendship or neighborhood primary associations, the nature of their behavior will vary quite irrespective of personal preference and particular activity. That is, persons have activities, such as camping, fishing, moviegoing, not necessarily because of some personal preference or some inherent force in the activity, but because that activity permits the consolidation and maintenance of the primary bond. Thus Britt and Janus (1941), in their excellent summary of studies on play, find that adult preferences may include as many as 1,000 activities, and although persons might desire tennis or golf,

Activities			
Hunting or Fishing	Driving for Pleasure	Driving Off-road Vehicles	Number of Families
60	86	14	94
66	87	09	243
65	76	18	252
53	72	11	282
44	60	05	211
26	64	—	221
35	69	15	615
29	82	05	688

these "desires are not necessarily the determinants of their play behavior." They report that home is the center for most adult play.

It would seem that group characteristics, rather than individual characteristics, are given their highest saliency for behavior in primary associations. The presence of a spouse or children (of a certain age), or of other adult kin, or of friends will affect the nonwork pattern. For example, the British National Survey (Mass Observation, 1970:4) of camping and caravanning (trailering) indicates that presence or absence of children was a crucial factor. Only 41 percent of all British households had children, whereas 61 percent of the camping households and 62 percent of the caravanning households had children. Mandell and Marans (1972) 1970 national survey of the United States also found the presence of children important in 5 of their 6 family recreation activities (see Table 26). Only driving for pleasure seemed less influenced by presence of children. Also, most of the activities are linked to the stage of family life cycle, thus the highest proportion of families participating occurs when the head of household is in the 25 to 44 age period, or the usual middle stages of the family life cycle.

The life cycle influence seems to be consistently supported by the research literature. King's (1965) study of Midwestern campers seems typical. He found that about 80 percent of the families had children.

TABLE 27 PARTICIPATION IN LOCAL PARKS AND
RECREATION AREAS AND PROPORTION OF SAMPLE
WHO PARTICIPATED WITH WHOM

Activity	Percent of Sample Who Participate	With Whom		
		Friends	Alone	Family
Picnicking	55.5	27.1	2.1	26.3
Walking and hiking	45.9	18.1	5.4	22.4
Baseball	36.4	25.0	1.8	9.6
Swimming	24.0	16.0	1.5	6.5
Using playground equipment	23.8	15.5	2.7	17.0
Fishing	22.1	11.0	3.1	8.9
Boating	15.7	8.0	0.7	5.6
Horseback riding	12.1	7.2	1.7	3.1
Tennis	12.0	8.2	1.7	2.1
Golf	7.2	6.5	0.0	0.7

Source: Yancey, Britt, and Snell (1971:84).

Of greatest interest is his finding that variation in participation is related to variations in children's age classes—1 to 5 years old, 25 percent; 6 to 12 years old, 49 percent; 13 to 18 years old, 26 percent.
Thus the stage of family life cycle seems to reflect participation in
camping. Families with very young children and those with adolescent children are not as highly represented in camping as those with
children aged between 6 and 12. As we discuss in Chapter 7, family
outdoor recreation seems to be the social arena where any member
can influence the behavior of the group. The special demands of
young children and the changing interests of adolescent children
would seem to be important constraints upon the activities of the
kin group.

The stage of family life cycle as an influence upon recreation behavior has been documented in a variety of studies (Burch, 1966,
1969; West and Merriam, 1970; Etzkorn, 1964; Anderson, 1953; Bossard and Boll, 1963; Cunningham and Johannis, 1960; Duvall, 1962;
Foote, 1963; Stone, 1963; Hawkins and Walters, 1952; Yoesting and
Burkhead, 1971). Further a leisure locale often attracts these same
primary associations of family, friends, and/or neighbors. Hutchison
(1973:4) found that 54 percent of his recreation groups were nuclear
families with small children; 13.1 percent, family and friends; 24 percent, just friends, with this latter group being largely composed of
adolescents.

The Yancey, Britt, and Snell (1971) study indicates a similar mixture for a wider range of activities. Table 27 suggests that some activities are more typically done with friends, while others are more

TABLE 28 GROUP COMPOSITION BY LEISURE PLACE

Place			Percent			N
	Alone	With Friends	Family	Family & Friends	Other	
Neighborhoods, at home or the house of a friend or relative	31	11	43	14	1	340
Parks	4	22	51	22	1	268
Playgrounds, Schools, Tracks, Stadiums and Ballparks	9	28	44	16	3	347
Beaches, Lakes and Rivers	3	20	50	26	1	529

Source: Field (1973:8).

typically kin related, and hardly any activities are typically done alone. Still, the mixture is such that we can assume that the timing and meaning of doing some things with friends is quite different from doing something with family, even if the activity remains the same.

The nature of an activity and its setting seem less important than the interaction opportunities for the participating group. Spaulding's (1937:5) study of recreation use at a Rhode Island beach found the same primary associations as were found in the western wildlands studies by Hendee et al.:

> *Slightly over half, 52.8 percent, of these were family groups; 56.8 percent of the family groups were nuclear family members, while the remainder were extended family members. Friendship groups accounted for almost all of the non-family groups, and most of these 53.5 percent had both male and female members. The remainder were all-male or all-female groups or males or females alone at the beach.*

Though individual respondents or group members might list the primary purpose of the visit as "going to the beach," it seems certain that the actual social purposes were quite different. A study by Field (1973) provides further clues. His data (see Table 28) suggests that there are some leisure locales where persons are more likely to participate alone and some where family or friends are the predominant organizing unit. Still, like the Yancey, Britt, and Snell (1971) study, all locales have some mixture of the different units of social organization. Given this mixture of social groups, it would require some stretching of credulity to believe that inner psychological forces or the particular locale were the primary sources of behavioral meaning. Thus, O'Leary, Field, and Schreuder (1974) report that social groups remain consistent, though activities may be interchanged or substituted as the nature of the group alters. That is, the activity is a facilitator for social interaction, while social group characteristics determine the specific form of the activity.

Finally, there seems to be some reinforcement (Burch, 1969; Hendee and Campbell, 1969) of nonwork patterns by the convergence of primary association norms and values. For example, a study by Klessig and Hale (1972) of Wisconsin hunters indicates the importance of such convergence. Most hunters in their sample grew up in hunting families, began hunting with family members, and have spouses who approve of hunting. Seventy-one percent of their sample had fathers who hunted while they were growing up. Ninety-two percent began hunting between ages 10 to 19, or younger. Only 10 percent of the sample first began hunting with a nonrelative. Over 85 percent of the sample had mothers and fathers who approved of hunting while they were growing up. Only 5 percent have spouses who disapprove of their hunting participation, 4 percent who dislike their hunting friends, 11 percent who are opposed to killing animals by hunting, and 12 percent who feel their spouses spend too much time hunting. Thus, in the majority of cases, both the family of orientation and the family of procreation provide positive reinforcement for most hunters.

This pattern continues during the actual hunting trip, where the kin influence remains significantly strong. Forty-seven percent of the hunters are accompanied by their spouse on some hunting trips. While only 12 percent went hunting alone, 52 percent went with some combination of kin or kin and friends. Further, hunters were likely to associate with other hunters; thus some 71 percent of the sample reported that most or all of their close friends were hunters (Klessig and Hale, 1972).

A similar pattern to that found in the use of beaches, parks, boating and other water activities, and hunting is found in the supposedly large solitudes of wilderness hiking and forest camping (Merriam, 1963; Burch and Wenger, 1967; Lucas, 1964; Moss, 1966). A major study of Pacific Northwest wilderness campers by Hendee, Catton, Marlow, and Brockman (1968) reports typical findings: 47.6 percent participate with their families only, 38 percent with their friends, 7.7 percent with organized groups, and only 6.6 percent go alone. This pattern also reflects a continuity.

Nearly 70 percent indicated their first trip was before they were 15 years old. Forty-four percent of the respondents also indicated that 3 or more of their 5 closest friends participated, at least occasionally, in wilderness type recreation.

The convergence and reinforcement of a set of norms by various primary associations and the continuity of values and nonwork activities between generations (Yoesting and Burkhead, 1973; Burch, 1969; Witt and Bishop, 1970; Sofranko and Nolan, 1972) are patterns found in most nonwork activities, rather than being confined to exotic varieties of outdoor recreation. Goodman (1969) found similar transference of time conceptions. While Hodge and Treiman (1968:739) found that "for both males and females there is a relatively high degree of intergenerational transmission of membership in voluntary associations." Indeed nonwork seems to follow the same cumulative pattern that maintains occupational differences between the social strata (Slater, 1960). However, there is the significant difference that occupational structures are shifting and only involve individual participants, while primary associations, which organize many forms of nonwork, are enduring structures that involve social groups. As Litwak and Szelenyi (1969) demonstrate, even in the technological society, which supposedly has little need for primary associations, such associations persist and continue to provide maintenance and protective functions that other institutions and groupings seem unable to fulfill.

Some idea of the stability of these continuities is gained from a careful study of the Detroit metropolitan area which replicated certain key questions from 1950s surveys in a 1971 sample survey (Duncan, Schuman, and Duncan, 1973). They found significant attitude changes in regard to child-rearing, divorce, religion, race, and so forth. As the media remind us, the 1960s were a decade of great social change—urban riots, student rebellions, assassinations of leaders, new forms of radical rhetoric and morality, moon walks, dramatic changes in foreign affairs, and significant alteration in the economy and relations between the legislative, judicial, and administrative institutions. Yet amidst all this change, there was a remarkable stability in the patterns of informal social participation. Table 29 illustrates both the regularities and stabilities of social participation. As one moves from the late 1950s to 1971, the percent distribution for the various frequency of participation categories remains remarkably stable. Of equal interest are the regularities in the patterns of participation with the various categories of associates—relatives, neighbors, work-mates, and friends. For example, the smallest percent in the "never" (1959–1971 columns) category is relatives, the

TABLE 29 SOCIAL CHANGE IN A METROPOLITAN
COMMUNITY (INFORMAL SOCIAL PARTICIPATION)

Frequency of getting together with—	Percent Distribution			
	1957[a]	1971[a]	1959	1971
Relatives (other than those living at home with you):				
Every day; or almost every day	4	7	7	6
Once or twice a week	32	31	35	31
A few times a month	20	20	21	20
Once a month	12	13	12	14
A few times a year	17	20	14	20
Less often	6	5	4	5
Never	9	4	7	4
	100	100	100	100
Neighbors:				
Every day; or almost every day	10	13	13	12
Once or twice a week	18	16	19	17
A few times a month; or once a month	18	19	23	20
A few times a year; or less often	19	22	22	23
Never	35	30	23	28
	100	100	100	100
People you or your husband work with:				
Once or twice a week; or more often	17	15	15	14
A few times a month; or once a month	22	24	22	24
A few times a year; or less often	30	33	36	34
Never	31	28	27	28
	100	100	100	100
Friends who are not neighbors or fellow workers:				
Once or twice a week; or more often	28	29	25	29
A few times a month; or once a month	38	35	37	36
A few times a year; or less often	23	28	29	28
Never	11	8	9	7
	100	100	100	100

[a]Wayne County only.
Source: Duncan, Schuman, and Duncan (1973:46).

next smallest with friends, the next with neighbors, and the last with work-mates. Even in a world of radical social change there is a substantive realm of social life that is radically unchanging.

SUMMARY

Indeed the consistency of these associations found across a broad range of studies, regions, activities, cultures, and times suggest social regularities of more than passing interest. Might it be that our grand and elaborate theories of social change and stability have unduly favored the drama of work, war, and rational order over the mundane trivia of nonwork, life cycle forces, and the emotional order of primary associations? Talmon (1972), in a brilliant, long-term study of the kibbutzim, finds its ideological traditions (myths) moving from the primacy of community and egalitarianism toward emphasis upon individualism and familism. Interestingly it is women, as mothers, who reemphasize the values of familism and affirm the individual rights to comfort and personal gratification. Some understanding of this pressure is provided in the ultimate contrast between the "ideology" of primary associations and the "ideology" of work (Davis, 1937:749):

> Within a group organized for bearing and rearing children bonds tend to arise that are cemented by the condition of relative permanence and the sentiment of personal feeling, for the task requires long, close, and sympathetic association. Prostitution, in which the seller takes any buyer at the price, necessarily represents an opposite kind of erotic association. It is distinguished by the elements of hire, promiscuity, and emotional indifference— all of which are incompatible with primary or gemeinschaft association.

In this chapter we have given most attention to nonwork activities that are organized by primary associations of neighbors, friends, and kin. Obviously, there are numerous nonwork activities that persons participate in alone; the porno-strip locales of the world's metropolitan centers suggest a market where alones can imagine they are with others. And then there are the worklike nonwork activities, such as painting, reading, and gardening, which are primarily individually organized. We will examine some of these variations in Chapter 6, which deals with matters of taste.

6

TASTE –
FROM
SOCIAL
BOND
TO
SOCIAL
SOLIDARITY

6

In Chapters 3 and 5 we talked about the kinds of groups that organize nonwork activities and the various factors influencing nonwork patterns. We suggested that nonwork is an important element in maintaining social unity. In this chapter we wish to look more closely at the nature of social unity and particularly at a matter that will be touched upon in our discussion of sport (Chapter 9) concerning the links between small primary associations and the larger human associations, such as the various types of community—ethnic, religious, and regional.

In human societies the establishment of a close bond with a small number of others seems essential in binding these small units into a larger social entity. Our interest is in the mechanism that permits the intergroup bond to be a component of intragroup solidarity.

In this discussion we will argue that taste serves both as a boundary-maintaining mechanism and as a means for establishing and sustaining intragroup solidarity. We will do this in two ways. First, we will consider how taste opens certain social boundaries by closing others, then we will look at a variety of studies that view taste as a boundary-maintaining mechanism.

SOCIAL SOLIDARITY—
INTRAGROUP AND INTERGROUP

Human beings, like other primates, are born into a small social group in which their formative years are ordinarily spent. In this group, requisite skills are learned, which enable continued social development in later phases of the life cycle. However, unlike other primates, human beings do not pass all of their lives within the same social group, except perhaps symbolically. Postpubescent males and females leave these initial groups and establish new breeding groups distinct from the originals. Into the new social groups, offspring are born and the procedure continues in cyclic fashion.

One of the interesting aspects of primate social life is the formation of social bonds between individual animals. A social bond is an attachment among individuals of the same species so that they react differently to each other than they do to others in similar situations. An important aspect of social bonds is the affective component, which seems always to be present. Recall Professor Washburn's (1961) statement that *Homo sapiens* have evolved to where they care intently about only a very few other conspecifics. This suggests that affect is not a necessary component of all social behavior among *Homo sapiens*. Yet there is hidden within this discussion a rather fundamental aspect of human social orders.

First, primates other than *Homo sapiens* tend to pass their lives within the same social group into which they were born.[1] Social bonds are formed, over time, with all other individuals in the group. Depending, in part, upon age and sex of the individuals these bonds will vary in form and content. There are, if you will, no strangers in a primate group. In fact, whenever conspecifics residing in the same general area casually appear on the peripheries of group territories, they are usually attacked and driven off or killed regardless of sex. In contrast, most individuals are strangers in human societies. That is, no social bonds exist among individuals, except for a limited few, in a manner comparable to other primate social orders. The presence of a culture permits nonexclusionary actions to remain at a minimal level. It is not that *Homo sapiens* are indifferent to conspecifics, it is merely that they recognize, through symbols, that they are all members of a larger class of similar social beings. In other words, the social meaning of being a stranger varies within primate social systems. One consequence of this, as mentioned earlier is that people form social groupings that are much more numerous than observed among other primates.

Second, assuming that culture enables *Homo sapiens* to create social persons and that human social orders are articulated through structured relationships between social persons, there remains another level of integration that must be examined. Although sociologists such as Cooley (1964) have shown a concern with the problem by indicating that human societies are comprised of primary and secondary groups, the mere labeling of a phenomena is but a first step of inquiry. The question remains as to what, if any, the relationship is between primary and secondary groups as structural components of human societies? What are the relationships between secondary groups? Finally, and most importantly, what are the relationships between primary groups? To date, sociology has infrequently addressed itself to the last query; and has given considerable attention to the second and somewhat less to the first. The reasons lie

---

[1] Except when the troop reaches a certain size and must split into separate units.

in part within the theoretical formulations employed. In particular neither functionalism nor social action theory can formulate acceptable answers within their respective schemas. Social psychology, particularly the Meadian school, has come closest, but it has bypassed the issue in its interest in the individual and how the individual becomes a social being.

To summarize, we must analyze human societies as representing variations of primate social systems and cultural systems. When we include the primate biosocial heritage of human societies, we may better understand the nature of social ties within and between social groups.

SOCIAL GROUPS

An intriguing aspect of *Homo sapiens*, which clearly distinguishes the species from other primates, is the sharing of food among individuals (Tiger and Fox, 1971). Thus, although primates may exhibit fairly complex social systems, individual foraging is characteristic; all members of a group fend for themselves, save infants at breast. Access to food stuffs is largely determined by the dominance hierarchy. Unlike among other primates, food gathering is distributed among *Homo sapiens* in a group. Those who have, share with those who have not. Within tribal societies the importance of food sharing is great. Indeed, the sharing of food in any human society is worthy of considerably closer study than it has received thus far.

We know that individuals share food within the group into which they were born and that among other primates this does not occur, certainly not to the same degree. We also know that social bond formation among individuals is an affect-laden phenomenon and that the number of individuals who share food on a regular continuing basis will be strongly affective toward one another. Comparatively speaking, no other social relationship shared with others will have precisely the same character. Although anthropologists have indicated the importance of commensal activities for the study of preliterate human societies, they have failed to note the significance of the activity for the study of all human societies. Sharing of food in human social orders may be an indication of social status; but who may eat with whom is of a somewhat different order than who regularly gives and receives food from whom. The distinction between individuals and social persons is particularly important here. For example, tribute in the form of foodstuffs is the act of giving and receiving food *not* among individuals but among social persons (or in some cases among social groups). The food is a symbol of deference not an act of affection as among individuals.

While *Homo sapiens* appear to build upon the common patterns of social bonding that exist among primates—that is, male/female, male/male, female/female—they develop these bonds within the additional structural constraints of numerically small social groups. One of the means through which these affect-laden bonds are cemented is the sharing of food. Solidarity within human social groups cannot help but build upon such biosocial patterns, but the binding of individual to individual may not create the ideal background for the manufacture of social persons. Indeed, the informal organization that operates within complex organizations is an acknowledgment of the fact that it is difficult for humans not to respond to conspecifics *qua* conspecifics, even when effciency, rationality, and the collective good are at stake.

ON THE CHARACTER OF HUMAN SOCIETY

The formation of social bonds among individuals is an emotional event among primates. Since the nature of human social orders is largely symbolic, what is the emotional cement that binds individuals in nonhuman societies? Is there a reservoir of emotion from which the overflow, in its intensity, overpowers rationality? Is this why man seemingly enjoys killing? Is this why a person who mistakes a social person for an individual responds so emotionally to what he or she perceives of as betrayal? Perhaps it is all or none of these. But what is noteworthy is that one consequence of the evolvement of culture as an adaptative mechanism for the species has been to restrict the number of individuals with which an affective bond is formed. It is conjecture as to whether this reduction in number has been accompanied by an intensification of affective arousal among some. Thus while culture enables one to recognize similarity among many more conspecifics, it alters the saliency of these shared characteristics.

Human social orders require individuals to contact and interact with a larger number of their conspecifics than is the case among other primate social orders, but without providing the individuals the certainties of primate social bonds. The affect problem must be dealt with on at least two levels: one is that of social solidarity between individuals and among social groups; the other is that of social integration between social persons and between social collectivities or assemblages.[2] "Taste" may resolve the social structural

---

[2]A social assemblage is an aggregation of social persons unified by virtue of the role relationships existing among and between them, for example occupational associations. Social assemblages are essential for an understanding of the social organization of work.

problems that emerge from the duality of the human being as bio-social species and the human being as cultural species.

SOCIAL SOLIDARITY—INTRAGROUP

Earlier we defined a social group as a number of individuals who identified themselves and were identified by others as members. The reciprocal nature of this identification process is particularly important in distinguishing a social group from a reference group. An important underlying aspect of this reciprocity concerns the social bond common to a primate species. The major variable that analytically distinguishes individuals in a social group from other conspecifics must be the affective arousal associated with the recognition of each other. These affective states are not idiosyncratic but are social in character; moreover, they are the products of particular transactions sustained initially among a very small number of conspecifics. Social groups are comprised of the several major categories of social ages; and within the social organization of nonwork infants and juveniles are especially important for an understanding of how social solidarity develops.

Social solidarity refers to the degree to which members of a social group share a common definition of a situation (Young, 1965). Social solidarity is, in the Durkheimian sense, an aspect of "consciousness of kind." It is a recognition of "belongingness" among individuals. Social solidarity refers especially to those social bonds formed between young and old within the social groups into which the individual is born and in which the individual undergoes initial socialization experiences. Indeed these social bonds are so resilient that the individual's biosocial nature creates problems for the emergence of the individual as a culturally socialized animal. A two-fold dilemma exists: (1) how to bring about affective neutrality so that social personages can be developed and (2) how to make it possible for the individual to leave the social group, physically though not symbolically, while establishing new breeding groups. It is at this point that the sexual maturation processes of a biological nature are harnessed to the social system. Some theoreticians, incorrectly we believe, see the problem purely in cultural terms when they examine the difficulties of the transference process. Our point is simply that among *Homo sapiens* biological sexual maturation is a mechanism for enabling individuals to desire to form social bonds with strangers. Such action does not necessarily attenuate the bonds previously existing between young and old in the group, except perhaps those among individuals of the same sex. Or as Davis (1964) argues, biology sets up certain functional demands, which the social system solves in a variety of ways; however, over time these solutions become deter-minants.

SOME MECHANISMS OF SOLIDARITY

A particularly knotty problem lies in how intergroup solidarity (that is, solidarity between two or more social groups) arises in the face of the biosocial nature of *Homo sapiens.* In large part it is here that culture as an adaptive mechanism becomes especially impor-tant for the development of shared definitions of situations. To un-derstand how this phenomenon arises, we turn to a consideration of taste. Given our earlier discussion of food as a biosocial mecha-nism for building interindividual social bonds, combined with the affective character of such experiences, it becomes clear that mat-ters of taste are cultural analogs for the emergence of intergroup solidarity.

Consider the power in social transactions among individuals of such matters as whether one eats tomatoes with salt or sugar sprinkled upon the fruit. Do you peel the fruit before you slice it or do you eat it with the peel? What is important is that these matters of taste are substantially learned as an aspect of social bonding among members of a social group. As such they are aspects of culture that are affectively conditioned. While it is only perhaps between cul-tures that matters of taste become symbolic, within a culture such variations, while not defined as matters of moral turpitude, do sepa-rate individuals and groups. Matters of taste, then, enable individ-uals to perceive the special nature of the affective ties of those with whom they are bonded. Social groups that share similar patterns of common usage consequently share common definitions of situa-tions. Since social solidarity is the degree to which such definitions are shared, taste can be seen as one mechanism, at the cultural level, that strengthens relationships between groups. This, of course, is one aspect of the study of life-styles.

In human societies there exist a limited number of opportunities for individuals to develop social ties outside of social groups anal-ogous to those shared among its members. Yet such ties must clearly develop if we can speak of a social organization of nonwork. One of the means through which such ties are brought about is the rec-ognition of kinship among individuals who are not members of the same social group. Another is the residual resiliency of same-sex bonds between siblings after departing the family of orientation. Thus food sharing becomes both a cultural and a biosocial mecha-nism. Recall our discussion in Chapter 5 on the influence of the elemental variables of age, sex, and number for the form of social groups and the linkage between taste and these structural properties becomes readily apparent.

TASTE AS A SOCIOLOGICAL CONSTRUCT

Culture provides a variety of potential responses to common situations. Within the set of alternatives available, individuals exercise a choice conditioned by various social opportunities. In short, the exercise of choice reflects the operation of preference among alternatives. This comes very close to a dictionary definition of taste, that is, taste is an individual's aesthetic preference or liking. But this is too narrow a definition for sociological purposes.

Matters of taste extend into all aspects of human social life. As Parsons (1937:678) noted: "It applies not only to matters of food, dress, daily personal habits, etc. but is a very prominent element in "art," "recreation," etc." Moreover, the exercise of taste in such aspects of everyday life are clearly sociological in nature. It is not merely the operation of whim in an idiosyncratic sense, but it is preference exercised in response to felt normative pressures.

What is the source of the normative order underlying matters of taste; if it is not efficiency or legitimacy problems, it is also a matter independent of such concerns. The confusion arises, in part, from the character of symbols per se; that is, a symbol may have more than a single meaning attached to it simultaneously. But it also arises from the failure to consider the problem of affect as inherently a sociological phenomenon that is canalized as precisely as other normative questions.

The norms governing matters of taste are, to use Parsons' (1937) terminology, particularistic in character; that is, they arise only within small social groups based upon kinship and friendship. They are transient in the sense that they govern preference among a limited set of individuals for a limited set of time. When individuals move out of their original social groups to form new groups, they may modify the content or discontinue conforming to such norms. However, norms peculiar to the new group tend to emerge for reasons previously considered, and these norms usually govern substantive matters similarly as did the norms no longer actively employed as standards of taste. In a sense these norms are somewhat similar to what some scholars have considered family rituals (Bossard and Boll, 1963), but they remain more pervasive.

Given the transient character of such norms, it is not surprising that sanctions are not uniform or universalistic. The violation of a matter of taste does not, therefore, normally evoke a negative sanction of the same character as would the violation of those norms concerned with legitimacy and efficiency matters. Though violations of matters of taste are perceived and recognized, the disapproval is largely affective in character and individualistic in administration. The wrinkled nose, indicating momentary displeasure at another's apparel, is not the same as the sergeant's admonition to his subordinate "You're out of uniform, soldier!" The former is a matter of taste; the latter is a matter of legitimacy.

To summarize, taste is inherently social in character, arises in small social groups around affect-laden matters, and is often connected with biosocial properties of the species. The norms governing such matters are transient, with the consequence that sanctions are not codified. In short, matters of taste are the social property of small groups, and as such they may provide useful indications of group boundaries. Intergroup solidarity requires that such boundaries be permeable.

GROUP BOUNDARIES AND MATTERS OF TASTE

As we suggested earlier, matters of taste are aspects of the social bonding occurring among members of a social group. Therefore, the presence or absence of norms of taste may provide a useful guide to the cultural boundaries of a group. This is a more efficacious index than those associated with aspects of social roles. Norms of legitimacy and efficiency apply to matters among social persons.

We have suggested that norms of taste are acquired by individuals as an aspect of bond formation among individuals in a group. We need to specify further how they become the basis for emergent solidarity between social groups. We noted two basic mechanisms: (1) the recognition of kinship (and friendship) among individuals (really a special case of response to conspecifics as representatives of a social category, but different by virtue of the affective component) and (2) the differential attenuation of bonds among age and sex classes in the social group. Particularly important are the bonds between siblings. We are not concerned with the psychological mechanisms through which learning may occur; we take these as given. Important to this argument is what is learned not how it is learned in the technical sense of reinforcement schedules. Permeability of group boundaries occurs through the mechanisms of kinship recognition and differences in bonding among age and sex classes. Without such patterns of permeability there could be no social circles and no sharing of common interests.

Indeed, the reciprocal influence between social norms and biological factors in linking social groups seems clearest in the changing practices of infant feeding. As women in the advanced industrial societies are now beginning to return to breast feeding, women in urban areas of developing societies seem to be shifting to bottle feeding (Wade, 1974). Women in developing societies are abandoning breast feeding to indicate their rejection of "vulgar, peasant customs" and to validate their own acceptance as sophisticated urbanites. Ironically, this change is contributing to severe malnutrition for the children of the poor, which may have ultimate long-term effects upon the brain development of these children. Therefore, the diffusion of certain taste norms becomes a means by which primary associations participate in larger social circles and which in turn may have this shared taste reinforce life situation inequalities through unanticipated biological pressures. Understanding some of these processes will involve the remainder of this chapter.

SOCIAL CIRCLES AND TASTE

Georg Simmel's (1955) notion of social circle seems the best concept for understanding how social groups form into larger social units, with respect to a particular aspect of life-style. The utility of the concept seems clearest in Charles Kadushin's theoretical and empirical development of the social circle concept. He has used the idea in studies of friends and supporters of psychotherapy (1966) and power elites (1968). He describes a social circle as a collection of people who share common interests, are informally organized (have a low degree of institutionalization), and a high proportion of whose interactions are indirect. As Kadushin (1966:788) notes:

> In an uncharacteristic burst of systematic exposition, Simmel offered some propositions about the functions of circles. First, he says, social circles can destroy tribal and neighborhood types of social organization, [sic] Historically, there is a development from these groups to associations based on free choice. Second, for social circles to develop, there must be focal points around which they can form. There are six such focal points: age and sex statuses (a more primitive type of circle); self-interest; family; religion; and sundry other statuses. Third, in modern societies individuals tend to belong to a number of different circles, partly because some circles are outgrowths of others, partly because each person through a variety of means (not clearly spelled out) acquires a unique configuration of circles to which he belongs. Fourth as the previous quotations imply, Simmel sees social circles as having both integrative and conflict-producing properties.

Kadushin's own work, as the ideas of Simmel, indicate how circles serve as points of traffic between small social units such as kin and friendship groups and the wider social order. While Mark Granovetter's (1973) study of "weak ties" provides an even clearer link between microlevel interactions and macrolevel patterns. Using data from collective behavior studies, diffusion and adoption studies, and his own job finding studies among professional workers, he builds a convincing case that acquaintance ties permit the bridging between social networks. Because networks of strong ties require considerable investment of time and emotion they become self-contained in keeping certain relevant information to themselves ("information management"), thus there is the need for noninvolving bridges between small groups. As Granovetter (1973:1378) notes:

> Weak ties are more likely to link members of different *small groups than are strong ones, which tend to be concentrated within particular groups. . . . weak ties . . . are here seen as indispensable to individual's opportunities and to their integration into communities; strong ties, breeding local cohesion, lead to overall fragmentation.*

We have suggested that taste may be the essential mechanism for establishing and maintaining these weak ties that bind social circles.

Polsky, for example, argues that in spite of all attempts to make pool playing a family activity—that is, include women—it will not work because every attempt to make the pool hall acceptable to female participants inhibits its appeal to the steady, all-male, participant groups. The pool hall has traditionally been a place where social circles based upon gender (male) are provided a routine activity and a regular locale for gathering. Polsky suggests it was largely a place where nonhomosexual, unmarried males remained the core of participants to be regularly supplemented by married males escaping from the "gentle ways" of females. With the decline of bachelorhood as a widespread social role and with the incorporation of male nonwork activities into family life, Polsky argues that the pool hall has lost its major function as a male refuge. It is important to note that Polsky's study illustrates how a social circle based upon gender is held together on the basis of a common taste, which crossed most geographic regions, social strata, and ethnic differences.

Popular music seems to provide a similar example, although here age (adolescence) is primary and gender is secondary as the basis for establishing a social circle. Johnstone and Katz's (1957) survey data illustrate how a small clique of friends reinforces particular tastes in music and disc jockeys. Yet these same primary patterns serve, with the disc jockey and the music as brokers, to stabilize taste in such a way that there is an overlapping into larger circles of youth, which cut across neighborhood and social strata. In a sense the weak ties to the music and the disc jockey serve as the basis for transcending the strong ties of the clique.

The linkages between small, intimate associations and the norms and values of larger, secondary associations based solely upon taste seem to have been best described in the many studies of the mass media audience, and particularly the television audience. Horton and Strauss (1957:587) provide a useful summary as to how such indirect interaction can sustain a circle of taste:

> Over the course of time direct and indirect interplay between performers and audience binds them together in a common institution or, better, a common "world" of entertainment which has its own well-understood values and norms of reciprocal behavior derived from the common social matrix, its own history and course of mutual development. Any one program on the television screen is but a single episode, for most viewers, in this history. The relationships built up, and the understandings that sustain them, seem no different in kind from those characteristic of normal social life; and the symbolic processes mediating them are likewise the same, though their operations are modified somewhat by the special conditions of television broadcasting.

The complicated patterns of interaction within a face-to-face primary association as it is joined to other similar, but separate, groups in vicarious or parasocial interaction to form a circle of taste—say the fans of a particular television show—can in turn lead to the formation of a formal organization, which may attempt to perpetuate or to alter a given fictional account of reality. For some participants this formal organization can serve as the node for forming new primary associations based on friendship. In such a way do circles of sociation flow into one another.

Ennis (1968) provides some useful examples, from spouse swapping to ocelot owning, of some of these patterns of organizational evolution in the circles of nonwork. Yet in all these complicated patterns of interaction, the larger social attachments remain firmly dependent upon the strength and continuity of affective, intimate bonds. An impressive study by Kasarda and Janowitz (1974:335) provides evidence that

> . . . number of friends is the overall most important type of social bond influencing community sentiments. Other types of local social bonds also exhibit some specific and significant partial effects. Number of relatives living nearby, for example, has a strong effect on a person's sense of community as well as a moderate effect on his desire to remain in the community.

However, as much as taste serves to link groups so does it equally serve to set apart such linkages. As we noted earlier, the issue of maintaining a group's boundary is as essential a problem as binding it into the larger social order. Taste serves as a boundary mechanism in a variety of ways and for a variety of social entities. Even a cursory glance at the literature suggests that various authors have seen taste as bound into matters of social inequality, social differentiation, and invidious comparison; that is, taste is seen as regulating social structure relations, interpersonal relations, and cultural relations. Though more refined distinctions could be created, these seem close enough to the intent of the various authors; and they still permit us to explore the sorts of boundary conditions that involve taste. We will begin with authors such as Karl Marx and Max Weber, who emphasize quite different structural aspects of taste.

TASTE AND SOCIAL STRUCTURE

For Marx, "taste" is a derived manifestation of economic domination and a means for sustaining this domination. Ruling classes, such as feudal landlords and capitalist entrepreneurs, not only expect economic dominance but control government, the world of ideas, and social institutions. For the deprived classes of the capitalist order, the constraints of factory production "would destroy their family life, religious beliefs and national characteristics," and this loss would forge their class unity. Out of the respective class situations of the bourgeoisie and the proletariat would emerge a consciousness of kind and the development of class organization for the inevitable struggle. Thus bourgeois art and culture would be replaced by the creative arts of the masses. In this sense, taste is a means for maintaining structural identities and mobilizing action for those sharing certain economic attributes. As such, taste plays no independent role in social change or in maintaing social stability.

As T. B. Bottomore (1964) notes, Marx was attempting to analyze the social relationships that underlay the economic relationships expressed in monetary values and prices. That is, he was concerned with property institutions that affected control over the means of production. Still, these social relations were conditioned by utilitarian necessity, the need to create survival out of the scarcities and vagaries of nature. All other matters such as art or faith or love are seen as embellishments of this fundamental necessity. For Marx all social action can be accounted for by understanding the relations that persons and groups have to the means of production.

Azrael (1961) indicates how this ideological underpinning continues to enforce a work ethic even as Marxist leaders are attempting to provide workers more nonwork time. Weber (1966:27), on the other hand, does not deny the importance of economic factors, he simply points to the empirical reality that people live and associate on bases other than their relation to the means of production. He states that

> ... "classes" are stratified according to their relations to the production and acquisitions of goods; whereas "status groups" are stratified according to the principles of their consumption of goods as represented by special "styles of life."

A "class situation" is based on ownership of property and on the market system. Although a shared economic attribute may lead to community formation, there is no assurance of this because of the existence of fragmenting tendencies, such as membership in diverse ethnic, religious, or occupational groups. Ideals of this prestige system are found in aristocratic groups of traditional societies, such as the estate system of medieval Europe or the caste system of India. Thus "status situation" is a natural community because it is rooted in the family experience—its religious, ethnic, educational, occupational, and historical heritage. And this is as much so for a family of household servants, stonemasons, or university professors as it is for the landed aristocracy.

For Weber, status honor is expressed through a life-style pattern that is only shared within a particular circle. To retain this distinctive pattern, a variety of restrictions relating to marriage and other social exchanges are created, closing the circle and making it impermeable to others. Thus life-styles grow out of and reinforce a particular social bond, for only by being a member of the circle does one know all the nuances, and only by knowing all the nuances does one demonstrate acceptability within the circle. This pattern is in direct contrast to the class situation, as Reinhard Bendix (1975: 153) notes:

> Even in the absence of concerted action, families share a style of life and similar attitudes. Classes without organization achieve nothing. But families in the same status-situation need not communicate and organize in order to discriminate against people they consider inferior. Weber understood that their solidarity against outsiders may remain intact even when they are divided by intense rivalries.

Finally, where Marx has a linear, inevitable thrust social evolution and Pareto (1966) has a circulation of elites (lions and foxes), Weber sees a circulation of conditions. These are some historical and cultural conditions where class position is most crucial, while at other turning points status position is the crucial determinant.

Again, Weber posits no terminal condition, but only an on-going flow of adaptive responses to change. Weber (1958:193–194) notes:

When the bases of the acquisition and distribution of goods are relatively stable, stratification by status is favored. Every techno-logical repercussion and economic transformation threatens stratification by status and pushes the class situation into the foreground. Epochs and countries in which the naked class situation is of predominant significance are regularly the periods of technical and economic transformations. And every slowing down of the shifting of economic stratification leads, in due course, to the growth of status structures and makes for a resuscitation of the important roles of social honor.

Thorstein Veblen (1953) saw the productive members of society as being those whose "instinct of workmanship" led them to pro-duce quality goods at reasonable prices, thereby reducing material inequalities. However, these persons had been displaced by the "leisure classes," who took the fruits of machine production and spent them on "conspicuous consumption," which increased in-equalities because even the working class began to emulate a cer-tain form of wastefulness. For the men of the leisure classes, women and servants were chattel whose prime function was to consume wastefully and thereby enhance the prestige of the pecuniary lord of the household.

Inefficient attempts at archaic activities, such as hunting or using candles instead of electric lights, are made to evoke a pseudopast. While in universities, the humanities are emphasized over the prac-tical sciences because they further distance the leisure classes from the lower classes. For Veblen, taste is a weapon consistently used by the leisure classes to inhibit the development of useful practices, objects and ways of life that would contribute to the life of ordinary persons. Although he always begins with economic forces, for Veb-len, taste is not simply a representative of a class situation nor com-pletely a manifestation of status situation, rather it becomes a causal force in its own right.

Of course, as C. Wright Mills (1953) observes, Veblen was record-ing the peculiarities of his time when the Goulds, the Fisks, and other *nouveaux riches* were attempting to consolidate their wealth. As Weber might say, they were attempting to convert class situation into status honor through the mechanism of life-style or taste. Mills (1953:xvi) argues that Veblen ignores the role that leisure activities play in securing "coordination of decision between various seg-ments and elements of the upper class."

Mills's (1951, 1956) own work is an exploration of how elites, primarily corporate and military leaders emerging in the 1950s, were incorporating into their class certain life-styles and persons from the world of professional celebrity. In this way these elites were attempting to convert their power into authority so their positions would remain unchallenged. Although Mills's ideas were condemned from a variety of fronts, and it was assumed that he was not reporting on long-term trends but only the decade of the 1950s, his observations remain empirically real. Certainly in the 1972 U.S. Presidential election, the endorsement of Richard Nixon by celebrities such as Frank Sinatra and Sammy Davis, Jr. and the endorsement of George McGovern by Paul Newman and Jane Fonda were seen as important elements in the campaign. Indeed, in the McGovern campaign, a person, who acted as a working-class conservative in a television situation comedy, acted in campaign advertisements as if he were a working-class conservative endorsing McGovern. Apparently a middle-class actor was considered more real than a real worker in a factory. While celebrities such as John Glenn or Ronald Reagan become politicians, old-time stump politicians such as Hubert Humphrey and Gerald Ford assume the stance and cosmetics of media actors. It would seem that the use of celebrity as a form of legitimation continues to be important in the "affluent" society.

Stephan Linder (1970) shares Veblen's premise that the leisure classes conspicuously waste time rather than enjoy it, however Linder assigns the cause to the necessities imposed by continued economic growth. Thus taste in developed economies is ruled by a time famine. Because of the glut of goods, so much time is required simply to maintain and consume possessions that there is little time for rational purchase; for self-maintenance; for enjoying eating, drinking, lovemaking, or child care. Under such conditions, taste must be standardized and managed by the advertising media. In Linder's view, taste becomes a manifestation of an entire economy with relatively widespread material affluence forcing a dismemberment of the more intimate social bonds.

TASTE AND INTERPERSONAL RELATIONS
Taste has been seen as a property of class aggregates and status communities. It can also be seen as a property of the social person. In the two former cases, Marx and Weber see taste as a touchstone for creating a community out of an economic aggregate or as a means of maintaining an impermeable boundary to outsiders. In the case of taste as the property of the social person, taste serves as a means for shaping social transactions. Thomas Carlyle's (1954) discussion of the role clothing plays in shaping behavior, Charles

Cooley's (1964) "looking glass self," in which we have a sense as to how we appear in the eyes of others, or Harry Stack Sullivan's (1940) notion of "reflected appraisals" as a means for guiding the course of ensuing social transactions are all pointing at ways in which we shape our *personae* for certain kinds of responses. Systematic research and theory on these nonverbal gestures by G. P. Stone and E. Goffman illustrate the importance of such gestures in regulating daily social life.

Goffman (1959, 1961b, 1963a, 1963b, 1971) has studied a variety of settings—Crofter Islanders, mental hospitals, street pedestrian traffic, and small social groups. He demonstrates how verbal and nonverbal cues function to regulate social discourse and to manage our strategies of self-presentation. Of particular interest is his study of stigma (1963b), in which persons who have certain unalterable characteristics—skin color, stammer, defective limbs—must develop strategies for managing their appearances before "normals." There is also the tendency for those who have a certain stigma to join together and convert the stigma into a positive attribute of taste; thus those with a particular stigma will agree they are more sensitive or creative or attractive than "normals." Social stigma seems an exaggerated case of how taste serves to exclude some persons, to include others, and to regulate the nature of the transaction.

On the other hand, attention to personal grooming and the use of cosmetics is the opposite of converting a stigma into a positive attribute of taste. In grooming, as Murray Wax (1959) convincingly reminds us, the person prepares to conform to a given social situation. Although his essay deals with women, it should be obvious that the general principles of managing one's appearance hold for both sexes. Wax (1962:593) notes:

> The situations that require the most careful grooming are those
> in which her peers or social superiors will be present and which
> are not defined as informal (casual). The woman who is isolated
> from men who are her peers, for example, the suburban housewife,
> can "neglect her appearance." Her dress and grooming tend to
> be casual. When questioned, she replies defensively that she is
> "too busy" to worry about her appearance; but the career
> woman has far more demands on her time, newspaper feature
> editors notwithstanding. The point is that the career woman
> always has an audience of male and female peers alert to her
> appearance, while the housewife seldom has one.

The purpose of grooming is to transcend eroticism and to manage one's gender so that social status becomes the central identity.

Or as Wax (1962:593) notes: "Cosmetics and grooming serve to transmute the attraction between the sexes from a raw physical relationship into a civilized game."

Stone (1962) has argued that appearance is an essential element in social transactions because it establishes the "identification" of the participants. Persons exchange not only verbal symbols but also natural signs, which establish and shape the interaction: gender, age, bodily size, clothing. Stone (1962:101) gives most attention to clothing, pointing out that "whenever we clothe ourselves, we dress 'toward,' or address, some audience whose validating responses are essential to the establishment of our self." Costumes and appearance become important statements about ourselves because they reflect our taste throughout life. Stone's data emphasize the importance of dress in our continuing socialization. His male informants were most concerned with escaping the clothing dictated by their mothers and adopting the dress of their peers. Women did not express the need to reject, but simply moved at an earlier age into adopting the "uniform" of their peer circle. In both cases, his data suggest how taste permits individuals to move from intimate primary associations to larger associations.

For Harold Nicolson (1955), good manners (mostly British and certainly not American) are the means by which we demonstrate our consideration for others. It is civility in interpersonal relations that raises humans above the other animals, and civilized persons above the savage. Civilized persons manage their egos to create individual styles at the same time as these styles adapt to the styles of others. Such standards, however, are not a creation of the masses of the emerging welfare state. Nicolson (1955:283) notes:

> I do not believe that all the citizens of an alert community can, even by the most ruthless economist, for long be rendered identical in possessions, intelligence or physique. Differences of temperament, which as I have shown exist even among hens, will create among human beings differences of taste and desire. It is generally agreed that in any society it is a minority only (whether it be hereditary, elective or co-opted) which is fit to govern. Similarly it will be a minority only that will mould the manners of the future.

Nicolson illustrates how manners serve to reinforce certain interpersonal relations and to attenuate others. Manners are a behavioral address to another that announces an identity, a history, and a probable course of action for the transaction at hand. Taking Nicolson's aristocratic ideals, we suggest that all groups sharing a particular status condition have a minority who creates standards of good behavior that permit inclusion and exclusion of persons. This pattern seems clearly illustrated in a recent study in which drug addiction was analyzed as a miniature social system. The researchers (Mc-Auliffe and Goron, 1974:832) note:

> *Our analysis pointed to an addict stratification system built around the two major psychopharmacological phenomena of opiates: withdrawal and euphoria. Addicts who can barely succeed at tending to their daily needs to avoid withdrawal occupy the lowest prestige positions. In the higher prestige ranges, addicts are stratified by success in achieving euphoria. Apparently, much of the prestige attached to addict occupations (the "boss" hustler) derives from the significance of their relation to the achievement of euphoria. Thus, the social system and the value system of addicts are closely related to the hedonics of addiction at the individual level. Since the reinforcers that are universally considered, within the subculture, to be most fundamental operate at the individual, psychopharmacological level and their hedonic effects seem rather robust in the face of social influence, it would appear that the major values of this subculture emerge from these personal values, rather than vice versa. This should serve as a needed reminder that cultural values are not necessarily the autonomous, ultimate origin of all that they contain, while the relation between competence as an addict and success at achieving euphoria provides an important demonstration of the extent to which competence may underlie stratification systems generally, deriving its legitimacy from consensus on personal values and from direct personal familiarity on everyone's part with the demands of the task in hand.*

Russell Lynes' (1949) delightful historical study of American taste provides ample illustration of similar patterns among persons whose occupation is not with drug euphoria. As Lynes (1949:4) notes: "Taste is our personal delight, our private dilemma, and our public facade." He traces, from the 1820s to the middle 1950s, our public, private, and corporate attempts to make invidious comparisons within an ideology of democratic equality. Not surprisingly, his description of the emerging taste strata of low-, middle-, and high-brows suggests that a certain personal competence underlies the system. Thus a purely social creation such as taste, in which standards ambiguously float without any objective means for testing and about which a range of professional tastemakers issue contradictory pronouncements as to the absolutely right standard, still becomes a creation which can erect the strongest of boundaries for regulating social relations.

TASTE AND CULTURAL RELATIONS

The culture of a particular society, ethnic group, or occupation is primarily a symbolic product. It is a set of prescriptions and proscriptions regarding the behavior, beliefs, and values of its members and the myths, language, and rituals of the collectivity, which distinguishes one social entity from another. Since these elements of symbolic solidarity must be given some material form, poets, painters, sculptors, architects, and other aesthetic groups, arise to create and maintain these material symbols. However, the very emergence of these aesthetic communities establishes a strain between art and society. For who is to be responsible for judging whether the creations are accurate representations of social value? As Lynes points out, the strain becomes even greater in large, diverse, and democratic societies. In such societies, cultural creations are to serve and be appreciated by the masses, yet only a minority of persons are given the right to approve or disapprove such taste.

There are numerous examples of such strains. Kenneth Clark (1961: 74), the noted art critic, argues "that all image art of any value has been made by, or on behalf of, a small minority; not necessarily a governing class in a political sense, but a governing class in an intellectual and spiritual sense." In discussing ornament Clark (1961: 74) says:

> All art is waste in a material sense; and the idea that things
> should be made more precious looking in accordance with the
> status of the use seems to me entirely fitting. I think that a bishop
> should have finer vestments than a deacon and that the portal
> of a cathedral should be more richly ornamented than the door
> of a warehouse. I would go further, and say that ornament is
> inseparable from hierarchy. It is not only the result, but the cause
> of status. The carving on the corner capitals of the Doge's Palace
> and the central window of the Palazzo Farnese confer a kind of
> kingship on those points of the building. In democratic buildings,
> where all the windows are equal, no ornament is permissible;
> although I understand that the higher executives may have more
> windows.

Later Clark (1961:74) states his first law of the relationship between art and society:

> . . . visual art, whether it takes the form of images or ornament
> is made by a minority for a minority, and would add this rider, that
> the image-making part is usually controlled in the interests of
> a system, and that the ornamental part is usually the index of
> status.

Noting a decline in the bond between art and society, Clark (1961:81) implies that strains toward equality are partly responsible for such severing of former linkages:

> The bright new towns in our welfare state are an achievement of which humanity may be proud. But do not let us suppose that this peaceful, humdrum, hell-free, de-Christianized life has been achieved without loss. And apart from the unlikeliness of art being forged at such a low temperature, the doctrine of equality and the drift toward equality, on which such a society depends, run counter to one of my first laws. We have many reliable indications of what Mr. and Mrs. Honest Everyman really want. We don't need surveys and questionnaires—only a glance at suburban or provincial furniture stores and television advertisements. There we see the art of a prosperous democracy—the art that is easily unwrapped—the art of least resistance. This would not matter much, were it not that Gresham's law—that bad money drives out good—is equally true of spiritual currency.

Later he indicates that when an elite minority loses its basis of legitimation it tends toward sect-like exclusions. Clark (1961:82) says:

> During the last hundred years values in art have been established by a minority so small and so cut off from the sources of life that it cannot be called an elite in my sense of the word. Let us call it a priesthood, and add that in preserving its mysteries from the profanation of all conquering materialism, it has made them rather too mysterious. There is something admirable in all forms of bigotry, but I do not believe that we can return to a healthy relationship between art and society over so narrow a bridge.

It is apparent that Clark's evaluation of the loss of connection between art and society is not attributed to mass popularity of art. Clark's argument stresses exclusion as an element in maintaining collective stability. He stresses that socially important art is art made by and for a minority, which the mass may appreciate but not judge because the more access and judgment are opened on an equal, rather than an unequal, basis, the more the value of this form is diminished.

Georg Simmel (1950:295–296) provides insight as to why Clark and others tend to stress an aristocratic distance as essential for artistic endeavor:

> In view of the actual differences in the qualities of men—differences eliminable only in a utopia—certainly, "dominion by the

*best" is that constitution which most precisely and suitably
expresses the inner and ideal relation among men in an external
relation. This perhaps is the deepest reason why artists are so
often aristocratically inclined. For, the attitude of the artist is
based upon the assumption that the inner significance of things
adequately reveals itself in their appearance, if only this appearance is seen correctly and completely. The separation of the
world from its value, of appearance from its significance, is the
anti-artistic disposition. This is so in spite of the fact that the artist
must, of course, transform the immediately given so that it yields
its true, supercontingent form—which, however, is at the same
time the text of its spiritual or metaphysical meaning. Thus, the
psychological and historical connection between the aristocratic
and the artistic conceptions of life may, at least in part, be based
on the fact that only an aristocratic order equips the inner value
relations among men with visible form with their aesthetic symbol,
so to speak.*

In art one does not weigh the worth of the artistic production by
the number of persons buying it, the price it brings, or the number
of admissions paid to view it. In art some judgments or votes are
considerably "more equal" than others. Art and aesthetics are highly
personal affairs in which the individual quality does count and,
therefore, it seems preposterous to call for an equalitarian decision.

Simmel's discussion of the influence of group size upon radical
political movements also adds insight to our general problem. Simmel (1950:205) states that "solidarity decreases in the measure in
which numerical increase involves the admission of heterogeneous
individual elements." That is, the more one expands membership in
an art elite to include diverse elements such as businessmen, politicians, and bureaucrats, the less coherent will be the standards and
the greater the tendency to fragment.

Though Clark (1961) is attempting to keep both the necessary social reforms of the welfare state and the aristocratic standards of the
past, he insists on couching his social analysis in aesthetic rather than
political terms. In a sociological sense, the material manifestations of
welfare state myths or collective representations are more likely to
be found on its billboards, television commercials, and newspaper
advertisements. It may even be that art has not been debased, but
that it truly reflects the nature of the society in which it exists, and,
socialist good will aside, it may be this political reality that Clark rejects. Indeed, within the world of art there may be artists—Andy
Wharhol, for example—whose image is as pure as the taste of the
masses. Or there is Tadzio D'allegro, the "sensitive" critic of slop
art, who sees the major threat to his street art in persons such as
John Lindsay, former mayor of New York City. D'allegro argues that

Lindsay's "WASP stiffness" makes him unable to appreciate old coffee containers and papers whirling in the wind as "nature complementing what man has made."

D'allegro who gained some recognition as a sculptor, has the vocabulary to develop the means for seeing art where others see garbage. As Freeman (1972:22) quotes him:

> *Once you see it as art—. . . all the junk and crap of the*
> *city—all the garbage cans and the graffiti, the dog turds and*
> *candy wrappers, . . . you know that it's not morally objectionable*
> *at all. You have to rediscover your basic instincts. Sometimes the*
> *old verities are best.*

It should be noted that D'allegro and Wharhol are far closer to "popular" art than the conceptualists. The masses could be expected to find some difficulty in relating to an art style whose mode of expression ranges from demolishing houses, filling a gallery with dirt, digging up the street in front of a gallery, mailing the artist's excrement to the gallery, closing the gallery at the artists' showing, or having oneself shot (Bongartz, 1974). Interestingly, elites in the world of art have found a way to establish trading prices for such art. For example, Chris Burden received $1750 for photographs "authenticating" his art form of being shot, and apparently such authentication is now bringing an even more handsome price at art auctions (Bongartz, 1974).

While we can be certain that D'allegro's "old verities" are different than those Clark might think are best, both seem to reflect a modern confusion over the sources of authority. Such confusion would seem most characteristic of a social order where social strata permeability is continuous rather than segmented. Kaare Svalastoga (1965:39) suggests:

> *A social system is considered more or less permeable depending*
> *upon the ease of entrance to and exit from any position in the*
> *system. Thus a minimum of permeability is indicated when birth*
> *determines entrance and death determines exit. A higher level*
> *of permeability is indicated where entrance and exit proceeds*
> *independently of birth and death.*

On this basis Svalastoga (1965:40) identifies five distinct models of differential permeability. They are:

1. Caste model—permeability zero.
2. Estate model—permeability very low but not absent
3. Class model—permeability about 40 percent of maximum

4. Continuous model—permeability about 80 percent of maximum
5. Egalitarian model—permeability perfect (represents certain tribal societies)

A continuous system is characteristic of a high-energy industrial society. "The model assumes that for any person of given status it is possible to find another as near him in status as desired without equaling him." (Svalastoga, 1965:59) Societies with a tertiary economy, such as the United States or Sweden, have a continuous system of stratification.

In a continuous system of social differentiation, the establishment of authority (intergroup dominance pattern) reflects the recombination of social circles in such a manner that they function as a means of establishing certain conditions of impermeability. As Lionel Tiger (1969) might suggest, where the attention structure for dominants is less clear because differentiation in the wider system is evident only at the ends of a continuum, then there will be a tendency to manufacture marginal differences. In the more articulated and rigid systems of differentiation—such as caste systems—it is more likely that social circles are isomorphic with class and status position. We doubt if the questions raised by Clark or Tadzio would ever occur in caste or estate systems.

In continuous systems there is a constant struggle to maintain the symbolic purity of the social circle, yet overlapping, invasion (commercialization), and succession are equally strong counterpressures. The authority of esoterica, final solutions (censorship, wilderness or park bills, licensing, professionalization), high personal costs (that is, time investment) serve as protective barriers. Because life-style roles and values are more ambiguous and commercially convertible than functional economic roles and values, the clear-cut inclusion or exclusion becomes difficult. For example, hippie costumes, rented, affected, or serious; artists and pseudoartists, conservationists and nonconservationists are all cases of unclear discrimination. Unlike a journeyman or apprentice machinist, these roles of hippie, artist and so forth are matters of self-identification and proclamation. Although a critical inner circle may attempt to arbitrate membership, its standards are always threatened by deterioration. In a caste or estate system the authority of the larger society supports the judgments of the inner circle; in a continuous system, the only guarantee is in institutionalization. Ironically, institutionalization of life-styles in a continuous system seems to more quickly open the standards to deterioration. For example, long hair as a banner of protest becomes a norm; universities as sorters for hierarchy are pressed to modify modes of discrimination and become ordinary; far-out music of one cohort becomes normative and "classical" for the succeeding cohort.

Thus producers, consumers, and maintainers of a life-style in a continuous system of differentiation are always in an uneasy relationship as they attempt to establish division where none clearly exists (Davis, 1971; Wilensky, 1964; Greenberg, 1953; Toffler, 1965). We suspect their problems mirror the problems of authority and social order in the wider society. At what point on an age continuum is one mature, or ready to be an adult? How are the sexual roles to be differentiated when conditions, ideology, and data suggest a continuum? Where is the city and where is the country in functional terms? Who is really a black and who is really a white? Or is this another continuum running from Cleaver to Wallace, with self-identity rather than objective or clearly understood criteria placing one in a dichotomous bin.

Problems of authority and social order in continuous systems are not likely to be resolved by appeal to traditional patterns of legitimation. Rather the building of estatelike conditions in life-styles seems a potential pattern. The re-creation and positive value of crescive and enacted ethnic life-styles among Afro-Americans, Italian-Americans, Spanish-Americans, and so on seems one attempt to close circles. For WASPS, the conservation movement may reflect one possible similar attempt.

Our basic argument is that life-styles serve to maintain a given level of social permeability: social circles are the fundamental social mechanism for maintaining life-style, and it is the combination of life-style and social circle that insures the maintenance of a given form of permeability in the wider society. For example, it would seem that all five of Svalastoga's (1965) forms of permeability prevail in an ethnically diverse, large, continental industrial society, such as the United States, Canada, or the Soviet Union. There may be a balanced tension between these forms of permeability, with one being the predominant force in the larger social order, while the other variations are tucked away in fringe, local, or organizational settings.

SUMMARY

We have considered how traditional working-class culture (Chapter 3) uses localism to tighten the permeability of its circles, while some professions provide occupational milieu that have most social circles converging around the job. In Chapter 5, we considered the elemental factors of age and gender, which still serve as focii for social circle formation. Also in Chapter 5 we saw how many of these forces are ordered by kin and other primary associations. And in all of these associations, taste serves to validate membership and to give a sense of stability in a world of change.

Taste, then, provides a generic fix of time and symbol, which connects and maintains the social loop. This is especially so for social units smaller than a society and larger than intimate associations. Ethnic, mystical, deviant, or counterculture groups are social units that seek to survive beyond the moment of an encounter or a single generation of existence. Yet under certain conditions, there is the press toward extinction, absorption, assimilation, or commercialization by the larger social environment. Therefore, the distinctive routinization of taste becomes a primary property for sustaining a collective identity, and the retention of "ownership" becomes a constant struggle.

Finally, the trickle down of taste standards from elite groups to the masses may have larger social implications than simply driving elites to seek evermore esoteric fashion. Lloyd Fallers (1966) suggests that the trickle effect gives the illusion of success to those who fail to achieve in the expected manner. He notes that there are always more persons qualified than there are higher positions. In a society whose myths emphasize achievement this illusion can be an important factor in keeping people efficient in their immobile work roles. Fallers (1966:404) states that if such a factor does operate then

> . . . new goods and services must be developed and existing ones must become more widely available through mass-production. Average "real income" must constantly rise. . . . Were the productive system to shrink, the pay-off would become negative for most and the unrealism of the motivation to achieve would be compounded."

The decade of the 1970s may provide the crucial test as to whether the dazzle of fashion change can confound the economic realities of a shrinking resource base in the Western industrial societies. If so it will certainly demonstrate the strength carried by the symbols of taste.

In summary, we argued that by including the primate biosocial heritage of human societies we can better understand the nature of social ties within and between social groups. We argued that taste serves as a means for persons to leave the tight bonds of family and friends and to participate in larger social circles.

However, we suggested that the process of linking some groups also served to set apart other groups. We considered studies where taste served to differentiate at the structural, interpersonal, and cultural levels. In this way we hoped to outline an explanation as to how microsocial interactions might be linked to macrosocial patterns.

In this argument we gave most attention to aesthetic representations. Here we attempted to go a step beyond Weber's seminal analysis of status communities, to argue that in continuous systems of social permeability the differences of aesthetic taste become essential in maintaining sharper cleavages than are available in the larger social world. Indeed, such trickle down of taste through the consumption of copies of former elite tastes may serve to maintain larger social stabilities.

Though much of our discussion remains speculative, we do feel there is sufficient evidence that taste, as other symbolic constructs, plays a larger role in social life than our materialist visions have heretofore led us to consider. This chapter has attempted to take our earlier discussion of the way nonwork serves to establish intragroup bonding and to illustrate how these bonds and other forms of nonwork can sustain intergroup unity. In the next chapter we will consider the interdependence between group characteristics, the physical design of places, and certain behavior regularities. While in Chapter 8 we will consider how myth as a natural elaboration of taste may serve to sustain larger societal systems. In each of these chapters we attempt to place the social person within a particular realm of overlapping social circles whose structure and continuity are both unique and isomorphic to the total person.

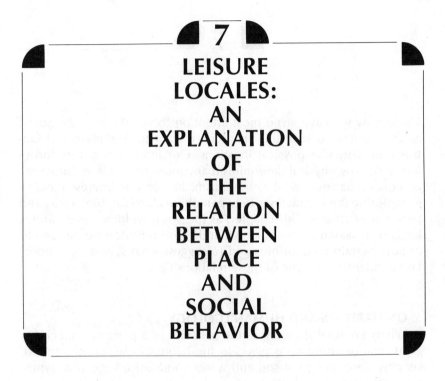

7

LEISURE LOCALES: AN EXPLANATION OF THE RELATION BETWEEN PLACE AND SOCIAL BEHAVIOR

Up to now we have given most attention to variations in the social aspects of nonwork. In this chapter we want to fit these social factors into particular physical locations. Our interest is not in "proving" a narrow physical determinism any more than it is in "proving" an equally narrow social determinism. Rather our interest remains in exploring the interactions between physical, social, biological, and personal variations. This chapter, as the entire volume, uses various kinds of research data—our own and those reported by others—to explore certain relationships and to suggest what seems like important regularities in some of these relationships.

ON HABITATS AND HUMAN ECOLOGY

When a naturalist describes the behavior of a particular species, a great deal of attention is given to the habitat in which it is found. Lengthy descriptions of soil and water conditions, vegetative types, topography, climatic factors, seasonal variations, related species, and other factors fill such reports. One seldom stops to ponder the relevance of such data, for it is understood that the object of inquiry is the species. Variables associated empirically with the presence of the species tend to be considered as potentially relevant to its presence. Thus almost all aspects of the biosphere that have survival potential for the particular species are routinely reported. This, in its broadest sense, is an ecological perspective.

Sociology has had such a "naturalistic" orientation. Otis Dudley Duncan, Amos Hawley, and William Catton are recent proponents, while Robert Park, Ernest Burgess, Howard Odum, August Hollingshead, and others established the early school of human ecology. For these scholars, the environment of *Homo sapiens* is an important focus for understanding its behavior. Moreover, the environment is comprised not merely of cultural objects or related consequences. There is an appreciation for the characteristics of the land, the spatial distribution of human activities, and the relation between demographic patterns and resource flows. For a number of reasons, not germane to this argument but considered elsewhere (Burch, 1971a), the ecological perspective has not passed much beyond its initial flowering. However, it may experience a rebirth if current overtures to rapprochement between sociology and the biological sciences proceed beyond the first flirtation.

Curiously, despite its concern to place human social behavior into a naturalistic perspective, one seldom encounters in "human ecology" the analogous descriptions of "habitat," which one might have expected to find. In part it is a reflection of an appreciation for the mediating influences of culture in the daily affairs of *Homo sapiens* and the attempt to document the operation of the basic processes of competition, conflict, accommodation, and assimilation occurring therein. But it also reflects the generalized absence of theoretical appreciation for the biosocial aspects of human behavior. Hence even within the theoretical perspective of human ecology, the conceptualization of the social group as a biosocial unit in addition to a cultural unit is not emphasized. We have suggested that cognizance of this fundamental property is necessary for an understanding of the manner in which the social organization of work and nonwork complement each other as aspects of human societies. Moreover our recognition of these differences suggests that the habitats commonly associated with various aspects of the respective social organizations ought to be distinctive.

Earlier (Chapter 5) we suggested that as a consequence of the institutional order of human economies, social age categories were segregated in places of work, schooling, homemaking, and so forth. The habitats in which such behavior occurs are different from others. Among students of the social organization of work this has been recognized implicitly in the many studies of factories, offices, hospitals, prisons, advertising agencies, insurance firms, and so on. Very few have approached such settings as a naturalist would have approached the study. Perhaps William Foote Whyte's (1948) study of the restaurant industry comes closer than others. Yet even his astute observation regarding the cultural dimensions involved in the interactions between waitresses and cooks, did not conceptualize it as Edward Hall (1959) might. That is, to what extent were the difficulties experienced in interpersonal relations between waitresses and cooks conditioned by the basic nature of interindividual social spacing? One cannot help being struck with this feature when Whyte's work is read from a background of recent ethological research.

Unlike the study of the social organization of work, the study of the social organization of nonwork necessarily directs our attention to the habitats where such behavior occurs. In this chapter we will outline our general approach and then direct our attention to two specific nonwork locales—parks and wilderness areas.

LEISURE LOCALES

For reasons discussed above, it is likely that the habitats where leisure behavior occurs will be distinct from those where other behavior occurs. Hence we may expect that human social behavior will be distributed differentially in an environment. Indeed such distributions tend to be characteristic of many primate species. Seldom do bathing, resting, eating, defecating, sleeping, and relaxing occur in the same place. *Homo sapiens* tend to also reflect this characteristic pattern of separation of behavior within space.

We may consider a leisure locale as a place where people engage in behavior not ordinarily associated with instrumental or work aspects of existence. Our emphasis here is a relative one. Some worklike activities go on during a golf match, just as playfulness and flirtation take place at a job location. Yet, in both nonwork and work situations, there are certain appropriate times and places for certain nonconforming activities. The nineteenth hole is likely to have a denser pattern of business talk than is found on the putting green; while the lunchroom or the water fountain are more likely places for a higher density of playfulness to occur than at the assembly line. The home would appear to combine a variety of activities, yet even here there is a sharp segregation of spaces appropriate for certain activities. The children are told to not play in the shop, study, sewing room, or sitting room, but to go outside or into the "family" room. One of the things that must have astonished Byington (1910/1974) in her study of steelworkers homes, was the attempt to separate the functions of sleeping, eating, cooking, bathing, and socializing by the workers' wives even though they had only one or two rooms. Even in economies where home and work are closely entwined, such as agrarian or hunter-gatherer, the home is primarily a place of social and personal maintenance, with places of work, ritual, and play nearby, but distinctly separate.

Polsky (1967) gives a graphic account of the varieties of action and social groups that can be contained within a relatively small space, yet which can remain highly segregated and almost unaware of the mutually occurring "other" action. Yet, in spite of this diversity of groups, there remains the common thread of nonwork, which the locale defines. As Polsky (1967:177) observes:

> The intersection of beat and "ethnic" circles, and indeed of
> Village social circles generally, can be seen at its warm-weather
> wildest in the hundreds of people who on Sunday afternoons
> gather round the children's wading pool in Washington Square
> Park. The circles here are as much concentric as intersecting.
> The inner circle consists of people who arrive by 1:00 P.M. and
> thus get seats on the rim of the pool and on the steps leading

*down into it; this circle is a mixture of early-rising square Vil-
lagers, many of whom have brought their children to wade, and
beats who get there early because they've been up all night.
(The beats used to get high and roll around in the pool with the
kiddies, fully clothed, until the Park Department enforced the
rule restricting the pool's use to those under 12 years of age.)
Surrounding this is a second, standing circle of clusters of folk
and hillbilly performers and their listeners; uptown tourists and
new-style rich Villagers, "ethnic" teenagers, Italians, a few beats.
Around this is a third circle, also quite mixed but consisting
mostly of beats asking each other what's happening, tourists with
cameras trying to elbow their way into the second circle for a
good shot, and tight-trousered Village homosexuals walking their
dogs and cruising each other.*

Further, although all places of work share certain similarities in
terms of the general moral order, measures of input and output,
functional social units that are involved, and so forth, each particular type of work has its own special variations. Like places of work,
leisure locales share certain general moral properties common to all
forms of nonwork, yet within this order there is a diverse range of
functions, each with its specialized moral order, physical design, and
social structure to ensure particular behavioral responses. Lee (1972),
for example, found considerable variation in the *manner* and *mechanisms* of normative enforcement in various types of urban open
spaces. However, in all areas that he studied there was a consistent
normative system operating.

For a number of years Burch and his students have been exploring the ways in which design variations provide "environments"
whose physical and spatial cues attract and shape a certain range of
nonwork behavior.[1] They have done systematic observation in a variety of locales—large urban open spaces, neighborhood parks and
playgrounds, museums, nature centers, children's camps, shopping
centers, beaches, sports stadia and cocktail bars, and so forth. Their
work suggests the following tentative classification of leisure locales.

1. *Transitional*, such as waiting lounges in transportation depots,
   courtrooms, theaters. These are locales where large numbers of

[1]As these studies are exploratory forms of data collection, most are unpublished
or in the form of working papers. There are over fifty of the latter represented
by: R. Allen, H. Black, P. Blanksma, J. Boyers, D. McCaffrey, P. Nemir, T. Pearce,
M. Shelstad, S. Shotland, J. Stockade, B. Young, F. Ziegenfus. Burch (1964, 1965);
Young, Shelstad, and Burch (1974); Lee (1973); and Greist (1975) are representative
of more formal papers. An important complement to this work is Klausner's (1971:
131–166) typology of vacation forms, which combines topographic relations, direction of social movement, and psychological orientation.

strangers are aggregated together to dissolve or to rejoin certain other human associations.

2. *Integration*, such as village greens, school playgrounds, club swimming pools, which serve as central interaction nodes and symbolic focal points of certain functional social units. The ecology of such locales permits a wide diversity of social units to be spatially and temporally segregated. As these are associations primarily based upon propinquity, the homogeneity of ethnicity, social class, and age seems characteristic. The effect of critical distance as discussed by Schmitz-Scherzer and Bierhoff (1974) is a significant ecological factor.

3. *Bonding*, such as large open-space territories, sports stadia, zoos, parks, beaches, where large aggregates of strangers are parceled into many small intimate social groups. It seems that already existing intimate associations such as kin groups come to such locales to reenact and sustain existing bonds.

4. *Solidarity*, such as occurs in indoor open spaces like museums, galleries, and specialized shows. Sculpture gardens, cemeteries, and certain parcels of urban form such as a historic square, street, or group of buildings can serve similar functions. Characteristic groups seem to be bonded pairs and organized groups, such as school children and tour groups. Such locales serve to reaffirm the larger social order through the display of artifacts that give physical shape to collective representations or myths.

5. *Custodial*, such as golden-age clubs, youth clubs, scout camps, day-care centers, where recreation is a means of managing certain populations through occupying them in "useful" activities. Such locales have clear organizational hierarchies and design environments that reinforce such management patterns. These settings are remarkably like work settings and, like work, the characteristic social unit is an individual.

6. *Exchange* includes a variety of indoor functional spaces such as singles' bars, shopping centers, foyers of banks, post offices, and unemployment offices. In such locales, personal futures are traded and exaggerated claims assume a certain currency. Individuals seem to be the most characteristic social unit.

7. *Fantasy*, such as fairs and amusement parks, where make-believe and vertigo are collective goals. Bonded pairs and kin of different ages seem the characteristic groups.

Each of these locales seems to have their own particular design and activity cycle constraints. For example, transitional locales such as waiting lounges in bus depots, railway stations, and airports, although attracting persons from different social strata, have a high degree of behavioral regularity. All such settings contain rows of fixed seating that inhibit face-to-face interaction, the indifferent food vendor, the newspaper vendor, the arrival and departure schedule, the ticket vendors, the ubiquitous clock, and the routinized cycles of crowding and emptiness. These are such universal features that, whether in Baroda, Gujarat; Cambridge, England; Wellington, New Zealand; or Naples, Italy, the stranger would recognize the locale and behave appropriately.

Such transitional locales represent highly routinized rites of passage in which the joining of one set of relationships requires the closing of another set; and all must be effected within a crowded public place. Further, the duration of the interaction cycle is short, intense, and rather devoid of content, and, therefore, must be guided by highly stylized greeting and leave-taking rituals. Thus social order is maintained by the ebb and flow of external events, which are contained by elaborate social rituals. Some idea of the pervasiveness of this external order can be gained by finding yourself caught on the high tide of a crowd that is arriving or departing and then, as that flow recedes, discovering that you and the stranger next to you are still waiting for the next arrival or departure. Suddenly what was a perfectly acceptable seating position in the crowd is now mutually seen as overly intimate within the embarrassing emptiness of the waiting room. This is in direct contrast to local park situations, where order is maintained by intimate social groups looking to their own needs and managing the behavior of their own members.

Relations between design and behavior could be explored for each of the locales we have identified and for those yet to be identified.[2] However, in the ensuing discussion we are going to use data on local parks and wilderness areas to illustrate some of the more salient properties of leisure locales and some of the factors that distinguish them from one another and from other kinds of social settings.

THE PUBLIC PARK AS A LEISURE LOCALE

Both historical and ethnographic studies emphasize that most societies have areas of land that are primarily used for expressive purposes rather than instrumental or economic purposes. Among such are sacred areas symbolizing religious values shared among the

---

[2]In recent years a great deal of research has been done on the relation between design and behavior. The work has involved a wide range of disciplines from architecture to zoology; however, work which is closest to our perspective is represented by Sommer (1969), Wohlwill and Carson (1972), Hall (1959), and Goffman (1971).

members of the society; areas where the sick and diseased, as a leper colony, were maintained to isolate such problems within a society; and areas where the morally unfit, such as criminals, are separated from the morally fit. The park appears to be another example of such land areas.

It is not altogether clear whether the public park as presently found in many industrial societies is solely a phenomenon of the postfeudal period or not. We do know that throughout recorded history there have been large land areas that apparently shared the characteristics of contemporary parks. In general terms, such areas served the functions of ornamentation, preservation, or recreation. However, until the end of the feudal period such lands were usually private property and were not open to any member of a society as a right of membership. Apparently, game parks, for example, were maintained for purposes of hunting. The animals killed in the chase were not necessary as a food supply for the household; nor were persons not attached to the retinue of the lord permitted to hunt these beasts. Punishment for poaching was serious and remains so in some societies even today.

Not all parks that contained animals were for hunting; some were for the pleasures of viewing or leisurely study of the fauna. In fact, a not inconsiderable amount of relatively sound zoological information and knowledge has been received from the observations of the owners of these animal parks. Still these were private preserves not available generally to anyone who wished to enter.

In a somewhat analogous manner, there existed large parks where the cultivation of flora for purposes of pleasure in viewing, leisurely study, and so forth were undertaken. These are perhaps more accurately thought of as gardens and arboretums. Different societies seem to have different social norms regarding who might enter these places, although the vast majority remained privately owned. Thus, in Rome, citizens could stroll a private garden providing they did not damage its contents or disturb the activities of the owners. Near the end of the feudal era, the public was granted access to some of the royal parks in Europe and Great Britain, but not as a right. The Roman example is suggestive that in some societies the appreciation of beauty was not considered the capability solely of the upper social strata. Perhaps the concept of noblesse oblige or its analog encouraged the opening of gardens as an indication of beneficence or to educate the masses in things of beauty. Whatever the reasons, there is evidence that some private gardens were available to the masses under certain conditions. These conditions were apparently revokable unilaterally.

It appears that such land areas, privately owned and maintained, were primarily symbols of social status in all of the societies where they occurred. In a like manner today, some land areas continue to serve the same function. The estates of the wealthy in industrial societies appear remarkably like those of earlier eras and serve many of the same purposes. Limited accessibility to such estates reduces the social visibility of the day-to-day lives of an elite, making the contradictions between the cultural imputation of moral superiority to such persons and the vulgarity of their behavior easier to avoid.

Sociologically, what is noteworthy is that these parks and gardens, though privately owned, were symbolic of beliefs and values shared among the members of a society. Public parks in contemporary societies continue this symbolic function as an important aspect of a sociocultural entity. Another aspect of the park throughout history is the association of pleasure with it. This association derives in part from the noninstrumental character of these land areas.

The park as a large land mass, privately owned, to be appreciated at the whim of the owner for noninstrumental purposes has carried over to the public park. Whatever the symbolic character of a public park or garden, one of its essential sociological ingredients is pleasure for the people.

Sociological Characteristics of Local Parks

Parks are thus symbols of beliefs and values commonly shared among members of a society and also essentially pleasurable places for those with access to them. Clearly not all parks are equally accessible to all members of a society. But for the moment we will ignore this practical reality and examine some of the sociological characteristics of local parks in the United States. In the study from which these data were drawn, a local park was any kind of public park located within a 2-mile radius from the home of the respondent.[3]

First, it was ascertained that among subadults, adults, and mature adults the majority go to a local park as members of a social group. Approximately 85.9 percent of the sample so indicated. Considerably less go alone (12.4 percent).

Second, it is particularly instructive that the social groups were organized and nonorganized. An organized group is more like a social assemblage, (see Chapter 6) than a social group as we have defined it. However, it is comprised of subunits some of which are social groups and some of which may be individuals previously unattached to the grouping until this occasion and, perhaps, never again. An example would be a tour group. Approximately 7.3 percent of the respondents were at the park in such organized groups. The remaining respondents in groups were in nonorganized groups (78.6 percent).

---

[3]For details of universe, sample, study design, and so forth, see Cheek (1971).

TABLE 30 RANK ORDER OF ACTIVITIES
IN LOCAL PARKS AND STREETS COMPARED

Activity Remembered	On Street	In Park
Observing people around me	1	1
Just sitting and relaxing	—	2
Looking at the scenery	2	3
Helping someone in trouble	7.5	—
Eating or picnicking	—	4
Feeling how beautiful life is	4	5
Doing just what I want to do	—	6
Being annoyed at litter on ground	3	—
Sharing my experiences and feelings with someone	6	7.5
Speaking with someone I haven't met before	5	7.5
Remembering a childhood experience	9	—
Being alone and thinking	7.5	—

Third, the nonorganized groups were divided, in turn, between social groups in which all individuals were related through kinship (57.1 percent) and those in which all individuals were friends (21.5 percent). In short, local parks appear to be places where a substantial proportion of the humans therein are present as members of social groups. It would appear likely local parks can qualify as places where social solidarity may be developed. To enlarge our understanding, we can now examine the respondents' reports of the kinds of activities in which they engaged while in the park.

Behavior While at Local Parks

Each respondent was provided a list of 25 different activities that might occur while in a park and asked if during the last time at a local park, he or she had done any of the 25. The purpose of this list was to enable the identification of common elements used by respondents in distinguishing among various locales. For comparative purposes we also show how the same respondents report on the same list of 25 activities when asked about the occurrence of such activities while they were walking down a street.

Table 30 shows the rank order of each activity from those activities that more than 50 percent of the respondents reported. For our present purposes, it is the comparative *dimensions* between the two locales that are instructive. Hence the use of rank order.

Notice that the local park differs from the street in that respondents report three activities that occur at the former, but not the latter: just sitting and relaxing, eating or picnicking, and doing just what I want to do. Conversely, they reported as major activities on streets, but not in parks: helping someone in trouble, being annoyed at litter on ground, remembering a childhood experience, and being

TABLE 31 RANK ORDER COMPARISON OF
GROUPS IN LOCAL AND NONLOCAL PARKS

Social Group Expected	Local	Nonlocal
College students	7	5.5
Parents with children	1	1
Groups of teenagers	3.5	5.5
Adults with a lot of free time	3.5	3.5
Young people on dates	5	7
Groups of school children	2	3.5
Groups of people who come by bus	6	2

alone and thinking. As can be seen, a number of activities are shared between the locales, but with somewhat different saliencies. It is to be emphasized that what is important about these data for our purposes, is the pattern associated with each locale. In short, the local park appears to be distinguishable empirically from other social settings in which similar actions may occur. Other differences also exist.

Group Structures
Leisure locales are not only distinguishable in terms of their characteristic patterns of activities but also in terms of the patterns of social beings present therein. Clearly not all leisure locales are the same, but, as before, it is the patterns produced by the relative presence or absence of various elements that make them distinguishable one from another. For example compare the rank orders of various expected groups of social beings between two types of parks—local and nonlocal. (See Table 31.)

Rank order is based on the frequency with which the respondents indicated the group was to be expected to be present in that locale. That which is instructive about the data is the comparative rankings of similar elements in two locales. In particular the "ties" are instructive. Difference "scores" between and within each locale provide some indication of the saliency of particular elements for a pattern. Thus comparing local and nonlocal parks, college students are a somewhat less dominant element in the pattern than is true for parents with children. However, within each locale the saliency of the element varies. In local parks its presence is considerably less salient than in nonlocal parks. It is important to notice that this element, college students, tends to be an anomaly in that it contains individuals who share nearly all the same social age grade—that is, subadult. This unitariness is in contrast to the dominant element of mixed age grade social groups. We will return to this point. It is interesting to notice that the category in which old and young are common members of the group is the first rank in both locales.

TABLE 32   WHO SUGGESTED GOING TO THE PARK?

	%
Respondent	35.0
Someone else	50.7
Don't remember	14.3
Total	100.0

To summarize, we have suggested that leisure locales can be distinguished both from nonleisure locales and among themselves by examining the presence or absence of certain common elements essential to a pattern. Having provided data to substantiate our claims, we now examine several other essential characteristics of such locales.

Sexual Composition of Groups

Primate social groups are characteristically mixed sex. The ratio of males to females varies among the several species, but the actual number is not as relevant as the observable social age categories and the ratios that hold among these. We have already noted the theoretical importance of the elemental variable of social age (Chapter 5) for the understanding of the social organization of nonwork. In our study of local parks we investigated the sexual composition of the social groups. Recall that 12.4 percent of the respondents had gone alone. Among the 85.9 percent who had gone as a member of a social group, only 12.4 percent reported that the sex of the group was the same as that of the respondent. Thus about 73.5 percent of the groups were mixed sex.

Number in Group Composition

Among the nonorganized social groups (that is, other than school and tour parties) found in the local park (78.6 percent), the mean number of the groups was 4.3 individuals. In terms of a distribution, 42.7 percent were groups with less than 5 individuals in them, 24.5 percent ranged between 6 and 9, and 11.4 percent had more than 9 members. The nature of the social relationships among the individuals will be discussed later; for the moment it is sufficient to note that the social groups present were comparatively small in size.

To summarize, we know that the local park, as a leisure locale, is characterized by the presence of small social groups, which are based predominantly on kinship and friendship ties, are of mixed sex, and are represented by a variety of social age categories. It would appear that the local park is a strategic research site for the

TABLE 33 THE INDIVIDUAL, OTHER THAN
RESPONDENT, WHO SUGGESTED THE PARK VISIT

Individual	%
Spouse	23.0
Child	27.2
Relative	22.3
Friend	19.3
Other (neighbor)	7.2
Don't recall	1.0
Total	100.0

investigation of affect and social bonding. Some additional data strengthen this interpretation.

Aspects of Intragroup Bonding

Leadership within social groups, particularly kinship groups, often tends to be traditional (except in some rationally contrived social collectivities that may appear to be social groups). We know that in patriarchal societies males are often the leaders; however, the male-female division of labor often makes the effective decision maker in a group someone other than the traditional leader. We wanted to ascertain the leadership structure of the groups going to parks.

First, we asked who suggested going to the park the last time the group went. As can be seen from Table 32, someone other than the respondent most often made the suggestion. Irrespective of the sex of the respondent, someone else most often was the effective decision maker.

Second, we wanted to ascertain who the effective decision maker was when it was someone other than the respondent.

As shown in Table 33, among those groups in which someone other than the respondent initiated the action of going to the park, there is a remarkable openness to suggestibility. This characteristic of the group suggests that with respect to going to parks, age grade and sex-linked norms, which are often found in other groups, may be inoperative. It may be that this apparent openness engenders the development of social bonds across age grades and among sexes and fosters an appreciation for individuals and their behavior in ways seldom occurring in other situations.

One of the important conditions which may explain these characteristics of the social groups is the continuity of going to the park with the same group. Accordingly, we asked if the respondent had gone to the park with this group before. (See Table 34.)

Only a small number had not been to the park with the same

TABLE 34   PARK VISIT WITH SAME OR OTHER GROUP

Have You Been in a Park with This Group Before	%
No	17.3
Yes	78.7
Some of the same group	2.6
Don't remember	1.4
Total	100.0

group. A small percentage had been with some of the same persons, but not all. Apparently going to the park with the same social group of significant others tends to remain stable over time. This suggests again that the range of people who are considered appropriate to go to a park with may be quite circumscribed.

The persistence of leadership patterns in any group depends upon the willing obedience of the followers. That is, those who follow must grant legitimacy to the suggestions and orders of the leader. We have noted that the social groups that go to parks apparently are characterized by an equivalency of decision making. In an attempt to ascertain the degree of social support accorded the suggestion of one member that the group go to a park, we asked the respondents to indicate the extent to which they had gone to the park because they wanted to do so. (See Table 35.) Apparently most respondents went because they wanted to do so. Even the 11 percent who reported feeling other social pressures also wanted to go.

These data suggest that the social group is the basic sociological unit around which the behavior of going to the park develops. Among the characteristics of these groups are the limited number of persons considered appropriate to participate, that is, kinsmen and friends; the continuity of membership in the group; the equal saliency among members as effective decision makers regardless of age grade or sex differences; and the degree of social support readily accorded the suggestion to engage in going to the park.

The social group of kinsmen and friends who go to parks may or may not remain physically together once they actually enter the park. Younger members may split away from the older members only to rejoin them at some later time just prior to departure from the park. On the other hand, the social group may remain together throughout the entire period in a park. Thus far we have ascertained that going to the park is something engaged in by social groups. If the groups remain together while in the park, then it may suggest that one of the social functions served is to facilitate a particular kind of social interaction essential to group stability. Suffice it to say that the park may be more than a setting in which persons partici-

TABLE 35   PARK VISIT AS VOLUNTARY OR OBLIGATORY

Went to Park Because	%
Wanted to do so	79.7
Felt had to do so	8.6
Both	11.0
Total	99.3

pate in a set of recreational activities. We asked the respondents whether the group with which they had gone to the park remained together throughout the period there, or if it had dispersed then reformed later. The data indicate that about 90 percent of the groups in which the respondents had been participants remained together while in the park. (See Table 36.)

Thus our data suggest that leisure locales like parks may be conducive to the development of social bonds among social age and sex grades. Parks appear to be settings where species-specific bonding transpires. Of particular importance for a species using culture as an adaptive mechanism is the bonding that occurs across social age categories. This is not to deny that the male-male bonds and female-female bonds, which are also facilitated in such leisure locales, are not extremely important. Indeed the male-female bond is facilitated, but again usually mediated through the social age categories. It is essential to notice that these basic bonds are emergent within situations where *Homo sapiens* are individuals and relate to each other as significant others not social persons.

SOCIOLOGICAL
CHARACTERISTICS OF WILDERNESS AREAS

Parks, and particularly local parks, provide a mixture of controlled nature and loosened social constraints. They are settings that sharply differ from the usual enclosed arenas of human action; and they attract certain well-defined social groups. Nature is managed to fit human ideals of aesthetics and to suggest, in Olmsted's term, a people's pleasuring ground. The planned order of grass, trees, foli-

TABLE 36   GROUP TOGETHERNESS

Did Group Remain Together	%
Yes	89.5
No	9.2
Don't Recall	1.2
Total	99.9

age, and play equipment establishes the mood for role release—children can run and shout with greater freedom, adolescents have more options for courtship rituals, and adults can unbutton from the constraints of their everyday costumes and social relations.

Of course, in most times and most societies, urban parks also provide convenient places for prostitutes, dope dealers, muggers, and other persons working in illicit occupations. However, illicit activities are found in but a small proportion of the total number of local parks, and our discussion is directed to the majority of parks that continue to provide local park satisfaction. Indeed, because local parks attract primarily kin and friendship groups, they can exhibit freedom because normative understanding and control are so secure. It is only when significant and rapid changes occur in a local park's catchment area population[4] that norms and sanctioning agencies become askew. Then formalistic brokers of control, such as policemen and park rangers, become the only thin and ineffective line of social order.

Though local parks are fairly universal locales, wilderness, as embodied in legislative concern, rhetoric, and political action seems a social definition uniquely confined to Canada and the United States. In other developing societies, such as Brazil, wilderness is a locale for heroic visions of national destiny rather than a romantic repository of lost innocence (Nash, 1973; Burch, 1971a); while societies with long histories of settledness, such as Europe or Asia, consider managed nature the only appropriate aesthetic. Such contrasts underline the fact that wilderness exists only at the suffrance of human society.

Certainly something sociologically important is occurring when highly urbanized and industrial societies such as Canada and the United States devote so much media and legislative attention and such substantial research budgets to lands that contain no permanent residents, voters, taxpayers, workers, factories, and not even a good likelihood that such developments are possible. The recreation clientele in these areas reflect only a small and select proportion of the national population.

A wilderness area turns local park notions inside out. The management goal in a wilderness is to emphasize natural processes and to compel human visitors to observe a planned order and organization. That is, a wilderness trip is not something that one does on the spur of the moment, but requires considerable advance planning and coordination. Entrances to such areas and the literature describing them consistently emphasize the potential danger, the need to

[4]The area whose population provides the highest proportion of activity days for the park in question; similar to the term used to describe traffic regions and watersheds.

be in good physical condition, the need for adequate planning and emergency procedures, and the need to advise others as to one's planned route. All such warnings close by listing the number of persons who have lost their lives by failing to so constrain and order their actions, and in recent years there has been much emphasis concerning the cost and imposition upon those who must rescue the ill-planned traveler. The social image thus produced seems intended to select only robust individualists, whose behavioral order is inner rather than other directed. Yet the fact is that most persons enter the area with the usual weaknesses and in small groups; they must continually monitor their behavior in terms of these others and the presence of other small groups such as their own.

Intra- and Intergroup Bonding

Therefore, wildland locales may provide a useful setting in which to examine embryo and emerging relationships between intra- and intergroup bonds. For example, data collected by George Stankey (1972, 1973), Robert Lucas (1964a), and others permits us to see the processes involved in intragroup bonding, where being part of a group is largely determined by being set apart from other groups. There are, also, intriguing possibilities for measuring how wilderness and similar type experiences affect the nature of the intragroup bond, under conditions of no contact, some contact, and frequent contact with other groups. These and other questions concerning the structure and function of small groups and their relationship to larger wholes seem most appropriate for wild land situations.

These questions can be dealt with because the prime behavioral unit in wild land recreation is an established social group, with its own history, future, and set of norms. Though nature and solitude are the central motives offered by most wilderness visitors, their verbal and acting behaviors are seldom isomorphic. As we noted in Chapter 5, only around 2 percent of the wilderness visitors are alone, certainly a far lower proportion of solitariness than is found in an innercity "wilderness." The bulk of the people go into the wilds with relatives or lovers or friends. Leisure choice and behavior seem to be primarily determined by these small, intersecting, and intimate social circles (Burch, 1969; Field and O'Leary, 1973).

Of course, nature as a goal is important; but it is important primarily as a setting for reaffirming and strengthening already established social bonds. Solitude is a euphemism for keeping one's group together, while the greatest proportion of time is devoted to interaction and adjustment within one's group, rather than with pristine nature.

However, all of this intensive interaction takes place in a setting where none of the customary physical and institutional screens are available. Unlike golf and other organized sports, which have normative mechanisms for including strangers in the play, wilderness camping is especially fluid. Wilderness camping has no clear and consensually validated rules regarding roles, goals, and relationships, *except* those already established within the intimate group. Consequently, strangers are disruptive because there is no context within which they can be fit. In this sense, wilderness has none of the order found in daily life, where patterns of inclusion and exclusion are routinized by walls, gates, turfs, ghettos, districts, streets, or zones; and where segregation permits the regular fulfillment of expectations (Greist, 1975; Lee, 1972). In daily life, diverse ethnic groups seem to routinely and effectively interact in work establishments, shopping districts, and entertainment districts, where abstract rules and segmental roles prevail; but collide in residential neighborhoods, where contrasting life-styles challenge unquestioned values and intimate relations. In the latter situation, like the wilderness, the small, intimate social circles seem vulnerable to strangers who may not hold similar values and behavioral patterns.

Management of Strangers

George Stankey's (1972, 1973) survey data for four distinct wilderness areas provides a set of satisfaction curves for what he calls "purists" and "nonpurists." His curves are generated on the basis of tolerance for encountering other parties with various kinds of equipment and at various places and times. His interest is in developing a "psychological carrying capacity" similar to the ecological notion used by range managers and other applied zoologists. Although his effort has positive rhetorical value, it seems more useful to convert his "satisfaction curves" into "discrimination curves" under conditions where regularized solutions to managing strangers have not occurred. The issue at stake is not really the number of encounters that can be tolerated, but who is encountered, or, as one of his respondents put it, "It's not the number, it's how they behave." Taking the data he gives us, encounter tolerance is defined by group size, number of groups met, mode of access by the groups—hiking, horseback riding, or motorized means—and moral deviation in the form of littering. Apparently wilderness travelers are most intolerant of large groups and riders (unless, of course, they are riding and/or members of large groups), so we will give first attention to these two factors.

Group size violates the expectation that intimate social groups rather than aggregates should predominate in the wilderness. And, as in a homogeneous residential district, there is a sense of personal freedom because one's neighbors seem pretty much like oneself. Swinging singles would naturally find suburbia dullsville; they do not share its stages of family life cycle, which is the prime mode for ordering such communities. We should recall that wilderness purists prefer contacting even greater numbers of small groups than any large groups (see Table 37). This is not surprising given the fact that small groups are most like the kinds of groups purists travel in.

The intolerance of riders by wilderness purists suggests that the way one pays costs of admittance to the wilderness serves as a social discriminator. This is similar to a report by Burch and Wenger (1967) in which they found that all types of campers, from those in motor home comfort to backpackers, were favorable to meeting hikers, somewhat less favorable to meeting horsemen, and almost totally unfavorable to meeting trail scooters. Most visitors to the wilderness and its fringes have stereotyped expectations about the behavior of groups using distinctive modes of access, and these stereotypes have an evaluative mode as to what is appropriate and inappropriate. This is not unlike studies of social distance and stereotyping between ethnic groups in which interpretation of ethnic behavior is based on the stereotype, even though the actual behavior runs counter to such a view. In relatively unstructured situations of intergroup contact we naturally use gross clues regarding the similarity or dissimilarity of the other group to our group and adjust our tolerance or intolerance accordingly. Gottlieb (1957) found similar processes in contrasting the leisure locales of the neighborhood tavern and the cocktail lounge. In the former, a consistent awareness of shared norms informally controlled disruption; in the latter, the management of strangers required much more formal and abstract controls. Those taverns whose neighborhoods were undergoing rapid ethnic change shifted to much more formal controls.

Stankey (1972), also, found encounter tolerance influenced by the number of other groups met, where they were met, and the evidence of littering. There is a certain point where further increase in the number of groups intensifies competition for scarce and desirable space, and such densities demand urban-type social controls. Therefore, it is not too curious that purists of all sorts prefer encounters on the trail rather than in the camp. The trail is public territory, like a street or a sidewalk, and for it to function properly access must be open to all. The allocation of trail space is ordered and familiar, while that of the campsite is not. The camp is a temporary home, a private property, yet it, too, is permeable to all and sundry; it, too, functions as a public street, although this is clearly not the expectation. While evidence of littering is but one more breakdown in one's moral expectations (Campbell, Hendee, and Clark, 1968; Clark, Hendee, and Campbell, 1971; Heberlein, 1971). Interestingly, the purists, if forced to a choice, will take more people rather than littering, which is a further suggestion that the behavior of others is more crucial than their mere presence.

In the wilderness leisure locale we have small, close-knit groups

TABLE 37   TOLERANCE OF GROUP SIZE IN FOUR WILDERNESS AREAS

Area	One Large Party	One Small Party	Don't Care	One Large Party
BWCA[a]	7	70	23	15
Bob Marshall	4	79	17	24
Bridger	4	88	8	16
High Unitas	3	73	24	14
Average	5	77	18	17

[a]Boundary waters canoe area.

concerned with maintaining the intragroup bond through temporarily owning some wild territory. When they contact other groups in areas where there are existing norms of intergroup contact, such as the trail, they remain satisfied with their experience; but where there are confused or unclear norms to regulate intergroup contacts, such as at the campsite, then satisfaction declines. At the campsite they attempt to use space as a means of maintaining social distance within a loose and ill-defined social order, which has none of the customary intergroup moral brokers: policemen, traffic signals, psychiatrists. Given these conditions, the typical means of recognizing and responding is stereotyping. Those groups that are most like one's own, in terms of likely structure (size), values (means of paying costs), and behavior (no littering), and who are not in direct competition will be the easiest to tolerate. Such patterns are not unlike the visual symbols of counterculturalists, soul brothers, and decal-flagged Middle Americans, who announce a shared value system that brings them together by setting them apart from other social groups.

The avowed interest in wilderness camping is its "freedom," but ironically this is possible only when there are clear guidelines and regulators of behavior for intergroup contact. In the absence of an enacted structure, the tendency is to evolve surrogate patterns that are not unlike everyday life in urbanized societies and may even reflect certain basic characteristics of the species.

SOCIAL EVENTS AND PERSONAL IDENTITY AS ASPECTS OF A LEISURE LOCALE

The general concern over the nature of other groups and the passionate descriptions of the wilderness experience suggest another dimension of leisure locales—that is, their contribution to the occurrence and well-being of social events. Social events are those inter-

Five Small Parties	Don't Care	One Large Party	Ten Small Parties	Don't Care
60	26	19	48	33
47	28	36	33	31
68	16	23	56	21
57	29	25	43	32
58	25	24	46	30

action situations that are distinctive from more routinized patterns, such as regular occasions, ceremonies, celebrations, and chance encounters, but that provide the substance for reaffirming one's identity. For example social events such as sexual encounters are fraught with great symbolic importance, though the objective amount of time and energy invested seems unimportant considering the larger time investment in all the other activities that fill a day and a lifetime.

Undoubtedly there is a researcher who would find out the going rate for local prostitutes and "scientifically" generate for us a cost-benefit analysis of satisfying sexual relations. Clearly these dollar terms would not measure the values we are talking about nor what our actors were engrossed in. Social events are unique, emotion-filled, set-apart occasions, which scramble the usual cost and benefit estimates. In such a context the central interest is not personal gain but rather the well-being of the event. And for its duration there are no other trade-offs. We suspect social events are significant elements in cementing the intragroup bond, and we may find that the larger social web is best-knit by such events, which establish strong and clear identities.

For example, Burch (1964) found an involvement with the experience and a sense of threat by wilderness campers, which was far beyond the usual concern over simply preserving the purity of the rules. The concern over permeability of the experience was regularly expressed by his respondents from quite diverse social backgrounds and with quite different frequencies of wilderness participation.

A well-to-do, well-educated, 53-year-old camper argued:

We do, however, sincerely believe that at least the present wilderness areas should be preserved in as nearly their primitive state as possible.

Open them up to automobiles, motorscooters, and motorcycles, and they will have lost most of their enchantment.

It just seems that there should be some areas left that require just a little effort to get to. It helps the individual to appreciate their small accomplishments. I would not think of climbing Mt. Hood any more. It has been made too easy. It is not like hiking from Government Camp to Timberline the night before—bed down and talk until 2 or 3 and then get up and climb the mountain.

I must sound like I'm about 80—but really I'm not. I'm really rather progressive in my thinking. Mainly I get just awfully tired of people and it is like a tonic to get as far away as possible for just a couple of weeks.

We know a lot of people that would like to do what we do but are quite frank to admit they are afraid to be alone.

A 38-year-old dentist responded to an item asking whether "If the majority of people want changes or improved recreation facilities they should get them" by saying:

LET US REMEMBER THIS IS A LAST FRONTIER OF WILDERNESS —NO MATTER WHOSE MAJORITY LET US SAVE IT FOR OUR CHILDREN—THERE ARE AMPLE TRAILS OUT OF OUR FORESTS FOR SCOOTERS—PLENTY OF WATER FOR BOATS AND SKIERS— LET US OUTLAW THESE PEOPLE FROM MORE OF OUR WILDER- NESS—LET US RESTRICT ROADS—PLEASE KEEP THESE THINGS FROM OUR FORESTS—FOR OUR CHILDREN.

A religious sense of placement in the cosmos through contact with nature was expressed by a 54-year-old, middle-income, business executive camper:

My true reward comes from renewing my contacts with nature: trees, plants, wildlife, insects, rocks, streams, lakes. These contacts improve my perspective. They make me realize (a) Man's essential insignificance in the total scheme, (b) The existence of a Higher Intelligence who has created the infinitely perfect balance we find in the universe.

A 48-year-old logger with a high school diploma, talking of possible changes that might discourage him from camping, says:

Continued rape of the natural resources by the monied interests and the adultery of the people who are hired to protect it. Giving it all to the flabby new type of "outdoor people" many of whom are apparently very unappreciative (but they DO spend money).

A 30-year-old graduate student in mathematics reported on his earliest experience in the out-of-doors at age 15 when he went "on a long hiking, camping trip with a favorite teacher and several school friends in a California redwoods area—an area which now, alas, is too full of people." Some of the most enjoyable things he did then were: "Hiking through the night, watching the sunrise from a mountain top. Wading through dew-covered ferns. Splashing in a secluded mountain stream." He says "We never go to auto campgrounds any more. We find ourselves seeking out more remote areas and unusual seasons—when fewer other campers are there."

Concern over the deterioration of a leisure locale is not a purely modern concern. Indeed Verplanck Colvin (1880) represents that peculiar American passion for both untrammeled nature *and* the progress of settlements. Colvin's (1880:6–7) reaction to the late nineteenth-century development of the Adirondacks seems to describe the classical tourist cycle:

> *While to the political economist these matters are of the first and most vital importance, to the lover of nature and of the wilderness, the progress of settlement, and the extension of civilization into the primeval forests, is recognized only with regret. To the explorer, also, it is pleasanter to imagine the wild mountain crest, or mirrored lake which he was first to reach, remaining as unvisited, in all its aspects as unchanged as when he first beheld it.*

He then describes how new trails had made Mt. Marcy easily accessible. Sadly he responds, "But the first romance is gone forever." However, unlike contemporary naturists, Colvin (1880:7–8) sees such costs as necessary for social progress.

> *And so, glancing over the field of former labors, I find following in the footsteps of my explorations the blazed-line and the trail; then the ubiquitous tourist, determined to see all that has been recorded as worth seeing. Where first comes one—the next year there are ten—the year after full a hundred. The woods are thronged; bark and log huts prove insufficient; hotels spring up as though by magic, and the air resounds with laughter, song and jollity. The wild trails, once jammed with logs, are cut clear by the axes of the guides, and ladies clamber to the summits of those once untrodden peaks. The genius of change has possession of the land; we cannot control it. When we study the necessities of our people, we would not control it if we could.*

Colvin's nineteenth-century optimistic rationale is seldom shared by modern primitivists. A variety of studies, as well as the journals of conservation organizations, indicate that wilderness purists consistently emphasize an almost mystical quality about the "experience," whose associated physical scene and patterns of social relations are profoundly personal, deeply involving, and which demand considerable physical and psychological expenditure. They expressly exclude those who do not wish to pay such a price of admittance. This deification of nature cannot be dismissed as simply an elaborate ritual of rationalization, but is, in Kenneth Burke's use of the term, highly poetic, for one of the individual's sources of identity is at stake. As Burke (1961) has said:

> If a man climbs a mountain, not through any interest in mountain climbing, but purely because he wants to get somewhere, and the easiest way to get there is by crossing the mountain, we need not look for symbolism. But if we begin to discuss why he wanted to get there, we do get into matters of symbolism. For his conceptions of purpose involve a texture of human relationships; his purposes are "social"; as such, they are not something-in-and-by-itself, but a function of many relationships; which is to say that they are symbolical. For eventually, you arrive at an act which a man does because he is interested in doing it exactly as he does do it—and that act is a "symbolic act." It is related to his "identity."

POPULATION STABILIZATION IN LEISURE LOCALES

Leisure locales not only exhibit varying patterns of group composition, behavior, intra- and intergroup relations, and normative patterns; they like other social habitats may also exhibit specialized mechanisms for stabilizing population growth. For example, Kottke (1975:18) concluded from a national sample survey study that there is a "camping-involvement cycle," whose stages are composed of potential, active, and ex-, or dropout, campers:

> According to our 1973 survey results, 9 percent of all U.S. households were in the potential stage, 21 percent in the active stage, and 20 percent were either temporarily or permanently out of the market. The remaining 50 percent were not involved in any stage of the cycle. Not only is the reservoir of potential campers relatively small, it has decreased from 7.4 to 6.1 million households between 1971 and 1973.

Some reasons for the unexpected declines in the supposedly ever-growing family camping market is provided in the Kottke (1975) study, in an analysis of an 8-year family-camping panel study by LaPage and Ragain (1971, 1973), and in a national survey study by

LaPage (1973). They suggest that nonwilderness campers are as concerned about the changes that have occurred in their leisure locale as are the wilderness campers. And a large part of that has to do with reaction to the "newcomers" in the locale. As LaPage and Ragain (1973:18) report:

A close examination of overcrowding comments revealed that they were almost always coupled with complaints about the consequences of heavy use, suggesting that those consequences may be fully as important as crowding. For example, more than 50 percent of the crowding complaints were associated with a comment about less desirable, and less friendly, campers. A great many crowding complaints went on to express concern about one or more of the following: poor campground maintenance and design, unsafe campground conditions, inability to be sure of getting a campsite at the end of a long-day's drive, and rising costs resulting from campgrounds providing "too modern" facilities and services for the crowds of "new" campers with their fancy equipment.

Of particular interest is their discovery of ways in which a recreation system tends to stabilize its own "carrying capacity." They found that "campers responded to feelings of overcrowding by reduced participation, by changing their style of camping or dropping out of the camping." However, many of those who remain within the camping system alter their style and follow two quite opposite strategies—a sizeable proportion move toward the wilderness while others move toward long-term rental in commercial campgrounds.

Therefore, though recreation bubbles may become booms, a prediction based upon extrapolation of the boom curve ignores the natural processes of population formation and stability in a given leisure locale. Stabilization occurs because only a certain proportion of any society's population is in a particular recreation "market" at any one time. Only a certain proportion of the population belongs to the social circles that would make a given activity a potential demonstration of appropriate taste. In addition, certain elemental factors, such as age and gender, render a given activity unacceptable; and certain social factors, such as stage of family life cycle, proscribe the potential population. And finally, as LaPage and Ragain (1971) demonstrate, every leisure locale has an alteration in the types of clientele, which over time so alters the experience that old-timers drop out, shift style, or move to a different activity system.

Indeed, participation in particular life-styles seems to follow a natural growth curve similar to that of other populations such as elk and deer introduced to new ecosystems or the various past epidemics such as the gypsy moth in the northeastern United States. There is a slow buildup, then an exponential period of growth, then stabilization of the population due to predators or disease.

In matters of human leisure there also seem to be mechanisms, such as occur in camping, which stabilize growth. For example, Du-Pont and Greene (1973) found that a mid-1960s heroin addiction epidemic had leveled off by 1971 and begun to decline by 1972, under the impact of control and treatment factors. Interestingly, they also note "It is probable, although difficult to document, that the development of an antiheroin attitude in the community also contributed to terminate the epidemic." (DuPont and Greene, 1973: 722) They report that the pusher is no longer seen as a glamorous individual but as a parasite. "As the appalling consequences of heroin addiction have become apparent, previously susceptible teenagers are no longer willing to take the risk of experimenting with heroin." (1973:722) Thus the at-risk population for a particular taste practice is always limited in size because taste awareness and practice flow through social circle networks and involve primary associations. And these constraining associations combine with the constraints of time, such that the potentially infinite range of activity options are narrowed to the limited one found in circles of kin, friends, and neighbors.

We have argued that all leisure locales have a similar array of symbols and persons concerned with maintaining them. Although the level of intensity may not be as strong as with wilderness campers nor the persons affected as articulate, the same processes of erosion are likely at work in the no-longer-safe local park, the neighborhood bar that no longer has any neighbors, the YMCA or Girl Scout program searching for its lost popularity. Though design of a locale is essential in the maintenance of a set of cues and behaviors, when the groups essential for establishing the norms and ensuring their observance are no longer present, then no amount of design excitements can recapture those moments of secure freedom.

SUMMARY

We have covered a great many issues in this chapter and engaged in an equal amount of speculation. We began by suggesting that analysis of the habitats of human action should be an important aspect of any form of human ecology. We defined what we meant by leisure locales and suggested a tentative classification. We then used data on local parks and wilderness areas to illustrate certain basic principles regarding leisure locales. As the discussion has been long and complicated, it may be convenient to outline some of our ideas.

We noted that some leisure locales re-present collective symbols, while others re-present personal symbols. Parks, for example, have a longer history and are far more widespread than wilderness areas. They tend to have closer connection to the collective symbols of status, history, or nationalism and to emphasize pleasure. Wealthy persons contribute their estates or purchase mountain ranges (the Tetons in the U.S.) or an island (Acadia in the U.S.) to become a national park and not a wilderness area. Wilderness areas tend to be leftover tracts of land whose economic utility remains to be found. Wilderness areas by definition minimize human elements while very often this is a prime reason for a park. Finally, wilderness areas emphasize nature and minimize pleasure. We can imagine pageants, ceremonies, and other routinized collective occasions occurring in parks, with persons in small groups coming to share in the pleasure of the spectacle. Wilderness areas, on the other hand, serve as settings for social events, where persons come with a few others to "find themselves."

We also argued that leisure locales can be distinguished among themselves and from nonleisure locales in terms of (1) whether a person comes alone or in a group, (2) the predominance of a particular kind of group—organized or unorganized, mixed sex or single sex, large or small, and (3) the predominance of certain characteristic behaviors and the absence of others. For example, a local park is characterized by the presence of small social groups based predominantly on kinship and friendship ties and composed of people of both sexes and a variety of ages.

Finally we suggested that some leisure locales may enhance the intragroup bond while others, such as the wilderness, may evolve means for dealing with the intergroup bond among strangers. This led us to speculate that there may be certain mechanisms in leisure locales that tend to stabilize the growth of certain recreation populations.

In the next chapter we will remain with our concern as to the role of nonwork in binding together person, group, and community, though our attention will shift from the realm of place to the realm of myth.

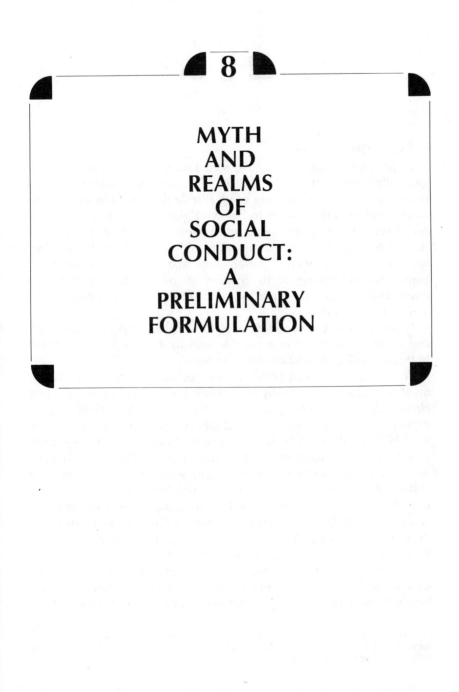

8

MYTH
AND
REALMS
OF
SOCIAL
CONDUCT:
A
PRELIMINARY
FORMULATION

8

EMOTION AND MYTH

In previous chapters we have said that work refers to behavior generally participated in by the *social person*, for which social approval is received in the form of wealth, honor, and power. On the other hand, nonwork refers to behavior generally participated in by *social groups*, for which social approval is received in the form of social favors, gestures of appreciation, and communion. Thus far we have looked at elemental variables of age, gender, and number; considered something of the nature of the relationship between inter- and intragroup solidarity; and considered the influence of variations in leisure locales.

It may now be useful to relook at some other ways in which work and nonwork relate to one another and to the larger social fabric. In this we will give most attention to myth.[1]

The process of social bonding involves the particularistic attachment among a comparatively limited number of conspecifics. Among *Homo sapiens*, affective states are learned, or conditioned, as a means of recognition of significant others. The bringing together of the few is simultaneously the setting apart from others. Yet societies could not exist beyond the "tribal" (that is, there exists a particularistic relationship among all individuals) without the element of a cultural mechanism to ameliorate the containing character of emotion. The biosocial nature of the human being creates an organism capable of a variety of states of arousal—subjective and objective. Rage, fear, cowering, and a variety of other behavioral manifestations are observed early in the life of the infant. Socialization is the canalization of such capacities. The "success" of creating particularistic attachment to conspecifics rapidly creates a dilemma. For the human must learn to differentiate between those conspecifics whom

---

[1]We use the term myth not in the pejorative sense of a false belief but in the sense of high social realism as Mircea Eliade (1960, 1963, 1965), Ernest Cassirer (1955), and Claude Lévi-Strauss (1969).

he or she may "love" and those whom apparently he or she may not "love," or at least not in the same manner.

Yet the inherent presence of subjective response to arousals persists within the individual. Taste acts to bind individuals in a particularistic manner. But human beings are not simply a biosocial species; if they were, then approach-avoidance learning would be sufficient to regulate approachability among conspecifics. Human beings are also a sociocultural species. Culture, as an adaptive mechanism, makes a much more complex response pattern possible for the individual. Since the world is responded to through symbols, individuals, as a consequence of taste formation, do not view it neutrally. They make moral judgments about it in a continuing process; and these judgments are rather simply understood as liking or not liking what is perceived. Yet it is this very act of making these moral judgments that requires enormously complex and prolonged cultural evolution in order to occur in a reliable manner. What cultural mechanism exists to protect the identity of the individual, so carefully nurtured in a particularistic fashion, during encounters with other persons with whom no previous social bonds existed but who are members of a particular tribe or community? How does one remain emotionally neutral towards these others when many of their actions are morally negative? Or in Talcott Parsons' (1951) terms, one is balanced between "affectivity and affective neutrality." If this dilemma has not been resolved, no human society as it is now known could have emerged. Broadly speaking we conceive of the mechanisms used to resolve such dilemmas as *myths*.

"Myth" is a sociocultural mechanism that presupposes "taste," a biosocial mechanism. This viewpoint suggests that what is different about *Homo sapiens* is not their ability to make tools but their creation of symbolic communication. The way in which this ability emerged is still a matter of some debate; but, happily, such knowledge is not central to our argument. Our argument suggests that the particular shape of contemporary and historical societies cannot be understood without equal attention to both the biosocial and sociocultural aspects of the species. Though the peculiarities of history have isolated the investigation of culture from the investigation of biology, our observations suggest that the study of society will be richer if both elements are unified in a single conceptual approach. We have found the study of nonwork to be a particularly fruitful area for examining and understanding how the biosocial and sociocultural elements are interrelated because nonwork seems to emphasize most clearly that the dilemma of sentiment, emotion, or affect is fundamental to the emergence of society.

In the balance of this chapter and in those to follow, we will suggest some of the ways in which such an integrated effort might be undertaken. We begin with some general comments on myth—how it relates to taste, and how myth and taste relate to other aspects of social conduct. We follow this with a chapter that examines how certain forms of nonwork (play, games, and sport) contribute to the elaboration of this conduct so that a society is possible. We then examine how one contemporary industrial society has evolved the new social institution of recreation in response to its own unique historical working through of these more universalistic matters.

MYTH—THE CULTURAL HARNESS OF EMOTION

Myth refers to a general class of explanations embodied in a culture. These explanations are of a special kind; they help explain why that, which should not occur on the basis of other beliefs, does in fact occur. Myths deal, therefore, with the incongruities and inconsistencies of social life. They are ingenious inventions that make it possible for men to simultaneously account for what will happen and what in actuality occurs, without questioning the adequacy of the previously accepted formulation. Thus whenever what is expected occurs, men and women tend to accept it as a matter of course and refer to a set of beliefs to explain it. But when the unexpected occurs and calls into question, logically or experientially, the adequacy of the former set of beliefs, another set of beliefs is often called into play to explain the unexpected. Taken together these form myth. Curiously, these new beliefs rarely destroy the former set of beliefs. Hence, whenever individuals, for whatever reason, continue to interact in social situations that they define as morally repugnant, myth acts to insulate their sense of worthiness in the face of defilement.

Alvin Gouldner (1970) has coined a most useful phrase for a certain category of beliefs. He refers to those beliefs about the way in which the world is ordered as *domain assumptions*. What happens when the domain assumptions held by an individual are continually called into question? One possible consequence is myth. In one sense, perhaps, the slippage from sanity into madness is the total embracing of myth by an individual.

Certainly a central function of myth is that it helps to explain the presence and persistence of incongruities in the behavior of others located in the same social situations. The content of myths may vary, but they always include normative direction for regulating social conduct between the individual and others. Since the individual is located in a social situation other than the confines of the social group, myth is seen as an inherent aspect of social organization necessary to the regulation of transactions occurring between social persons and social assemblages.

Incongruity is seen as a naturally occurring consequence of the exercise of taste—that is, the moral evaluations of the behavior of conspecifics outside of the social group as if they were individuals within the social group. Yet the very lack of "taste" in the others calls out a negatively loaded moral judgment. Continuing contact with such individuals is thus morally repugnant, but may be necessary for reasons of utility, as we will enlarge upon shortly. Myth "explains" that such contacts are not the same as those occurring between individuals bonded together by positive affect or sentiment. Perhaps the most insightful understanding of this fundamental social structural difference is to be found in the research of Erving Goffman. In particular, the limiting case is that of the role of nonperson, the case where an individual performing a functionally necessary role in the overall social situation is defined as not in existence. Goffman's most exquisite example is the case of the woman undressing in the presence of male slaves, perhaps the ultimate example of the insulation of emotion among humans. Thus myth makes possible the formation of larger social collectivities among species possessing culture—that is, symbolic communication—for it neutralizes the problem of affective arousals among individuals belonging to differing social groups.

We turn now to a more detailed analysis of the modes of attachment occurring among individuals and social persons. Broadly considered, we identify three basic modes—social bonding, social solidarity, and social integration—each of which can be characterized by a particular set of norms appropriate to that mode. We examine explicitly the question of the normative character of leisure, although our analysis thus far has implicitly rested upon such an assumption. Taste may arise as a consequence of bonding individual to individual, but it must be expressed symbolically if it is to have a social meaning. Hence, taste as well as myth is normative, but it does not obviously deal with all normative matters in a society.

LEISURE AS AN ESSENTIAL
ELEMENT WITHIN THE NORMATIVE SYSTEM

As Bennett Berger (1963:26) notes, the "concept of leisure must be normative . . . the meanings of work and leisure are inextricably related both to each other and to the cultural norms which define their moral place in a social order. A sociological definition which ignores this fact does so at the peril of becoming irrelevant." Later Berger (1963:28) says: "Students of leisure, however, do not study time, they study behavior. To contrast work and leisure—and we must contrast them, since they have sociological meaning only vis-à-vis each other—we must conceive of leisure also as a kind of action which, however, is distinguished from work." Still we have not really defined leisure in an operational sense; Berger (1963:29) suggests "any normative distinction between work and leisure as action should be a distinction between the kinds of norms which constrain them or a distinction regarding the extent to which norms have been internalized."

Berger's observation that leisure behavior, like work, is part of the social structure and, therefore, is not "free" but is constrained by the norms and values of society gives equivalency to the two dimensions of action. However, it soon poses questions as to what the relevant norms are, under what conditions they operate, and what their regulatory mechanisms and locus of enforcement and reward are? Thus students who would follow the wisdom of Berger's insight must make some attempt at classifying norms.

Human decisions are never made in a social vacuum; they are framed within the context of prevailing social values. Seldom are these social values neat and clear-cut guides to action, for they must cover a wide range of social situations; hence norms range between proscription and prescription—between must, must not, and maybe. Thus in *Homo sapiens* the behavioral regulators are not as neat and tidy as the genetic guides to conduct, which are the predominant factor in other species. In human beings, guides to conduct, or norms, are sentences or words that regulate behavior. They are standards or frames to which we refer in organizing our action in specific social situations. They permit continuity of interaction in that they hold discourse between what Greg Stone calls the limits of nonsense (absence of meaning) and boredom (total understanding); and norms generally manage internal social conflict.

Agreement as to the general nature and function of norms is reasonably easy. However, as Kingsley Davis (1949) noted, the many cross distinctions of norms makes a systematic classification difficult. In Davis's classification, the severity of sanctions serves to differentiate his classes. Though this is important, our purposes in understanding species universals and cultural particulars in work and nonwork requires a classification that gives central attention to the affected social unit. Obviously such a classification scheme is no final solution, rather it is a means of ordering that part of reality in which we are most interested. In the following discussion the reader might justifiably wish a more detailed elaboration; however, it should be emphasized that our main interest is in aligning classes of norms with classes of attachment patterns.

Our ways of social expression are not all of one piece, any more than is our expression of love. We love our country, our club, our school, our gang, our mother, our father, our child, and our lover in quite different ways. None of our loves really assume a hierarchy, but rather are distinct, even complementary, and often equal expressions of attachment. Our loves are not of different levels but of different compartments, whose sum is indeed greater than our many parts.

The social order of society is not unlike such a pattern. It must bind together a diverse set of individuals and have them perform a great diversity of tasks, many of which most individuals would prefer to avoid. It must provide a sense of permanence and continuity, and at the same time it must be open to adaptation and change. All of these cross tendencies and disruptive forces are unified in enduring societies by what would seem a miracle if it were not for their commonplace familiarity. Indeed we only become upset during those rare moments when our expectations are unfilled; while such gaps between expectation and fulfillment are seen as being closed by attributing them to accident, mistake, deviation, corruption, social problems, and sin.

The frequency of such gaps is kept at a minimum by at least three patterns of unity that sustain an edifice of continuity through change. Issues of value, utility, and sentiment are basic to any society as they order social motives for what we should desire, what and how we should fabricate our survival, and with whom we should have most frequent and intensive interaction. Thus social solidarity deals with the quest for symbolic unity, social integration deals with the quest for functional unity, and social bonding deals with the quest for interpersonal unity. We emphasize that these always remain quests rather than fixed accomplishments. Further, each of these have characteristic cycles: those of myth, which deal with fundamental life contradictions and the transition between them; those of work-nonwork cycles of production and consumption; and those of individual, family, and other life cycles of birth, growth, and demise.

LIFE CYCLE, SOCIAL BONDING, AND SENTIMENT

The nature of the human life cycle provides the individual a compelling sequence of challenges from birth to death. But important as such sequences are for the individual, they are even more important to those social units that must guide and respond to the individual's adjustment. It is here where social bonding among humans differs from that of other primates, for we can contemplate our own death, and other futures, as we can exist in much larger symbolic communities. Thus, male-female, male-male, female-female bonds are largely formed at the small-group level, but are manifestations of sentiment rather than simple adjustments of dominance and group protection. Kinship and friendship associations, as the smallest elements of human association, involve social relations composed of the highest levels of feeling.

For our purposes it is enough to note that the establishment and alteration of the social bond is affected by changes in the life cycle of the bonded participants, and that sentiment is a prevailing component of such bonds. It is here that the seriousness of play, the game, and leisure are given most clarity. At significant turning points in our life cycle we play with our future, we try on anticipated roles from child to youth, to adult, to mature adult, to aging, and to death. The intricacies of a whole complex of roles and rules—the game—also provide enduring issues as we move through the life cycle (Rapoport and Rapoport, 1974). At one point we must learn that mother's brother is the person of indulgence in contrast to father's stern authority. That is, our present role with its rights and obligations must be seen in its relation to a complex of other associated roles. And at the very point at which we are learning this interdependence, we must always be ready to shift positions—to be the nephew now but be prepared, in turn, for when we will be the uncle. And it is the conjunction of all these changes that orders the life cycle of the kin or friendship group.

It is in such a way that we learn the ways of our personal community and play our part in its perpetuation. All of this reflects the classic treatment provided by George Herbert Mead (1934) and students of his theory, our only alteration is that we would not extend his concepts beyond the relatively small size of the personal community (Henry, 1958).

It is also at those points where life cycle, social bonding, and sentiment prevail that leisure is likely to occur. Here is the core of continuity and consistency; in spite of changes in life cycle and social situation, the core sum of biography and behavior are unique to the individual. It is here where the motives identified by Roger Caillois (1961) assume importance as rationales to account for the consistency and variation of behaviors that make up our personal identity. Thus we reason that we are "that way" because we dealt with chance, or tried a contest, or imitated an admired role, or sought disequilibrium and a new consciousness. It is in such moments that we seek our "true self." It is here, as we noted in the last chapter, that the core of one's personal identity is established.

The codes of conduct most directly germane to such small units are those that maintain personal distance and those that have the most demanding sanctions. It is at this level that the highest degree of predictability is essential if the social unit is to endure. A fragile unit, such as the modern nuclear family, is totally dependent upon mutual trust and can be helplessly sent into disarray when an individual fails to fulfill expectations. This frequently occurred in industrial societies during the 1960s "generation gap." It had an impact not unlike that of a member with a mental or physical disorder who erratically "spoils" the regularity of the family's expected performance and the web of mutual trust. A unit primarily bound by sentiment simply cannot sustain the bond under such pressures. Yet the resiliency of bonds between individuals may persist, although interpersonal contacts may occur infrequently. Thus while a social unit may be rent with interpersonal tensions, calling into question certain domain assumptions, the unit persists simply because it is matters of taste that make it a unit and these are not easily replicated. Moreover, the ties of sentiment are not equally binding upon all members of the social unit. Individual is bonded to individual *uniquely*.

Thus, in one sense a family may be in disarray, but this is really only a convenience of speech. The calling into question of the trustworthiness of one member may or may not have equal consequences for the strengths of the bonds existing among the others. It is only a partial truth to say that a family is broken up by divorce, infidelity, and so forth. Our concern is not with special cases of a general phenomenon. Our examples should not lead the reader away from the focus upon primary associations and their resiliency. Matters of taste are enduring and influence human behavior long after their initial formulation has been learned. The dissolution, figuratively speaking, of a particular kind of social unit (for example, a family) does not destroy or attenuate the network of primary associations itself nor its defining properties (that is, matters of taste). Such a breakdown in interpersonal relations may change the rights and obligations of certain individuals to be evaluated uniquely as before, but it does not necessarily undermine those matters upon which such evaluations are made. In general terms we consider the norms that arise around such matters as local codes. They regulate interpersonal contact among individuals attached to each other through sentiment or affect.

There are other modes of attachment among members of a society. We consider next a class of norms called transitional codes. These are norms that regulate interaction among members of society where the certainties of taste are absent and the comforts of utility are not appropriate. This is the arena of myth. The problematic condition is: How does the individual interact with others with whom no direct social bonds exist but with whom others to whom he is bonded may be bonded? Local codes are inadequate, but standards for social conduct are required if social entities larger than the social group are to arise and be sustained. Myth arises in such situations; but, like taste, myth must be legitimated by others if it is to have consequences for a social order. Codified it becomes tradition and forms an important binding force in social systems—social solidarity.

We explore some of the conditions out of which such codes arise in this next section.

MYTH CYCLE, SOCIAL SOLIDARITY, AND VALUE

Talcott Parsons (1951:12) notes that "an element of a shared symbolic system which serves as a criterion or standard for selection
among the alternatives of orientation which are intrinsically open in
a situation may be called a value." Although this statement is close
to our intention, its detail is such that it applies to all levels of social
organization and, therefore, does not permit us to identify how
smaller units are formed into a larger whole. In this sense we find
most useful Durkheim's (1961) treatment of "collective representations," or the shared visions which transcend the individual and his
intimate associations. It is an emotional link that binds us to our
"people," and that expresses the solidarity of our ethnocentrism.
These are our myths. Burch (1971:57) states:

> *Myths, then, are the grammar and rhetoric of the social order.*
> *They not only regularize the flow of information, but also convey*
> *feeling. Like the calls of geese in the night, appeals to collective*
> *myth serve to remind us that we are together and heading in*
> *the right direction.*

Edmund Leach's (1967:3–4) summary of this approach is clear and
concise:

> *Binary oppositions are intrinsic to the process of human thought.*
> *Any description of the world must discriminate categories in*
> *the form of "p is what not-p is not." An object is alive or not*
> *alive and one could not formulate the concept "alive" except as*
> *the converse of its partner "dead." So also human beings are male*
> *or not male, and persons of the opposite sex are either available*
> *as sexual partners or not available. Universally these are the most*
> *fundamentally important oppositions in all human experience. . . .*
> *This pattern is built into the structure of every mythical system;*
> *the myth first discriminates between gods and men and then*
> *becomes preoccupied with the relations and intermediaries which*
> *link men and gods together. This much is already implicit in our*
> *initial definition.*
> *   So too with sex relations. Every human society has rules of*
> *incest and exogamy. Though the rules vary they always have the*
> *implication that for any particular male individual all women are*
> *divided by at least one binary distinction, there are women of*
> *our kind with whom sex relations would be incestuous and there*
> *are women of the other kind with whom sex relations are al-*
> *lowed. But here again we are immediately led into paradox. How*
> *was it in the beginning? If our first parents were persons of two*
> *kinds, what was that other kind? But if they were both of our*
> *kind, then their relations must have been incestuous and we are*

all born in sin. The myths of the world offer many different
solutions to this childish intellectual puzzle, but the prominence
which it receives shows that it entails the most profound moral
issues. The crux is as before. If the logic of our thought leads us to
distinguish we from they, how can we bridge the gap and estab-
lish social and sexual relations with "the others" without throwing
our categories into confusion?

Though myths function to stabilize social solidarity, the internal
and external changes of the social and nonhuman environments
must affect the viability of certain myths. For example, only small
proportions of the human community account for events on the
basis of the divine rights of kings or the flatness of the earth. Yet
such solemn social truth as contained by myth must require special
persons or events to challenge or ignore them. We believe that the
process is not unlike that involved in creating the "tradition" of
washing potatoes in salt water by a troop of Japanese macaques.
Such a tradition was started by a two-year-old female monkey
(named Imo by her human experimenters, it should be emphasized;
her conspecifics probably had less flattering names to call her). As
Kummer (1971:118) notes in his summary of the research:

The ease or resistance with which a monkey took to potato-
washing . . . was partly a function of sex and age. The class to
learn most readily was that of the juveniles between one and
two-and-a-half years, Imo's own age class. Male and female
juveniles learned with equal readiness. Five years after Imo started
the behavior, nearly 80 percent of the younger group members
in the age class of two to seven years washed their potatoes. The
adults above the age of seven were more conservative. Only 18
percent of them had acquired the new behavior and all of these
were females. The remaining adults never adopted the habit.

The other factor in learning the new practice was the regular
feeding with an intimate companion. "Thus, mothers readily learned
from their children and older siblings from younger brother and
sister," (Kummer, 1971:121). In this way the new practice spread
through an everwidening net of overlapping social circles until it became troop tradition.

It would seem that there are certain similarities in human society
where even the most tradition-bound are subject to innovation and
new processes of cultural evolution. As Allen Johnson (1972:157)
notes:

But the effects of experimentation carry beyond the short run of
protective variation, for those experiments which are successful

*add to the technology in that cumulative way we call cultural
evolution. At least some anthropologists have been misled by
their own colleagues on this matter. For example, Braidwood
hypothesizes that the highly innovative Neolithic in the Near East
must have been characterized by a unique "atmosphere of experimentation." This hypothesis is, I believe, Braidwood's puzzled
response to the apparent dilemma of the conservative tradition-
bound human being (as drawn from the literature) suddenly
doing something creative. A much more likely hypothesis, of
course, would be that the propensity to experiment is part of the
basic endowment of the human species, just as the propensity
to play with and explore the environment is a basic characteristic
of all mammals, and that particular epoch of high innovation
must be explained on other grounds.*

The myth cycle is comprised of the following: (1) a changed set
of conditions (potatoes for the macaque group), (2) a youthful innovator or other socially marginal persons—the aged, the eccentric,
or persons who are brokers between two cultures, (3) the innovation
is picked up by age peers and becomes a fashion, (4) the fashion is
adopted by a wider range of age and gender classes who form a
circle of taste that sets them apart from other social circles in the
community, (5) the practice becomes a tradition for the entire community as the older adults die and larger proportions of younger
adults have been socialized into the practice, and (6) such a tradition holds until a new set of conditions, a new innovator, and so
forth start the entire cycle over.

Obviously there are many innovations that never become fashionable, and many fashions that never spread beyond the peer group.
Further, there are many myths that will retain their adaptive power
with only slight modification. For example, although the myth of the
market has been shared by only a small proportion of those humans
who have ever lived, it has had remarkable durability when all empirical evidence and human response would suggest its failure to
operate as a purely rational and efficient regulator of supply and
demand. Employees of vast bureaucracies, such as vice-presidents of
General Motors, continue to invoke the myth of the free market as
if it alone brought oil flowing from Saudi Arabia or it alone regulated the prices of Chevrolets and Cadillacs.   .

It is useful to note that these norms are considered transitional;
that is, there is an element of passage and fluidity—for individuals,
for social groups, and for the society at large. Further, fashion, taste,
and myth are regulated by nonwork routines such as rites, rituals,
and ceremonies; and in this way, as Monica Wilson notes (1967),
the values of the group are revealed.

Our use of "sentiment" and "value" as coordinates of behavior implies that they are self-contained rather than being related to external goals. As Weber (1962:60) notes:

> *Value-related conduct is distinguished from affectual conduct by its conscious formulation of the ultimate values governing such conduct and its consistent planned orientation to these values. At the same time these two types share in the fact that the meaning of conduct does not lie in the achievement of some goal ulterior to it, but in engaging in the specific type of behavior for its own sake. Affectually determined behavior is the kind which demands the immediate satisfaction of an impulse, regardless of how sublime or sordid it may be, in order to obtain revenge, sensual gratification, complete surrender to a person or ideal, blissful contemplation, or finally to release emotional tensions.*

Thus value and sentiment are in direct contrast to the goal achievement of utilitarian concerns. Such concerns are a major dimension in binding together the social order through its institutionalized search for food and shelter, goods and services, and all other material means of survival that compose a group's economy.

The binding force of utility is extensively considered in sociology. Our focus has been to emphasize the alternate modes of attachment, but this does not imply that we ignore or do not recognize the importance of such issues. Attachment occurs among individuals in their capacities as social persons; here the dilemma of particularism and affect are clearly not operating. The engaging of local codes and some transitional codes are inappropriate. There are, however, norms to regulate social conduct in situations where one is clearly not bonded to others as individuals. We call these norms universal codes.

WORK—NONWORK CYCLES, SOCIAL INTEGRATION, AND UTILITY

In the quest for material survival, all societies exhibit some form of division of labor in which incumbents of certain social positions specialize in certain work tasks. Thus there is functional integration, or what Durkheim (1947) called organic solidarity, in that each task unit requires the specialization of others so that their combined product can mean better levels of living at less energy expenditure. With an elaborate division of labor, social integration is maintained because it offers each specialization mutual advantage.

It is important to note that in the realm of utility, persons do not exchange the totality of their *persona* as they do in the realm of sentiment, nor do they relate as social roles—such as bride and groom, the bereaved—and other social roles, as they do in the realm of value. In the realm of utility, persons represent social categories—for example, the men, the women, management-labor, children-adults, corporate business-government agency.

As suggested earlier, all human societies exhibit some regular timing of work-nonwork activities. Some may have a certain number of hours of each day devoted to work and a certain number devoted to nonwork, other societies may have rather intense periods of work around certain seasons. The important point is that all societies have some regular pattern of work-nonwork, whose cycle contributes to the social rhythm as do the life and myth cycles.

We have discussed the timing and meaning of work-nonwork cycles in detail in Chapter 4. Here our interest is in normative variations.[2] Studies by students of the sociology of work have rather consistently indicated that the nature of work influences the nature of the social organization (Caplow, 1954; Moore, 1951; Taylor, 1968). Thus work that primarily involves the manipulation of materials and things differs from that which primarily involves the manipulation of other human beings; and both, in turn, differ from those tasks that primarily involve the manipulation of symbols. Each of these types of work are recognized in our daily lives, some of us have "jobs," others have a "career," while still others have work that is a way of life, a "calling."

Given our central focus upon group properties that influence behavior, we are especially concerned with the different types of social unit that are associated with these different types of work. Laboring is most characteristic in work in which a high proportion of the workers have equal status, in which the division of effort is only marginally differentiated, in which the goal is specific and the attainment clearly perceived, and in which the basic behavioral unit is a social person bound into a social organization. An occupation is more characteristic of small business people and people in clerical and middle management positions. In an occupation there is a greater degree of stratification, a more highly differentiated division of labor, more diffuse goals, and the basic behavioral unit is a social person linked into a social assemblage.

Because the timing of laboring units is crucial for the tight interdependence that prevails, there is a much more rigid, formal, and elaborated code of conduct. In Mumford's (1967) phrase, they are

[2]In this line the reader should consult the important discussions by Roberts (1970) and Kelly (1972). The classic discussion of the difference between labor and creative work is still Arendt (1958). Green (1968) provides a useful application of Arendt's ideas.

part of a social machine, a megamachine. In an earlier era, the standard, replaceable social person was part of the military, the church, or a major public works (such as part of the work force constructing the pyramids of Egypt).

On the other hand, the timing and coordination for "occupations" are much less crucial, and since many of the goals and outcomes are ambiguous there is a fairly high turnover of metaphors and practices. The metaphorical shift from hunting to football clichés and from authoritarian economic practices of time and motion to the friendly therapy of Muzak and sensitivity training is often quite rapid. Thus codes of conduct largely follow the path of folkways and the flurry of fad.

The third category of work, "vocation," is most characteristic of the older, learned professions. Though the goals of the individual practitioner may be specific, the goals of the collectivity are highly abstract and nearly impossible of measurement; the search for health, justice, abstract knowledge, truth, and beauty are not likely to be qualified by even the most elaborate computer program or the most sophisticated multivariate analysis. And because the practitioner spends such a long period being socialized and screened and selected, most of the social control is built into the individual. Thus a body of colleagues—equals who are differentiated only on the basis of individual effort or creativity—aids in maintaining the appropriate dignity towards clients and colleagues and the appropriate social distance so that the mystique of collegial bodies may be retained. Though we are drawing from the learned professions for our discussion, it is obvious that we also include other cases, such as the shamans of the Navajo, in which vocation is based upon long periods of training, a high degree of selectivity, fairly abstract sets of goals, and some segregation based upon age and gender. These elemental factors seem most important. After all, a "young" medical practitioner, lawyer, or professor is nearly a decade older than a "young" laborer; and women furnish a higher proportion of workers to "labor" and "occupations" than to some "vocations," while other "vocations"—such as nursing, librarianship, and primary school teaching—have had high proportions of female practitioners.

In general, then, work-nonwork cycles deal with issues of "utility," or what Weber (1962:61) called "rational conduct." He defined such conduct as

> ... of the goal-oriented kind when it is engaged in with due consideration for ends, means, and secondary effects; such conduct must also weigh alternate choices, as well as the relations of the end to other possible uses of the means, and, finally, the

relative importance of different possible ends. The classification of conduct either in affectual or traditional terms is thus incompatible with this type.

Each of these work activities have their counterparts in nonwork. Labor and sport have similar patterns of regulation and similarly structured social units (the "team"). Occupations and recreational activities, such as participation voluntary associations, yacht clubs, and executive fitness programs, have similar direct personal payoffs and bureaucratic structuring. While vocations have normative structures and organizing units that are similar to those of hobbies and crafts.

SUMMARY

We have discussed how the major elements of social unity—sentiment, value, and utility—have both an appropirate locus of expression and appropriate guides to behavior. Our intent has been to demonstrate the varieties of norms that regulate our conduct and the ways in which nonwork is also a component of these normative systems. Finally, we have attempted to indicate that the norms that influence social bonding are not the same as those that integrate the utilitarian division of labor, nor are they the same as the myths that permit a sense of solidarity by neutralizing affective arousals.

We also argued that there are some codes of conduct that regulate exchanges between "whole" persons in small local situations of high emotional intensity. There are also transitional codes that regulate exchanges between social roles. Then there are universal codes that regulate exchanges between social categories. Each of these normative patterns also engross nonwork group structures and activities. Play, games, and leisure share the moral codes of small bonded associations; ritual and ceremony enact the mythical expression of value; while sport, recreation, and hobbies share the codes characteristic of labor, occupations, and vocations.

Chapter 9 will examine the ways in which play, games, and sport contribute to the stability of these differing modes of attachment and social unity. The final two chapters will examine the emergence of recreation and the social implications of this emergence.

9

INTERPRETATIVE DRAMAS – PLAY, GAMES, AND SPORT

9

In the last chapter we considered some ways in which nonwork activities may serve to bind intimate human associations into larger, more abstract societal entities. This chapter will give more attention to sorting out some theories and data concerning three specific forms of nonwork—play, games, and sport. We make no pretense that this is a complete survey of all the literature nor even an adequate synthesis of that which we consider. However, it illustrates how our general approach builds upon and differs from some of the more classical concerns. Also, there is an opportunity to clarify how a sociological approach to nonwork can complement the more traditional approaches.

REPRESENTATIVE THEORIES

Play, games, and sport seem to have attracted nearly as much philosophical and scholarly speculation as sex and money getting. Our intent is not to try and summarize all of this work, but rather to indicate those theoretical traditions that we share and those that run in different directions. Most of the classical theories of play in social animals concentrate upon the biological mechanisms in individual organisms. Thus Schiller (1875) and Spencer (1870) posited that play is essential for releasing the surplus energy that builds up in the higher animals. While Karl Groos (1911) combined interesting observations on play in animals and men with a general theory that there is a play instinct that functions to prepare the young animals for adulthood. Groos (1901), also, argued that play is a form of catharsis; it permits the release of energy that has antisocial possibilities. The psychologist G. Stanley Hall (1920) argued that play reflects the past as ontogeny repeats phylogeny.[1]

---

[1]There are a variety of studies that summarize the various theories of play, leisure, recreation, and other forms of nonwork. Some of the best of these are: Sapora and Mitchell (1961); Lehman and Witty (1927); Neumeyer (1949); Dulles (1965); Britt and Janus (1941); Lowe (1973); Ingram (1973); Ingham and Loy (1974).

These four types of explanations continue to recycle, in slightly altered form, through each generation of students of play. In our times the surplus energy idea will become the "compensatory hypothesis," which argues that a necessary function of recreation is to provide workers with sharply contrasting nonwork experiences that release energy stored from the tedium of work. The play instinct theory will encourage the development and support of learning games, playgrounds, and summer camp programs. Catharsis will support the "need" for secondary school sports programs and youth centers. While Hall's ideas seem to have some expression in simulation games and the general systems movement.

We find such individualistic and instinctive theories interesting, and certainly they are useful as rhetorical strategies for justifying particular programs and policy decisions. However, the causes they describe seem difficult to observe, and the theories about these causes seem difficult to verify and highly contradictory.

Other scholars such as Johan Huizinga (1955) and Roger Caillois (1961) give more attention to the cultural and social dimensions of play. Both Huizinga and Caillois use play as a general term, which includes all forms of nonwork—games, sports, gambling, fantasy, and so forth. And both see play as a culture-creating activity—that is, we can gain an understanding of a culture through understanding the nature of its play forms as readily, if not more so, as from descriptions of its economy, kinship, and other institutions. Huizinga (1955:28), for example, defines play as

> . . . a voluntary activity or occupation executed within certain fixed limits of time and place, according to rules freely accepted but absolutely binding, having its aim in itself and accompanied by a feeling of tension, joy and the consciousness that it is "different" from "ordinary life." Thus defined, the concept seemed capable of embracing everything we call "play" in animals, children and grown-ups; games of strength and skill, inventing games, guessing games, games of chance, exhibitions and performances of all kinds. We ventured to call the category "play" one of the most fundamental in life.

Caillois (1961), though acknowledging the importance of Huizinga, quite clearly recognizes the contradictory premises and limited analytic application of the earlier writer. Caillois develops a more operational definition of play and a taxonomy of such activities, which permits a more systematic approach. He (1961:9–10) defines play as an activity that is essentially:

1. *Free*: in which playing is not obligatory; if it were, it would at once lose its attractive and joyous quality as diversion;

2. *Separate*: circumscribed within limits of space and time, defined and fixed in advance;
3. *Uncertain*: the course of which cannot be determined, nor the result attained beforehand, and some latitude for innovation being left to the player's initiative;
4. *Unproductive*: creating neither goods, nor wealth, nor new elements of any kind; and, except for the exchange of property among the players, ending in a situation identical to that prevailing at the beginning of the game;
5. *Governed by rules*: under conventions that suspend ordinary laws, and for the moment establish new legislation, which alone counts;
6. *Make-believe*: accompanied by a special awareness of a second reality or of a free unreality, as against real life.

Caillois (1961) then goes on to identify four main rubrics of play —*agon* (competitive games), *alea* (games of chance), *mimicry* (simulation), and *ilinx* (where vertigo is dominant). He then divides the entire universe of play into quadrants that contain games of the same kind but that are arranged on a continuum between the pole of exuberant and impulsive forms (*paidia*) and that of a highly ordered and formalized action (*ludus*). A child whirling about to become dizzy is seen as expressing an impulsive form of vertigo (*ilinx*) while a tightrope walker would be expressing the *ludic* or ordered form of vertigo.

Caillois provides a rich set of ideas concerning the forms of non-work, while his six formal properties of play and the logical classification of games permit a systematic treatment of such issues. However his emphasis upon treating all play as primarily an interior experience of the individual and his blurring of the distinction between play and games are directions different from ours.

Another important set of ideas and empirical research on games has been done by John Roberts, Brian Sutton-Smith, and their colleagues. For example, an article by Roberts, Arth, and Bush (1959: 597) defines a game as a recreation activity "characterized by: (1) organized play, (2) competition, (3) two or more sides, (4) criteria for determining the winner, and (5) agreed-upon rules." They (1959: 600) argue that games are "expressive models" that are related to other aspects of culture:

> . . . *games of strategy . . . should be related to the complexity of the social system; games of chance which are models of interaction with the supernatural should be linked with other expressive views of the supernatural; . . . games of physical skill may be related to aspects of natural environments.*

They "tested" these ideas by examining 50 societies sampled from the Human Relations Area Files and, not too surprisingly, found general confirmation for their propositions.

Curiously, in their conclusion the authors accept a psychoanalytic notion that games are experiences in mastery with their three classes of games representing (1) training for mastery of the social system, (2) the supernatural, and (3) mastery of both self and the environment. Their use of an individualistic explanation is curious as their definition of game can only make it a phenomenon of collective behavior, while their cultural data deal with small tribal societies in which individuals are likely to have no or only limited options on playing or not playing certain age–sex peer games. A black male growing up in a North American innercity area who played chess rather than basketball would be distinctively different, but not nearly so different as a person in a smaller, more homogeneous, and isolated tribal society who sought games other than those considered normal for his age–sex class.

In a series of additional studies, Sutton-Smith and Roberts (1963) develop a more elaborate "conflict-enculturation" hypothesis, which builds a causal chain from childhood training programs to adult success and which presumes these create tension and conflict that games resolve.[2] When they treat game involvement in adults they support their ideas with survey data that found differences in recreation activities between men and women and upper and lower social strata. Sutton-Smith and Roberts (1964:14) argue:

> . . . game playing ensures periodic inoculations of manageable
> success and manageable failure, reassuring the participant that
> he is indeed one who can tolerate such pressures in his own
> psychic economy. . . . but it is doubtful that much important . . .
> social learning takes place through games after biological and
> cultural maturity has been attained.

Apparently "psychic economies" represent zero growth rather than the boom-and-bust patterns of the political economies in which they exist. Still, it seems strange that those who are most successful (high-status males) by all the everyday life criteria would need an inoculation of play success or failure. Further, as we demonstrate in Chapter 3, those most successful are those most active in *all* forms of nonwork activity. How much inoculation do they need? Perhaps it is simply that men and women, the old and the young, the upper and lower social strata, the developing and the developed political

---

[2]Some other reports are: Sutton-Smith, Roberts, and Kozelka (1963); Sutton-Smith (1971); Roberts (1966); Avedon and Sutton-Smith (1971). Important work in a similar vein is Anderson and Moore (1960) and Raser (1969).

economies have different patterns of social life because they are indeed different kinds of social reality.

The "conflict-enculturation" hypothesis seems to have some aspects of the modern compensatory hypothesis reworked from the Schiller-Spencer surplus energy hypothesis as well as the catharsis notion of Groos. A similar conflict-enculturation hypothesis has been proposed by Paul Hoch (1972:199–200). He notes: "In the society governed by the so-called Reality Principle of vicious sexual repression—or what is the same thing, repressive cosmetics-and-commodity sexual pseudo fulfillment-fascism seems still capable of galvanizing the emotions of men and women." This means, apparently, that sports serve as an outlet for the conflicts created in childhood socialization, "where the regime of vicious sexual repression, sado-masochism, love-hate for authority, and the distorted Oedipal conception of the American nuclear family begins." Needless to say, Dr. Hoch's solutions are somewhat different from the psychoanalytic solutions proposed by Roberts and his company of scholars.

Of course only a physiological individual can experience vertigo. However, the search for that experience and the ability to interpret such experience as joy rather than madness are meanings embedded in the social rather than the individual (Becker, 1963). Indeed, we would argue that one of the important questions raised by Caillois and others, but seldom given much attention, is how can persons spend so much energy and time in such nonutilitarian pursuits, many of which, in other contexts, would be seen as desecrating sacred deities, institutions, and persons? That is, an actor may assume the robes of God and yet behave with all the infidelities of mortals in a staged play, children may play at marriage or religious rituals, and football players are rewarded for aggressive behavior that can very likely lead to injury of opponents. Yet outside of these appropriate social contexts, the person playing at God is treated as mad, children playing with sacred ritual are punished for indecency, and aggression in the public streets is a serious criminal act. We feel that the significant questions regarding nonwork behavior such as play, games, and sport do not deal with something intrinsic to individuals. They deal rather with questions of social context—who is permitted to participate, what is the number and composition of participants in the case at hand, how is the participation organized, who is involved in the modification of the rules, and who is involved in enforcing sanctions associated with the rules.

PLAY AND GAMES

Without denying the importance of the psychological, aesthetic, philosophical, historical, and small-group approaches, we will explore a different viewpoint. We view play, games, and sport as sharing a commonality of interest in rules of conduct but serving as integrative representations of the different social units in which the individual exists. Play is the means by which the rules and roles of intimate association are given an idealized enacted form. Games relate to a "generalized other," larger than kin and friendship associations but smaller than the nation-state. A neighborhood, locality, or ethnic group provides the social nexus for games. Sport is a game played before spectators, indeed it requires spectators to complete its meaning. Thus the whole community or a nation-state is the social nexus for sport. The remainder of this chapter will detail these ideas.

For purposes of social analysis, play is a term best reserved for those social situations where the rules of conduct are created and sanctioned by the participating person and/or a few coparticipating intimates. Furthermore, play usually involves situations where new relationships are being explored. This most frequently occurs when the child, youth, or adult is anticipating new social rules or after a long duration of performance in the social role permits the individual a certain distancing, which confirms a high degree of competence. As these are moments of strain, exuberance, and exploration, the social cues must be clearly attended to and not misinterpreted. Therefore, intimate associates and/or familiar and secure settings seem essential.

In this sense, George Herbert Mead (1934) seems a more useful theoretical guide than most of the writers directly concerned with play. In regard to play by children Mead (1934:150–151) notes:

> *Children get together to "play Indian." This means that the child has a certain set of stimuli which he makes use of in building a self. The response which he has a tendency to make to these stimuli organizes them. He plays that he is, for instance, offering himself something, and he buys it; he gives a letter to himself and takes it away; he addresses himself as a parent, as a teacher; he arrests himself as a policeman. He has a set of stimuli which call out in himself the sort of responses they call out in others. He takes this group of responses and organizes them into a certain whole. Such is the simplest form of being another to one's self. It involves a temporal situation. The child says something in one character and responds in another character, and then his first character and so the conversation goes on. A certain organized structure arises in him and in his other which replies to it, and these carry on the conversation of gestures between themselves.*

In recent years the ideas of Mead have been given some confirmation in the studies of animal behaviorists. Play often involves characteristic display gestures that signal that a particular forthcoming act should be seen as nonaggressive. However, of most interest is the finding that "among bonded individuals, various non-aggressive contact activities are often initiated and sustained with little or no displaying" (Smith, 1969:148). That is, play would seem to be a regular and important form of contact among bonded individuals whose message seldom needs a display warning. While the important work done at the Harlow's primate laboratory suggests that "an extremely important basic function [of maternal love] is the management of infant play so that the infant monkeys play together effectively instead of in a disorganized manner" (Harlow, Harlow, and Suomi, 1971:541). Apparently for the vertebrates and especially the higher primates, play and games have a certain survival value in preparing individuals to function as mothers, fathers, and members of social groups. It would seem that in those species whose survival strategies are more dependent upon learning rather than genetics, the protective context of play and games would assume a corresponding importance.[3]

It is important to note that unlike Groos this behavior is attributed to social rather than instinctual processes. For example, the Harlows found that monkeys who were deprived of play relations with adult kin during their youth had a difficult time performing their later adult roles. It is the social community and ultimately the species that is disrupted, not the individual organisms that suffers from an unused instinct.

It should be clear that Mead is using the play and games of children to illustrate a self-definition process that occurs throughout the individual's lifetime. It is important to note that Mead's interest in the way the individual organizes patterns of behavior in regard to significant others and the larger social universe presupposes certain varying patterns of social organization in terms of size, intimacy, and sources of authority. Thus play behavior involves a different sort of social organization than does participation in games. With somewhat passing attention, he suggests there are significant differences in the rules for play and games, in who has the right to modify the rules, and in who has the right to impose sanctions. Mead notes (1934:151):

> If we contrast play with the situation in an organized game, we note the essential difference that the child who plays in a game must be ready to take the attitude of everyone else involved in that game, and that these different roles must have a definite relationship to each other. Taking a very simple game such as

---

[3]There has been some attempt at examining how games and sports might serve as means for adjusting to modernization. See for example, Stumpf and Cozens (1947, 1949) for the strength of the idea and the limited nature of the data.

*hide-and-seek, everyone with the exception of the one who is
hiding is a person who is hunting. A child does not require more
than the person who is hunted and the one who is hunting. If
a child is playing in the first sense he just goes on playing, but
there is no basic organization gained. In that early stage he passes
from the one role to another just as a whim takes him. But in a
game where a number of individuals are involved, then the child
taking one role must be ready to take the role of everyone else.
If he gets in a ball nine he must have the responses of each
position involved in his own position. He must know what everyone else is going to do in order to carry out his own play. He has
to take all of these roles. They do not all have to be present in
consciousness at the same time, but at some moments he has to
have three or four individuals present in his own attitude, such as
the one who is going to throw the ball, the one who is going to
catch it, and so on. These responses must be, in some degree,
present in his own make-up. In the game, then, there is a set of
responses of such others so organized that the attitude of one
calls out the appropriate attitudes of the other.*

For our species (and probably to a certain extent for other primates), play, games, and sport seem to be those social activities
most directly and continuously concerned with the nature of rules.
Though law and politics and commerce give considerable attention
to rules and their manipulation to obtain certain ideal social ends,
such attention is directed to encouraging social activity, rather than
the social activity existing to stabilize and reaffirm the sacredness of
the rules. That is, rules in law, politics, and commerce regulate imperfect and variable social rules, while rules for play, games, and
sport seek to regulate perfect and fixed social roles. The crucial distinction is that in daily life we expect imperfect outcomes, while in
nonwork we expect perfect outcomes to result from our tinkering
with rules. As Mead (1934:158–159) noted:

*The game has a logic, so that such an organization of the self is
rendered possible: there is a definite end to be obtained; the
actions of the different individuals are all related to each other
with reference to that end so that they do not conflict; one is not
in conflict with himself in the attitude of another man on the
team. If one has the attitude of the person throwing the ball he
can also have the response of catching the ball. The two are
related so that they further the purpose of the game itself. They
are interrelated in a unitary, organic fashion. There is a definite
unity, then, which is introduced into the organization of other
selves when we reach such a stage as that of the game, as over*

> against the situation of play where there is a simple succession of
> one role after another, a situation which is, of course, characteris-
> tic of the child's own personality. The child is one thing at one
> time and another at another, and what he is at one moment does
> not determine what he is at another. That is both the charm of
> childhood as well as its inadequacy. You cannot count on the
> child; you cannot assume that all the things he does are going to
> determine what he will do at any moment. He is not organized
> into a whole. The child has no definite character, no definite
> personality.

In play the high seriousness of rule observance is balanced by the
ease with which the rules can be altered to meet new conditions.
Thus whimsy is founded upon a bedrock of predictability. A group
of young male primates can play at aggressive displays because the
cues are presented in a social situation of secure predictability. Children can rapidly shift from playing house to playing war because the
fictions are shared by peers. The surgeons that Goffman (1961a) observed playing with their roles could do so because those copresent
for such displays are fully knowledgeable regarding the surgeon's
real competence.[4] In such a way, play permits the symbolic enactment of private lives and anticipated social roles. And those crucial
junctures in the individual's life cycle, which Anselm Strauss (1959)
calls turning points, would seem those moments with the highest
density of play actions.

Like Mead, Jean Piaget (1965) and his colleagues used the play
and games of children to develop general theories of human development. (They give most attention to marble games of boys and
"Ilet cachant" of girls.) However, Piaget and his colleagues did more
systematic empirical work and, therefore, permit a more detailed
understanding of the nature of games in social life. Using the rules
of the game as an index of change, they suggested a four-stage development continuum. The small child explores within a world of
external constraint, though it tends to ritualize certain behavior.
From two to five years of age the child is "egocentric." It has the
example of codified rules but continues to play by itself, or if it plays
with others there seems little interest in winning or other attempts
to "unify the different ways of playing" the game. Around seven to
eight is the stage they call "incipient cooperation." At this stage
each player attempts to win. There is general agreement on the rules
of the game, though these are consistent only for the duration of a

---

[4]Goffman's (1961a) entire essay on role distance is important, but see especially
pages 148–150.

particular game. The fourth stage occurs around eleven to twelve, and here the rules are completely codified. Indeed "the dominating interest seems to be in the rules themselves." Yet it is at this stage that "a rule is conceived as the free pronouncement of the actual individual minds themselves. It is no longer external and coercive: it can be modified and adapted to the tendencies of the group" (Piaget, 1965:50). Rules have gone from a vague set of guides sporadically observed, to highly sacred entities still sporadically observed, and finally to a clearly understood mechanism for aiding the collectivity in accomplishing its goals.

The changes between stage one and stage four are similar to those observed by Mead (1934:152):

> *Children take a great interest in rules. They make rules on the spot in order to help themselves out of difficulties. Part of the enjoyment of the game is to get these rules. Now, the rules are the set of responses which a particular attitude calls out. You can demand a certain response in others if you take a certain attitude. These responses are all in yourself as well. There you get an organized set of such responses as that to which I have referred, which is something more elaborate than the roles found in play.*

The data of Piaget and his colleagues also indicate that rules for games are elaborated by children alone, with older children passing on the rules and modifying those which they receive from prior generations. Further, the rules of games vary by locality—indeed, neighborhoods—and moments in time. Piaget (1965:16) and his colleagues reported that a fourteen-year-old who had given up playing marbles because "the customs of his generation are going by the board instead of being piously preserved by the rising generation." However, the hierarchy of materials composing marbles seem to remain constant as does the ritualistic use of words to gain control. Finally, there is a consistent emphasis upon sustaining equality, with various devices giving losers a legitimate claim upon redistributing the marbles of high winners.

The rules of the game constitute a well-marked social reality "independent of individuals." Piaget and his colleagues suggest these rules are like language, where the fundamentals are transmitted from one generation to another, yet the individual can innovate to meet the general needs of the collectivity. We would simply extend their insight to touch all crucial moments of transition in social life, with the socialization of the child being the most evident because the change is the most dramatic. Yet each significant passage from youth to married person, from nonparent to parent, from PhD student to professor, from schoolboy to worker, and so on would seem to require a similar moral continuum. There is the egocentric play and role fantasy regarding the anticipated role. Then there is the sacred respect and rigid conformity to the rules of the new role. And finally, Piaget (1965:65) and his colleagues note, there is the stage where

> *All opinions are tolerated so long as their protagonists urge their acceptance by legal methods. . . . he no longer thinks that every-thing has been arranged for the best in the past and that the only way of avoiding trouble is by religiously respecting the established order. He believes in the value of experiment insofar as it is sanctioned by collective opinion.*

That is, the person has confidence enough to practice "role distance"; to announce he is part of the present game or role, but, also, much more than that.

Something of the larger social implication is in a characteristically off-hand passage in which Mead (1934:152–153) observes certain similarities between both the play of children and the sacred rituals of "primitives":

> *A striking illustration of play as distinct from the game is found in the myths and various of the plays which primitive people carry out, especially in religious pageants. The pure play attitude which we find in the case of little children may not be found here, since the participants are adults, and undoubtedly the relationship of these play processes to that which they inter-pret is more or less in the minds of even the most primitive people. . . . This type of activity belongs, of course, not to the everyday life of the people in their dealing with the objects about them—there we have a more or less definitely developed self-consciousness—but in their attitudes toward the forces about them, the nature upon which they depend; in their attitude toward this nature which is vague and uncertain, there we have a much more primitive response; and that response finds its expression in taking the role of the other, playing at the expression of their gods and their heroes, going through certain rites which are the representation of what these individuals are supposed to be doing. The process is one which develops, to be sure, into a more or less definite technique and is controlled; and yet we can say that it has arisen out of situations similar to those in which little children play at being a parent, at being a teacher— vague personalities that are about them and which affect them and on which they depend. These are personalities which they*

take, roles they play, and in so far control the development of
their own personality. (emphasis added)

We think that Mead is hinting at an important characteristic of
nonwork behavior—that is, its idealization of social norms. A child
who plays at being a policeman, mother, or cowboy deals in representations not realities. The child's conception is as things might be,
just as rituals to deal with unknown deities represent expressions of
some idealized characteristics of the gods. The sun's warmth may be
symbolized by fire or the movement through the heavens may be
symbolized by a group procession and so forth. Yet as we observers
and those who are participating clearly understand, such symbols
hardly touch the complex behavioral reality of the sun. Play, games,
staged dramas, sport, and so forth are interpretative activities that
remind us of the social order and our place within it.

SPORT

Play and games are universal human activities because the characteristic social units that organize them are universal. On the other
hand, sport seems the only child of large, diverse, and independent
social entities, such as the industrial order of today or imperial systems of antiquity. Only such a social order has the necessary organizational patterns and technologies for the accomplishment of sport,
and, perhaps, only such an order has the multiplicity of large social
aggregates searching for a common coin to unite their many diversi-
ties. In this analysis we will treat the "participant sports," such as
hunting, fishing, bowling, and so forth as recreational forms. While
sports will be seen as occurring only in those games where spectators gain influence over the style of action, where participants no
longer have a significant voice in establishing and modifying the
rules of the game, and where the organizational system is nearly
identical to that of work. Examining these three dimensions of sport
will occupy the remainder of this chapter.

A continuing "management" problem in sport is its need for the
spectator yet its inability to keep the spectator from becoming over-
involved and attempting to circumvent the rules of the game. Sport
events always include a large contingent of police and other officials
whose primary function is to keep the fans in "their place," so the
game may continue. In small towns where the high school team is
"the only game in town," there is a pressure to win that equals or
exceeds the pressure upon college and professional teams. For example, a small Connecticut town with a single high school as its
"representative" apparently had so much trouble with its fans that
all postal boxholders in the town were sent a special set of rules for

appropriate conduct by the fans. The rules are sufficiently elevating so that we reproduce them:

High school students should set a good example in the matter of sportsmanship and quickly condemn unsportsmanlike conduct on the part of other students or adults. To this end they should—

1. Remember that their team, coach, and supporters are the official representatives of their school before, during, and after any contest or other activity.
2. Recognize that the good name of the school is more valuable than any game won by unfair play.
3. Not deride the officials whose responsibility is to control the game, enforce the rules, and protect the players.
4. Recognize and applaud an exhibition of fine play or good sportsmanship on the part of the visiting team.
5. Not boo nor jeer opponents, particularly during individual play situations such as: foul shooting, batting, speaking, etc.
6. Insist on the courteous treatment of visiting teams.
7. Remember that when visiting other schools and communities their conduct should be above reproach in all respects so as to reflect credit on their own school.
8. Acquaint the adults of the community and the grade pupils with the ideals of sportsmanship of the C.I.A.C.
9. Impress upon the community its responsibility for the exercise of self-control and fair play at all athletic and other contests.
10. Encourage the full discussion of fair play, sportsmanship, and school spirit through student councils, class work, and auditorium programs. GOOD SPORTSMANSHIP CAN NOT BE LEGISLATED BY PRINTED RULE. IT COMES FROM THE HEART.

Interestingly it is the high school students who are to educate the community, though by definition such students are the objects of intensive socialization by the community so they will eventually become "good citizens." Yet, as a subgroup of the community it is the good name of their sole official institutional form that is threatened by bad sportsmanship. Like the players on the sports team, the students have their work ordered by others but are expected to give this work a loyalty usually reserved for their own creations. The magic by which society is sustained is the fact that most students do what is expected of them.

School sports provide an interesting contrast to working-class spectator sports, such as stock-car racing (Radosta, 1974) or wrestling (Stone and Oldenburg, 1967), in which an important part of the game seems to be the performer's ability to cheat external abstractions such as rules. However, the cheating, to be "legitimate," must be done by the right performer, with the right style, and in public. Therefore, while high school sports attempt to sustain the purity of the game by managing the behavior of the fans, in stock-car racing and wrestling the game is managed to satisfy the fans. In either case the fan assumes a certain standing in shaping the nature of the play.

The fan is of a fairly standard statistical type. A U.S. national survey study in 1965 (Bureau of Outdoor Recreation, 1970/1974) found, not too surprisingly, that a higher percentage of men than women attend sports events. The attendance difference between men and women is fairly close during the secondary school years of 12 to 17, but becomes three times higher during the family formation years of 18 to 24. Spectator sports have higher appeal to younger persons and to persons with high incomes and high levels of educational attainment.

Most of these findings are similar to those Stone (1957) found in a much smaller Minneapolis sample during the late 1950s. While surveys in a variety of New Zealand communities (Robb and Carr, 1969; Congalton, 1954; Robb and Somerset, 1957) and the multinational time-budget study (Szalai, 1966, 1972) offer similar patterns. Stone (1957:16) found that males in his sample had formed team loyalties in adolescence and that these were retained into adulthood. He suggests that far from being a liability to sport, "spectatorship may have important consequences for promoting the solidarity of the larger society and its instituted relations."

In many cases a sports team is the only tangible expression of community life shared by all class, status, and ethnic groups. And certainly spectators are not an undifferentiated mass but attend in small groups of kin and friends and, therefore, add further dimension to the social bond.[5]

However, there are differences other than spectatorship between game situations and sport. In game behavior there is an almost tribal concern with equality among the players, rules emerge from the oral tradition of the locality, the players are able to modify the rules and sanctions, and there seems a consistent valuation surrounding the various game-associated materials. Like the penny-ante poker game, with its limits on pots, elaborate discussion of house rules, and other means of narrowing the range of permissible inequalities, differs from a Monte Carlo casino; so do games differ from sport. In games one earns esteem with the pride of doing a job well, rather than status with its rights to invidious distinctions. Indeed the "bing-

---

[5]Stone provides some data as does casual observation at a sports event. Of most interest is a 1910 study by Margaret Byington (1974) which reports similar patterns.

ing" taking place in the bank wiring room as reported in the famous Western Electric studies may have been as much of an attempt to build gamelike egalitarian forms and rules to protect the group from the larger hierarchical realities of Western Electric than it was an elaborate system of rewards and punishments to sustain internal group structure.[6]

Indeed the strategies of the Western Electric workers seem not unlike the "hanging around" of teenagers or others equally fit but not "gainfully" employed, where conspicuous inattention is "worked" to distance themselves from some of the realities of their deprived esteem (Liebow, 1967; Whyte, 1943). In factories the "playing" with one's circumscribed role builds esteem with one's work-mates that is contrary to the established system of esteem and status. Yet a hustle within the cavity of an establishment without a circle of admirers is as meaningless as a single hanging-around teenager whose studied contempt is now patently impotent.

These examples merely suggest the structure of seemingly formless events in which the person rather than the social organization is the display property. Hanging around is neither work nor play, it is a game that represents a systematic adaptation to social limbo and that shares its fund of meaning with the awards in Golden Age club dance contests, American Legion tribute banquets, offices in academic societies, prizes at "ladies" bridge club gatherings, and so forth. Here surplus persons band together to create esteem properties that they can then equitably distribute among one another, according to an agreed-upon set of rules.

In sport the emphasis upon equality is retained, but it is highly formalized, bureaucratically precise, and seldom directed to controlling the size and distribution of winnings. Certainly much of the juggling to maintain competitive balance reflects as much an interest in enhancing the "dis-plays" for the fans than in being a means to help advance the play and ensure the safety of the players. As Ingham and Loy (1974:41–42) note:

> . . . *constant attention is required to assume an uncertain outcome in ludic encounters. Strikingly uneven competition dulls the participant and bores the spectator. Thus various structural modifications of the form of ludic situations are made to ensure a semblance of equality. These efforts typically focus on the matters of size, skills and experience. Examples of attempts to establish equality based on size are the formation of athletic leagues and conferences composed of social organizations of*

[6]"Binging" occurred when one man hit another as hard as he could on the upper arm, the other had the right to retaliate with a similar blow (Homans, 1950:60).

similar size and the designation of weight classes for boxers and wrestlers. Illustrations of efforts to insure equality among contestants on the basis of skill and experience are the establishment of handicaps for bowlers and golfers, the designation of various levels of competition within a given organization as evidenced by freshmen, junior varsity and varsity teams in interscholastic athletics, and the drafting of players from established teams when adding a new team to a league as done in professional football or basketball.

Along with spectators and egalitarian rules construction, sport differs from games in the nature of its timing. As Paul Weiss (1969) suggests, a game is an occurrence and sport is a pattern.[7] Sport has schedules and closing seconds and playoffs, and endless hours of blocking, blocking, blocking or batting, batting, batting. Sport is action timed to a precision that time-and-motion experts can only dream about. Sport requires highly routinized, ordered, and abstract rules and regulations, arbitrarily created and enforced through centralized bureaucracies. In short, the normative system of sport is similar to work, and indeed sport can acquire certain organizational forms and become work for some participants. Professional, intercollegiate, and little league football have similar organizational patterns, which include large-scale intergroup compacts that transcend the locality and which define fairly specifically the rights and obligations of the social roles at each level of the hierarchy.

As Sage (1970) notes:

Sport is characterized by institutional organization, formal instruction for players and teams, and leagues with teams contesting for championships; it is further distinguished by commercialization and systematization of players into artificial rankings, i.e. amateur and professional.

His definition with a few modifications would seem appropriate for defining all large-scale social entities in the corporate-industrial world.

The athlete—the football player, the hockey player, the track star—does what everyone else in a corporate society does. He demonstrates a perfunctory loyalty to the organization, observes a specialized functional role, accepts and responds to the chain of command, is a semiskilled or skilled employee, whose highest hopes for advancement is a middle management position or the accumulation

[7]Other important contributions to sociology of sport are: Kenyon (1968), Loy and Kenyon (1969), Edwards (1973).

of sufficient capital to invest in a business of his own. The difference is that the athlete is (1) permitted to dramatize his work role, (2) permitted a sense of conclusion (final score) to timed tasks, and (3) able to develop a flamboyant life-style, which is conspicuously consumed by the media audience. And all of this is played out before an audience that fully appreciates the subtle style involved in the performance of routine tasks.

Or as Stone (1972:2) notes, "the simple mention of sport establishes the fact that play has become infected with its conventionally accepted contrast—work—for sport is working at play. Yet we can observe that sport occurs when non-players take time out from work to watch it."

The similarity between sports and work in industrial society was probably easiest to see during the Nixon era in the United States. Here Nixon and his favorite coach, George Allen of the Washington Redskins, regularly blurred the distinctions between the metaphors of football and the larger social values of their society (Lipsyte, 1973). The attitude of time-and-motion studies, bureaucratic organization, and the Protestant ethic were applied by Allen to his football team. While sports metaphors for the loyalty, struggle to overcome, team play, and most of all winning were applied by the President to the nation-state. Both saw sport, and particularly football, as a major means for linking together the diverse elements of their society. Allen thought his team had made Washington, D.C. a proud and unified community, and Nixon had "game plans" and fourth-quarter comebacks guiding his personal, domestic, and foreign policies.

Whether sport is the appropriate metaphor for guiding complex corporations and nation-states may be questioned. Yet it is difficult to see how the interest and use of sport by Nixon is a uniquely perverse expression of the "decline of the American empire" (Hoch, 1972). The use of the Olympic Games as a point of national pride was no more lost on Palestinian terrorists than it was lost on Hitler's Germany. The world soccer cup matches of 1974, which pitted the two Germanies against each other, were simply a continuation of the regional and national competitions that are played out in sport throughout Europe and Latin America. The use of the Muhammed Ali-George Foreman world heavyweight boxing title to enhance the prestige of Zaire suggests that President Mobbutu probably shared George Allen's view that "when you lose, you die a little." And, of course, there is the constant soul-searching about racism in sport. This seems especially heightened among world-class rugby nations since the two countries with the most consistently strong teams— South Africa and New Zealand—have officially diametrically opposed philosophies regarding native peoples (Thompson, 1964,

1969).[8] Descriptions of soccer in modern England and sports in Ancient Greece and Rome seem very much like those organizational conditions so often greatly condemned by athletes when leaving the professional hockey, baseball, and gridiron football leagues of modern North America.[9] Just as public pandemonium reigns supreme when the local team returns the victor whether it is the Pittsburgh Steelers, a Brazilian soccer team, or a national cup victor in Yugoslavia. In short, as an extension of the community, sport has a certain universal perversity that seems more attributable to the nature of its organizational form than the peculiar quirks of a particular nation-state. To be sure there will be certain variations attributable to a particular culture. However, these are only variations on a general theme, much as Japanese industry, which exhibits certain differences from American patterns but shares far more similarities as part of a worldwide industrial order.

As a business in America, sport was a growth industry during the 1960s. Thirty-four percent of all Americans (or 66 million) attended outdoor sports events in 1965, and there are confident projections of 150 million attending by the year 2000. New football leagues were formed and then absorbed by old leagues but with expanded numbers of teams. The number who paid to attend football games continued to increase, while the number attending baseball games stabilized or decreased. But in all of this growth, racing was far ahead. In 1968, horse racing had 68.9 million people who paid to attend; auto racing, 40.9 million; greyhound racing, 12.0 million; baseball, 33.5 million, and professional and college football, 37.0 million (Bureau of Outdoor Recreation, 1970/1974). It seems likely that gambling and its hope of unearned increment had an important influence upon these patterns of attendance, perhaps even equal to the moral uplift experienced in observing keen competition.

In the 1970s, sport began to follow the natural saturation curves we described in Chapter 7. The World Football League stumbled into a void of empty stadiums and empty banks. The difficulties of the World Hockey Association and of World Team Tennis, and the declines in profits for established teams indicated that sport was no longer a get-rich-quick investment. An important factor may be an Internal Revenue Service ruling that may prevent sport franchise owners from "writing off a huge share of their taxes in short term

[8]Of interest is a December 22, 1972, *New York Times* full-page advertisement on the last page of the "News in Review" section. The ad is entitled "South African Sports News" and has a variety of sports pictures with an interracial theme that support the idea that "sport should be played by everyone regardless of race, colour or creed." The hope was to retain South Africa's participation in international sports competition.

[9]For recent examples see Harris (1973) and Davies (1974); for an older example see Fox (1903/1968).

player depreciation and paying a small tax on the cost of the franchise itself. In the Atlanta case, $7.7 million was attributed to player depreciation and about $50,000 to the actual cost of the franchise" (Tuite, 1975:51). And so sport will no longer be quite like its corporate sisters in the oil business. Sport is organized like work, thinks of itself as cultural expression, and is staged as a theatrical production —which probably makes it closer to the automobile business.

Though the organizational system of sport closely resembles that of work, there is a constant evolution in these organizational forms which tend to match existing social and cultural environments. Football—soccer, rugby, and American and Canadian football—in contrast to baseball or cricket, seems better tuned to the ordered cadences of the industrial world. Baseball reflects the melting-pot era of 1890 to 1941, when immigrants thought that aspiring to WASP lifestyles as well as standards of living were useful goals. Baseball has less explosive and more measured patterns of action. (Football fans would say it is duller and drags incredibly.) The aim of baseball is to give full attention to the individualistic performers—the batter and the pitcher—with their seconds of aloneness before the fielders, basemen, and runners are again brought into the picture. All of this is in stark contrast to the flashy quarterback, who is totally dependent upon the precise, automatic, programmed behavior of his teammates, all of whom fulfill highly routinized specialist tasks.

It seems perfectly appropriate that Henry Aaron, a black Horatio Alger, should surpass Babe Ruth's home run record while playing for Atlanta, the major center of black middle-class America. Baseball seems part of the older American dream, in which hard work, frugality, and individual initiative earn their reward. Unlike in the world of the corporate state, accountability remains clear—namely, the rules prescribe the individualistic responsibility.

Baseball, cricket, and other "inner-directed" games reflect the precorporate world.[10] Their very social structure seems likely to inhibit their attempts at adaptation. Faster balls, wilder scoreboards, faster pacing, and all other attempts at making the game more of a spectacle are unlikely to save it from the inroads of football. The corporate world, inhabited as it is by images rather than personal responsibilities, seems more hospitable to glittering spectacles.

Though sport has a variety of social, economic, and physiological functions in society, we suggest it has two important roles for our daily lives. First, it permits dramatic enactment of our ordinary routines and thereby joins us to a larger social order. In Durkheim's terms, it is part of the collective celebration. Secondly, as Greg Stone

---

[10]See Reuel Denney's (1957:103–120) marvelous outline of the evolution of football.

(1955, 1957) has argued, it provides a coin of communication. That is, persons who are together have the need for talk, which reaffirms their copresence as strangers, lovers, and friends. In such "grooming" conversation, form is more important than substance, and the talk of sport is a form which, laden as it is with statistics, arcane anecdotes, and irrelevant asides, seems to have substance.

Sport, like other cultural games, is an opening of the collectivity to itself. Though it may be used for the personal social mobility of the individual athlete or team owner, it really is not bound into a reinforcement of the stratification system. Perhaps too much uncritical application of the Roman circus metaphor has affected our view of modern sport. Sport seems much closer to Geertz's (1972:26) description of the Balinese cockfight:

> What sets the cockfight apart from the ordinary course of life, lifts it from the realm of everyday practical affairs, and surrounds it with an aura of enlarged importance is not, as functionalist sociology would have it, that it reinforces status discriminations (such reinforcement is hardly necessary in a society where every act proclaims them), but that it provides a metasocial commentary upon the whole matter of assorting human beings into fixed hierarchical ranks and then organizing the major part of collective existence around that assortment. Its function, if you want to call it that, is interpretive; it is a Balinese reading of Balinese experience; a story they tell themselves about themselves.

In industrial societies, sport is one means by which we interpret and celebrate the prevailing forms of community structure and work. Therefore, sport remains essentially a realm open to all by virtue of their membership in the community. And, of course, commercial producers of spectacle attempt to capitalize upon this easy sense of community involvement by threatening to take their professional team franchise from this town to some other. Yet, as we have consistently argued, if the group structures are weak or nonexistent, then no amount of nonwork hocus-pocus is likely to alter the underlying social reality. Interpretive and celebrative functions infer structures worth interpreting and celebrating.

SUMMARY

We began this chapter by looking at some classical and contemporary theories and studies on play and games. We suggested that individualistic theories only present part of the explanation. We argued that play, games, and sport share a common interest in the nature of rules but serve as integrative representations for different social units. Play is largely conducted in the presence of intimates, and it serves to integrate the individual into such associations. Games generally involve peers, and they serve to integrate the locality, neighborhood, or ethnic community. Sport often involves persons from different districts, social classes, and ethnic backgrounds, and it serves to integrate an entire community or nation-state.

In play, the individual creates rules from the received models of his social world. In games, the players and local tradition are involved in the creation and modification of rules. In sport, associational committees of nonplayers create and modify the rules, though the press and fans are considered important elements. In play, the sanctions are enforced by the person. In the game, the players enforce the sanction, or create a nonparticipant social role to arbitrate disputes, though the incumbent is only chosen by the players. Sport represents a system of hierarchy in which officials of the play are professionals chosen by committees of nonplayers from which a variety of appeals can even enter the civil legal system and reach the highest judicial body of the state.

Finally, we argued that play, games, and sport are interpretive representations. As such they are rhetorical forms that bind us to the various collective dimensions that make up our lives. In play, the person assumes an idealized version of the kind of role being played, or, with the confidence of long-term performance, seeks to play an ironic counterpoint. As Simmel (1950:50) notes: "The more profound, double sense of 'social game' is that not only the game is played in a society (as its external medium) but that with its help, people actually 'play' 'society.' " In games, the ideal of social equality is played out, while sport represents industrial work ideally consumated. That is, like our daily lives at work, the players of sport observe mundane routines of seemingly endless practice hours, yet the significant meaning of this effort is given in the spectacular production of the game. And like the productions of our job, the sports game, too, folds into the cave of time as an artifact of the memory. To paraphrase Aristotle, the rhetoric of sport emphasizes the *pathos*, or feelings, of the audience; games emphasize the *logos*, or form and content, of the game; and play emphasizes the *ethos*, or character, of the individual person. In the next chapter we will focus attention on the relationship between recreation and its social organization.

10

RECREATION
AND
ITS
SOCIAL
ORGANIZATION

◀10▶

We have suggested that leisure is a ubiquitous aspect of human life. However, wherever and whenever it occurs, it does not necessarily occur in the same way in all societies or all historical epochs. We are not basing this observation upon any explicitly examined theory of human motivation, nor do we have some preferred implicit theory. Our observation is based upon the knowledge of the social structural aspects of human societies, those common persisting characteristics of everyday life worked out in the social relationships of a society. Among such aspects are the orderly distribution of goods and services, the training and replacement of persons in social relationships, the allocation and creation of power, the distribution of affection among individuals. Societies appear to differ in these and many other structural aspects (see Chapter 4).

Thus far we have alluded to several broad classes—literate/preliterate, industrial/nonindustrial. Even these very broad descriptive differences suggest ways in which societies differ. For example, literate and preliterate societies differ in terms of the presence of writing and associated skills like printing. Societies in which these skills occur have a means for preserving recollections of the past other than the recollections of that society's oldest members. Hence we might suspect that the power of tradition in societies would be different.

Industrial societies differ from nonindustrial in terms of the nature of the economy. Industrial societies employ machinery powered by other than animal strength for the production of many of the goods used by its members. Such societies do not cease to have other forms of production within them, but those societies that possess industrial modes in addition to other modes of production exhibit characteristic differences from those societies that do not possess industrial modes. We want to examine leisure activities in this broadened sense, focusing upon a particular aspect: recreation. We will examine its characteristics, its history, its emergence.

SOME MEANINGS OF LEISURE

Philosophers and theorists have conceptualized leisure in a variety of ways. As we noted in Chapter 1, few attempts have been made to validate conceptualizations empirically. One can argue, quite correctly, that conceptualization does not depend upon empiricism. As long as we are merely concerned with speculation about something, we do not need empirical support obtained in a systematic manner. Moreover, the presence of empirical evidence of a systematic nature is not, in and of itself, sufficient to destroy certain conceptualizations, which may be articles of belief and faith. Thus many conceptualizations of leisure exist from different historical eras and focusing on different aspects of leisure, which is especially confusing for an emerging field of interest, such as the recreation and parks field, because the field does not have a testable theory. The existence of systematic data based upon conceptualizations drawn from other disciplines are useful for evaluating the underlying principles.

One conceptualization of leisure, sometimes thought of as the classical one because of the writings of Plato and Aristotle, understands leisure as a state of being, experienced by an individual, in which all necessity is absent.[1] Another conceptualization understands leisure as discretionary time. This is a behavioral orientation attempting to conceptualize a residual category of all remaining behavior after the essentials are taken care of, such as work, family matters, and personal maintenance. A third conceptualization sees leisure as the differential access of wealth. Those having more can allocate it to goods and services not available to others in the same society (Veblen, 1953). Leisure has also been conceptualized as omnipresent—that is, present in all aspects of human behavior, bursting forth variously in work and on other occasions. This conceptualization deals with psychological dimensions. Other writers have codified the conceptualizations in their work. Comparatively few of these conceptualizations can marshall evidence of a systematic nature.

In a similar vein, while the debates about conceptualization of leisure have proceeded in the intellectual community, a similar concern has raged in contemporary times. This is the debate of leisure as a social problem. The concern with the problem of leisure presumes certain ideological commitments about people and their nature, about people and their inclinations, about people and their relationship to the means of production, and about leisure as an essential aspect of certain kinds of societies.[2] Interestingly, neither the

---

[1] The contemporary version of this conceptualization is mirrored in self-actualization, which is based on the "hierarchy of needs" theory by Maslow (1954).

[2] See Burch (1971b) for an analysis of this phenomenon.

TABLE 38 MEANING OF LEISURE ACTIVITIES TO ADULTS

Importance of Leisure	Percentage	
	Weekly	Monthly
Not at all	5.8	7.1
Slightly	11.5	12.0
Moderately	34.5	32.6
Very	48.2	48.3
Total	100.0	100.0

intellectual nor the ideological approach has often concerned itself with how persons in the everyday aspects of life think about such matters. Some assert that because the United States is a society in which the Protestant ethic has played an important cultural role, leisure and recreation are unimportant, if not unnecessary, aspects of everyday life. (An example during the recent "energy crisis" was a piece of nearly enacted legislation, sponsored by Senator Henry Jackson of Washington, which would not allocate fuel for nonessential activities such as recreation.) On the other hand, there is the folk wisdom embodied in the saying that "all work and no play makes Jack a dull boy." This suggests that relaxation, however it is conceived, is a necessity of existence.

The 1973 Continuing National Survey (see Chapter 2) provides some information regarding how adults in the United States think and feel about aspects of their leisure activities. Regardless of how leisure may be conceptualized, there is enough agreement on the meaning of leisure so that adults understand what they are being asked about when the word "leisure" is used. The respondents were asked how important their leisure activities were to them individually; the distribution of responses can be seen in Table 38. The distribution is shown both for those respondents who answered questions about participation in a weekly time frame and for those who answered in a monthly time frame.

In each distribution, slightly less than 50 percent of the respondents indicated that the activities were "very important" to them. Conversely, only about 5 to 7 percent indicated such activities were "not at all of importance." Approximately another 33 percent of the adults indicated that their leisure activities were "moderately important." Thus, these data suggest that regardless of the activities pursued, the majority of adults define leisure as of some importance to them. Apparently contemporary American adults do not follow the dictates of the Protestant ethic as interpreted by some observers, nor do they see leisure and recreation as nonessential. While these data do not permit comparisons with the indicated importance of various

TABLE 39 SATISFACTION OF
AVAILABLE LEISURE ACTIVITIES TO ADULTS

Satisfaction of Leisure	Percentage	
	Weekly	Monthly
Not at all	3.2	3.3
Slightly	5.5	8.2
Moderately	26.4	26.3
Very	33.1	31.8
Completely	31.8	30.4
Total	100.0	100.0

other categories of activities, such as employment, education, religion, health, it does suggest that leisure activities are recognized by many as important aspects of their everyday lives.

People deal with selected aspects of their lives in terms of various dimensions. Hence one cannot assume that when people indicate the importance of something for themselves, it simultaneously implies something about their satisfaction. For example, if one asked how important transportation activities were to someone, the respondent could indicate they were very important. However, the respondent may not be satisfied with his or her own available means of transportation. Perhaps he or she wants an automobile or would prefer another mode of transport to the one currently available. During the 1973 CNS studies, respondents were asked to indicate their satisfaction with the currently existing leisure activities that were available to them. The resulting distributions for those who responded in terms of weekly participation and those for monthly participation are shown in Table 39.

In both distributions, the modal category of response was "very satisfactory." Approximately 32 percent of each distribution is in this category. Moreover, an additional 30 percent or so of the respondents indicated they "were completely satisfied" with the activities currently available to themselves. While it is not to be denied that many persons are not as satisfied as others, the clear majority of respondents indicated substantial satisfaction with available activities, regardless of specific ones mentioned later in the studies.

Empirically it seems that substantial percentages of adults in the contemporary United States define their leisure activities as of importance and largely satisfactory. Given the diversity of leisure activities, these summary statements are of some importance for our understanding of the social organization of leisure and recreation in industrial societies. In one industrial society, in which activities related to employment are often thought to be the dominant source of social honor, activities not directly related to employment are defined by a majority of adults as being of great importance. We are unable to assert on the basis of these findings that the propositions about employment are not any longer accurate, but we need to inquire more thoroughly into the nature of leisure and work and in particular into the nature of leisure in industrial societies.

RECREATION AND LEISURE

We have noted that regardless of how leisure has been conceptualized, there exists in many cultures an understanding, by those experiencing leisure, of what the word "leisure" means. If one asks respondents to describe what leisure is and observes behavior that is normatively described as leisure, one finds that an essential characteristic of leisure is "pleasure." Regardless of the activity or setting, persons report experiencing feelings of pleasure, enjoyment, relaxation. Another frequently reported feeling is "being oneself," or, as it is sometimes reported in current argot, "letting it all hang out." While we possess material from a variety of contemporary sources that indicate the presence of these characteristics, we again lack similar data from empirical studies conducted at previous times.

Some definitions of leisure have included criteria that recognize the presence of enjoyment and have conceptualized it as implying spontaneity, voluntarism, and being free of constraints. All of these may be present or they may not, but this is an empirical question. One of the difficulties in reaching agreement regarding a unitary conceptualization of leisure is its multifaceted nature. There are perhaps as many ways to enjoy oneself as there are ways to earn a livelihood, but certain broad categories can be distinguished. One of these is recreation.

For the moment we will regard leisure as generally referring to behavior that is engaged in because of the enjoyment being experienced by those persons participating in it. There are a variety of leisure activities some of which we have examined in the preceding chapters. Many others not directly considered share this quality of enjoyment. But while enjoyment may be the major defining characteristic, there exists another important structural property —namely the characteristic of spontaneity. Usually one thinks of spontaneous events as occurring on "the spur of the moment." The idea seems to be that the behavior is not planned but arises as appropriate within the momentary context of surrounding events. To a certain extent, much behavior in which enjoyment occurs does possess spontaneity, more or less. But structurally, spontaneity is better thought of as aperiodic. Thus the behavior occurs in an unplanned manner. For example, people go to work or school in a known periodic sequence. If one asks respondents when they will be going to work or to school the next time, the occurrence of the events is quite likely to be as predicted. In contrast, if one asks respondents when they will be going to play checkers or fishing the next time, the event may or may not take place. Thus, leisure behavior tends not to be routinized. It is in this sense that it is spontaneous.

There is an additional element of the aperiodicity of leisure behavior. Each occurrence is complete within itself. This characteristic has been variously described as behavior set apart from other aspects of everyday existence, as behavior which is an end in and of itself, and as behavior in which one occurrence is not directly dependent upon similar previous events. It is behavior which is self-contained and detached; it is nonsequential in character. Whenever one is examining social behavior almost all statements must be relative. Thus our use of terms like aperiodic and self-contained to describe leisure are understood to mean "relative to other forms of behavior"; they are not absolute terms. In general terms, leisure behavior tends to be self-contained, aperiodic, and enjoyable. (It is understood that we are referring to social behavior.) All known societies exhibit such normative patterns, although the specific content varies as a function of culture. Thus, as far as we know, all engage in amusements, games, song, dance, sport. But some societies differentiate between some apparently similar normative patterns. Within industrialized societies these help distinguish between recreation and leisure.

ROUTINIZATION OF ENJOYMENT

Modernization has been studied extensively by historians, sociologists, economists, and other social scientists. As presently conceived, modernization is the study of the process of social and cultural change associated with the transition from nonindustrial to industrialized economies. Although its specifics are many and varied, most scholars agree that it involves several interrelated but identifiably separate subprocesses. These include the commercialization of goods, the commercialization of labor, bureaucratization and "technification."[3] As has been noted by many scholars since Max Weber identified it as a major distinguishing feature of certain societies, rationality is its hallmark (Weber, 1947). Weber argued that what transpires is the application of rationality to previously nonrationalized situations. By rationality, Weber meant the relation of means and ends in terms of accomplishing desired objectives of values. Ul-

[3]The discussion of these subprocesses their interrelationships, the adequacy of this formulation, and related matters is not the center of our interest in this exposition. Therefore, our discussion must be truncated and the reader is referred to the literature should more exhaustive treatment of the subject be desired.

timately the often-encountered concerns of efficiency and effectiveness of action so common in modernized societies becomes pervasive in many areas of everyday life not directly related to the particular modes of economic activity. Weber's genius was to recognize that once the process of modernization was underway in a society, it was impossible to limit its impact to any single institutional sector, such as the economy. Often conceptualized as secularization, rationality was observed in matters of religion, family, inheritance, and even music. Weber never intended that rationality was always to be construed as dominant or equally powerful in its intrusion into all institutional aspects of human life. He merely argued that no institution, sacred or secular, would be immune from its impact once it was operant in a society. He did not, of course, believe that the appearance of the rationality in everyday affairs ended the importance of tradition or charisma in the lives of people. He merely sought to point out that societies in which rationality existed were not the same as those without rationality. Weber's great concern with the many various ways in which particular combinations of rationality, tradition, and charisma could exist empirically is evidenced by his works on religions, the city, bureaucracy, science, and music. (In Chapter 6 we discussed his interest in taste as well.) Taken together these works constitute the investigation of the range of empirical limits of rationality. His efforts tended to substantiate his argument that the societies in which the rationality operates are different from those in which it is absent.

Men and women value many different things, including other humans. Each human stands in particular relation to others. Some relations are defined as means and some are defined as ends. The inappropriate application of a rationality to relations culturally defined as ends tends to be labeled exploitation or worse. Yet rationality pervades all of social existence to some degree. It is hardly surprising, therefore, that the institution of leisure should be similarly affected. Modernized societies tend to exhibit both an institution of leisure and an institution of recreation. Broadly conceived recreation is rationalized leisure; it is the routinization of enjoyment. Leisure activities and patterns, while retaining outward form, change in the meanings attached to them. Participation ceases to be aperiodic when games are engaged in as an aspect of education. Self-containment ceases when one participates in sports to demonstrate attractiveness as a mate or partner in other institutions. Enjoyment changes when one responds to the urges of being on time for the beginning of the candle-making class so as not to inconvenience others. In short, recreation is leisure activity engaged in for purposes other than enjoyment. Participation becomes a means to some other ends—for example, to make business contacts, to meet the right people, to build character, to improve physical conditioning, to learn self-reliance, to strengthen moral fiber, to sustain family tradition.

Routinized leisure becomes much like other institutions influenced by the intrusions of rationality. In industrial societies, recreation becomes a basis for employment, for market activities, for large-scale enterprises of both public and private endeavors, for technological improvements. We want to examine the emergence of recreation in the United States as an example of the process of modernization. Of particular interest will be the question of how recreation and leisure come to persist within the same culture, because it appears that the institution of leisure per se has changed little as a consequence of modernization, while the institution of recreation is solely its creation.

THE EMERGENCE OF
RECREATION IN THE UNITED STATES

From the beginnings of the colonization of North America the colonists engaged in leisure activities characteristic of the societies from which they originated. The sometimes overly romanticized depiction of the Puritans tends to cloud the diversity that actually characterized the colonial epoch. The proprietary colony of Virginia transplanted a miniature version of contemporary England, with its frivolity and energies. The Dutch in New Holland created a colony not known for its austerity. And, though the Pilgrims of Massachusetts are aptly portrayed as work oriented, they nonetheless engaged in leisure activities for it was not activity that was evil but idleness.

The Germans moving into the colonial holding of William Penn brought not only their farming and mercantile skills but also their leisure activities. The Scotch-Irish immigrants in New England and in the southern colonies added their impacts. By the time of the American Revolution, the diversity of ethnic groups in the colonies was great, although the Anglo-Saxons were predominant. There were many leisure activities pursued. Some were of the outdoor variety: racing, street games, hunting, fishing; some were occasions when communities combined to accomplish tasks beyond the abilities of a single family: logrolling, animal drives, house-raising, deer hunts. It is difficult to decipher whether these communal activities were mostly work or mostly play. As remains true today, cooperative events among neighbors are often opportunities for relaxation and enjoyment.

The events that transformed the fledgling colonies into an independent nation set the stage for the arrival of the nineteenth century. It was during these hundred years that much of what is today thought of as American came into being. The particular combination of events have seldom been equaled in modern history. It was the blinding speed with which these events unfolded that made it unique. Consider, within a century the nation expanded territorially from the Atlantic Ocean across more than 3000 miles to the Pacific Ocean. The immenseness of the Great Plains, which extends 1500 miles from Canada to the Rio Grande, is depicted by the phrase that "the only thing between the two points is a barbed wire fence," signifying its essential topographic similarity. The rapidity with which great wealth was acquired by people exploiting the natural resources of the new nation was unparalleled in history. Although the frontiersman is honored in myth and folklore as the ideal man, it has always been the man of commerce who made his fortune while residing in the city. The settling and subduing of the land mass and its indigenous inhabitants during the nineteenth century was accompanied by the emergence of the railroad, which linked the far-flung reaches of the nation; the resolution of political dominance through arms in the Civil War; the rise of industrialization; the growth of cities, both in number and size; and the attempts to resolve moral issues through means not amenable to those attempts. Throughout the century the steady flow of immigrants continued with but momentary respite. The richness of cultural diversity still evident in the United States derives directly from the immigrants. Indeed, it was this richness of diversity, occurring in this truncated time span, which called out the actions of the last part of the century and extended into the first of the twentieth century. This era is generally referred to as the Progressive Era. It was during this time period that recreation began to emerge as an institution. We will examine in particular the operating social forces that assisted its appearance.

The Progressive Era in the history of the United States covers the period of years between 1890 and 1917. The designation of any historical epoch is always somewhat arbitrary; hence the preciseness of the dates of inclusion are misleading. The Progressive Era is often thought to have been a period during which what was wrong with America was being put right. In one sense this was true; but in another, it is deceptive. (Perhaps the association of the term "muckraker" with the era aids the perpetuation of this not completely accurate interpretation.) The recognition of the excesses of a burgeoning industrialism and the attempts to regulate these excesses (for example, child labor), the difficulties of sprawling cities faced with increasing populations, and the reformulation of the politics of expansionism—these were but aspects of a larger and far grander design: the manufacture of the American! The forces marshaled and at work during this era were quite consciously trying to create homogeneity from the immense diversity extant in the nation. (Interestingly, this cultural product bore fruit in the 1950s, when the excesses of conformity, as depicted in the man in the gray flannel suit, came under consideration.) The necessary characteristics for such an effort included enlightened philanthropy and ideological commitment to the implicit principles of social engineering.

The passing of the frontier as a way of life or a goal took place between the cessation of the Civil War and the beginning of the Progressive Era. In a sense the Progressive Era could not have come about without the frontier. As long as there was the opportunity for passing through into unclaimed and uncharted spaces, the problems of existing communities, whether of a personal or a social nature, could be effectively surmounted. The phenomenon of "warning out" the undesirables in a community began early in the New England colonies and persists in modified fashion today. But once the territorial expansion was effectively terminated—both physically and perhaps most importantly psychologically—new mechanisms were likely to appear in the society. While much or little, depending upon various theories of history, can be made of the importance of the closing of the frontier in American history, it was a necessary condition for the emergence of the Progressive Era and the rise of recreation as one of its consequences.

The loss of the frontier began to be understood in a systemic sense as a recognition that the nation was indeed a limited, if not closed, system. While it stretched across the continent and occupied a considerable land mass, it began to be defined as a bounded system. This concept was important for later events.

The United States, while initially North European in terms of its ethnic makeup, was never solely that. The presence of African groups commenced early and continued. But with the exception of the Africans, substantial numbers of settlers of all ethnic groups moved through the cities and towns of the eastern area and went westward founding new communities. Most were welcomed, though one ethnicity, the Chinese, was not appreciated in the same manner. In 1882, however, Congress passed the first law to regulate immigration and its purpose was to control Chinese entry into the United States. At the same time the second great wave of migration was occurring in the eastern areas. These immigrants were largely from southern and eastern European countries. These new Americans were different in many ways from those who had come before. Their customs, languages, and food were at great variance from those of the early settlers. They never had to choose sides in the Civil War, and because of this they were somehow suspect. But perhaps the most important characteristic of these immigrants was their failure to follow the previously existing pattern of passing through. Unlike their predecessors, they remained in the nation's cities. Until their coming, only the Irish had tended to concentrate in the urban centers.

Consequently, the problems of housing, sanitation, transportation, and so forth quickly arose. While ethnic diversity enriched American culture in the long run, it was a difficult barrier for the society at the time. The awareness of the lack of cultural homogeneity was an important spur for the drive to create "the American."

The continuing influx of new immigrants and the growing appreciation of the limitations of the system made the issue of how permeable the boundaries should be one of increasing political moment. The regulation of migration, which commenced in 1882, continued until well into the twentieth century. It is of interest that until the revision of the underlying principles regarding migration during the late 1950s and early 1960s, it was ethnicity that formed its backbone. The historical answer to the permeability of the system was, in a sense, how close the potential immigrant would come to the "home-manufactured" product. The drive for cultural homogeneity was an important condition for the emergence of recreation.

Another important aspect of the latter part of the nineteenth century, which helped to bring about the Progressive Era, was the changes occurring in agricultural production, which resulted in the beginnings of the migration from the country to the city. Though it was to be the dominant migratory stream of the twentieth century, it had begun earlier. Into the cities came men, women, and children who were already Americans but who were undergoing perhaps a more profound cultural shock than the immigrant from abroad. The romanticism that lauded the country virtues, still in many ways the contemporary dream of Americans, received great impetus in the face of the living conditions of the cities and towns of the 1880s and 1890s. This ideology was an important component of the rationale underlying the emergence of recreation.

The vigor of the reformers of the Progressive Era was prodigious. The great outpouring of energies of many dedicated persons could not have occurred, however, without a devotion to the principles of social mechanics. Though the evolutionists were beginning to make their impact felt during this era, its flowering was of later times. (Indeed the significance of the environmental movement of the late 1960s and early 1970s may lie in the final supplanting of the mechanistic metaphor by that of an organismic.) The American experience was largely that of pioneering, which rewarded self-reliance but also made one acutely aware of the consequences of overestimating what one person or one family could accomplish without assistance. It also meant that social recognition went to those who did the job, regardless of other defining characteristics. Codified by scholars as pragmatism, it was the fundamentalism of rationality embodied in the mechanistic metaphor that epitomized Americanism at the juncture of the Progressive Era. The belief that the right amount of adjustment and tinkering with the social order could smooth out its operating problems was begun. The soundness of the belief was not to be seriously questioned until the decade of the 1960s. With the right know-how and the right amount of resources, Utopia could be constructed. Recreation was an essential institution in this grand order. Society was perfectable and the task was at hand. The work was begun eagerly.

Other scholars have detailed in great specificity the processes leading to the recreation movement (Dumazedier, 1967; Kaplan, 1960.) We will focus upon certain important aspects, which are noticeable from a macroscopic perspective but which at times are lost sight of in more limited formulations. We want to point out those forces and trends that eventuate in the empirical regularities reported throughout this volume. We shall move boldly from events in one era to those in another as we sketch in the details of the emergence of the institution of recreation. Underlying its existence today is an implicit set of assumptions that remain largely what Alvin Gouldner has termed "domain assumptions." To understand the contemporary organization of leisure and recreation, we need to examine these assumptions carefully. They explain much about the institution and they may suggest something about the future.

RECREATION AND EVERYDAY ENTERPRISE

The cultural riches of the newly forming society were everywhere evident in the nineteenth century. This was as apparent with respect to leisure as with any other sphere of everyday life. Children played near their homes under the watchful eye of parents and older siblings, as they do today. Adults engaged in amusements of brief or lengthy duration within and sometimes outside of the sight and sound of children, as it is today. The events of life were celebrated in various fashions, with appropriate gaiety or solemnity. The foods consumed, while plenty or sparse, were sources of pleasure. Meal times provided opportunities for recounting or planning the events of a day. Though the specifics of life were varied, the patterns were similar. And so they remain today. What was different was the interpretation given these similarities because they were bound into different cultural patterns, such as language and dress. The reformers of the 1880s and after saw the need for the establishment of common experiences for all. They saw, or at least thought they did, the erosion of the abilities of people to deal with the everyday challenges of existence. They based their program in recreation on a set of assumptions.

First, urban life was thought to be not as desirable as rural life. Certainly the conditions of many aspects of city life tended to force one to such a conclusion. Sanitation presented an important problem, disease was present in ways no longer understood by many contemporary Americans, slums and poor housing were increasing under the pressure of foreign and domestic migratory streams. Laws appropriate for small communities but inadequate for larger ones created peculiar situations—for example, children were arrested for playing in streets. The children, in particular, were seen as the most hard pressed yet valuable asset for a future.

Second, urban life was thought to create a major departure from the rural or previously existing leisure patterns of life. Families were no longer seen as units of toil, children were forced to work away from parents. Not all members of the family did the same kind of work nor worked in the same place. The hours of work were not regulated solely by natural time (that is, rising and setting of the sun in concert with the alternations of the seasons.) The previously existing locales where relaxation could occur were lacking. The distances to be traveled to reach open land for many previously enjoyed amusements were greater. Transportation was difficult. The local street was the open ground for many. Apparently the reformers did not understand that the place of activity, as contrasted with its meanings to the participants, was not the deciding factor for leisure patterns.

Third, it was assumed that it was possible to create acceptable substitute areas in urban environments for the rural openness. In New York the existence of Central Park predated the appearance of the Sand Garden in Boston by many years. The latter is often cited as the first accomplishment of the playground movement. Thus playgrounds were created in urban areas as places for children to play in safety and in conditions more conducive to appropriate development.

Perhaps the most intriguing assumption was the one that underlies much of recreation today. This was the assumption that it was necessary to teach and train people, especially children, how to play properly, so that areas like playgrounds could be used appropriately. Apparently the heterogeneity of urban peoples encouraged such a view, although the theories of men like Friedrich Froebel were influential in the thoughts of early leaders like Joseph Lee. Moreover, if one is to create Americans it would surely be necessary to insure early attention to shaping their cultural growth properly.

Of equal magnitude was a companion assumption that it was the responsibility of the community to make facilities, programs, and so forth available for the purposes of recreation. When the playground association was formed this was one of its major tenets. The proper training of children for play was not to be found in the family but in the community. In particular, it was the local community that was the focus of this assumption. Local government could be monitored more readily by the reformers to see that appropriate actions were being taken; and local governments were most likely to be amenable to the influence of many of the concerned citizens backing the growth of playgrounds. It was to be many years before the recreation movement would compromise its attachment to this position.

These assumptions were important ones encouraged by the mechanistic metaphor and appropriate to it. Of especial importance was the concept of children as "parts," necessarily molded in ways that the familly was not necessarily capable of accomplishing for a variety of reasons. Although the concept that play was necessarily related to adulthood was not new, it was stressed anew. It was to be nearly fifty years from the beginnings of the movement before the importance of recreation for adults was to become emphasized; and it was even later for the concern with special populations to appear (those of the aged, ill, infirm, and so on). Once play began to be defined instrumentally, then rationality had intruded into enjoyment and spontaneity. There were examples already for such formulations.

As early as the 1820s, German immigrants formed so-called *Turnerbunds* or *Turnervereins* as combination centers for gymnastics and social meeting places. Gymnastics for all ages was a part of maintaining health; for girls it was an aid in developing good posture and grace in motion. Gymnastics was always a serious business for some ethnic groups as it was when it was popularized in the 1880s by the Swede Nils Posse. Thus while controlled exercise was early seen as instrumental to health and formed the basis for the dramatic emergence of physical education after World War I, the fundamental character of defining play instrumentally cannot be overstressed. Moreover, that such definition occurred during the Progressive Era was not a matter of happenstance.

Once rationality penetrates previously traditional areas of social action, its spread continues apace. Recreation began with children and then was greatly expanded to adults with the aid of the mobilization for World War I and the creation of the War Camp Community Service, which operated off-post clubs for the soldiers away from home. The attempts to convert the wartime euphoria of community solidarity into a permanent condition through community centers serving the adult population failed, but that all ages needed assistance in the wise use of leisure was established.

The generally poor physical condition of the average American male at the time of induction into the Army led, in the postwar years, to the institutionalization of compulsory physical education for all children processed through the public schools. Mandatory physical education gained legislative approval during the era before the wars. The purposefulness of children of all ages participating in supervised activities (much like those they engaged in without supervision outside of the classroom) in the name of health, character building, stimulating ability to learn other subjects, and so forth, became a permanent part of the social institution of education.

Later, the purposefulness of recreation as essential to certain forms of work for adults emerged into what is now known as industrial recreation. Though begun in 1941, its major growth period followed the termination of World War II. Similarly, recreation as a means to improve health and rehabilitate persons actually ill (as contrasted with recreation for preventive reasons) came to be known as therapeutic recreation. So-called military recreation blossomed after World War II as well. Thus within a century, members of the American society have come to engage in activities which, though usually participated in for relaxation, are also done for reasons having nothing to do with relaxation. Though paradoxical perhaps, this mixture of duty with enjoyment is an everyday enterprise in contemporary American society.

RECREATION AS AN INDUSTRY

The routinization of enjoyment in industrial societies has the characteristics of other institutions in the society. In recreation, one may observe the commercialization of goods as well as labor, the bureaucratization of its activities, and the increasing technification of many of its aspects. While we have dealt with sport in the preceding chapter, we can use it as an example to illustrate these aspects of recreation.

The commercialization of goods as an aspect of recreation is readily observed with respect to sports. Especially team sports seem almost impossible to engage in nowadays without the purchase of the requisite equipment, uniforms, and so forth. The manufacture of these goods involves the whole panoply of modern industrial activities. Capital is provided by entrepreneurs to form a company, acquire machinery, establish production routines, ensure quality, train personnel, transport goods, distribute to wholesalers, establish bona fide sales agents, establish price regulations, and so on.

In a similar fashion the commercialization of labor is present. Some people earn a livelihood from the sale or manufacture of sports-related goods, many earn a living by instructing others how to participate, and some earn a living as regular participants (that is, professionals). Distinctions arise between professionals and amateurs in many sports, thus further rationalizing the activity. The continuing need for instruction so that people participate according to the rules is a particular indication of rationality in sports. Moreover, it is not just a matter of teaching skills, but the need for an expert to teach skills properly. Not only are there specialists who engage in the activities, but specialists who teach others as well.

The development of vast collectivities to regulate the occurrence of sports demonstrates the presence of bureaucratization. Organizations arise to establish regulations concerning how the sport may be conducted, how people may be recruited to engage in it, how to settle disputes between teams on and off the field, and so forth. The skills of industrial management are as necessary for operating a Little League as they are the National Football League. Hence for players, managers, as well as many others, the usual concerns of remunerations, labor management relationships, and so forth are evident.

There is perhaps no better place to demonstrate the presence of rationality than in examining technification in sports. Each day, it seems, some new item arrives in the marketplace to improve competitive advantage in the activity. Consider the exactitude of the weight of a baseball bat, the graphite core of golf clubs, the shape of the tennis racquet, the materials for a fishing rod, the curvature and materials of the protective pads used in gridiron football. Specifications of equipment become concerns of regulation and gain great prominence. The operation of all the aspects of mass marketing are let loose upon the public to convince them that the successful performances of particular participants are solely the result of the use of a particular piece of equipment, dietary regimen, or other technically developed item or routine.

Characteristic of the processes of industrial societies, the routinization common to recreation tends to spread into a variety of activities. Among sports, those known as team sports are obvious examples, but similar considerations occur in nonteam sports as well. Within recent history, few if any sports have remained immune to the process. Some that were largely amateur—for example, tennis, golf, bowling, car racing—now possess the accoutrements of professionalism. Indeed, the supposedly primitive and solitary activity of wilderness camping is a major growth market for technification.

Interestingly, activities not normally thought of as sport begin to be redefined, such as the game of chess, which recently moved into high visibility as a result of the world championship match between an American and a Russian. Activities not normally considered sports in the usual sense are undergoing the same processes—for example, dog showing, horse showing, rodeos, and parachuting. By now sport has a form of organization that permits the rationalization of many traditionally nonsporting leisure activities into such a mode and thus expanding the traditional definitions associated with it. It appears that wherever competition exists in leisure activities, it may become rationalized. Moreover, the creation of new settings for an activity may create new activities. Particularly good examples of this are waterskiing and sandskiing. Thus the cultural meanings of the activities are expanded. It is not enough to know that a person participated in a game of baseball. Much more information is needed to know what that participation experience was likely to be.

It is perhaps easiest to see the consequences of the rationalization of enjoyment in sports activities, but rationalization is not limited to sports. Many hobbies, from model building to collecting, share similar characteristics, with new forms appropriate to a culture tending to emerge. Technological diversification provides many opportunities. Recently, collecting has expanded beyond coins, stamps, and art to include electrical transmission pole insulators, barbed wire, and beer cans. Individuals show their collections in competitive events, acquiring trophies and sometimes money for rewards. The preservation of machinery and goods from previous eras no longer remains the sole province of museums. Automobiles, tractors, airplanes are collected, repaired, and exhibited by individuals. The commercialization of the arts is well documented and too well known to require further comment here. Thus the attachment of rationality occurs to many leisure activities in industrial societies. Of particular interest is that the appearance of recreation does not destroy leisure in such societies. The reasons why leisure has persisted constitute much of the previous sections of this book.

Since its inception, the definition of the community responsible for providing training and facilities for recreational activities has undergone substantial variation. Some facilities are provided through public expenditures of tax monies, for example, municipal stadiums, parklands, racing tracks. Indeed, in the United States, the history of outdoor recreation is largely the history of successive levels of government, from local to national, spending public funds on outdoor recreation facilities. (Peculiar to the United States, the conservation and preservation movements became important sources of legitimation for the expansion of public funding for facilities primarily utilized for recreational purposes.) Public educational programs and facilities are important sources of instruction for participation in recreational endeavors, for both children as they develop and later for adults who take classes for enjoyment or use the facilities outside of school hours for other purposes, such as playing basketball with a neighborhood group. An example, in the United States, of the impact of government on increasing participation in an activity is easily seen by examining how the creation of public swimming pools has greatly expanded participation among the population. While the public sector of the economy is especially important to recreation, the private sector may be most important to the institution of leisure (though not unimportant to recreation). In particular, the great variety of goods, services, and places associated with leisure activities for most people tend to be aspects of the private entrepreneur. From roller-skating rinks to dance halls, from bars to exclusive resorts, from etching acid to kilns for firing ceramics, private enterprise makes available the locales and tools for acquistion by individuals. The organization of leisure and recreation includes various means by and through which necessary goods and services become available and influence participation.

SUMMARY

We have noted that recreation emerges in particular kinds of social orders. Basically, it appears to be the rationalization of enjoyment. Yet the emergence of the institution of recreation depends upon the prior existence of the institution of leisure. Rationality operates upon tradition, and, indeed, presupposes its existence. But while its course may diverge once commenced, it does not destroy the existence nor the function of tradition in all human social orders. Recreation is different from leisure in an empirically verifiable fashion. It differs in patterned, knowable, and predictable ways. Though recreation presupposes leisure, the converse does not appear to be true.

11

THE TRENDS –
NEAR
AND
NOT
NEAR
FUTURE

The machine is the symbol of the industrialized, modernized society. Manufacturing is the overwhelming productive process of the
society. Its peculiar "logic" and rationale come, in time, to pervade
insidiously many apparently nonrelated aspects of everyday life. The
metaphor of the machine, clothed in various garbs, encourages the
appearance and persistence of a particular frame of mind. This casts
an interest in tomorrow so that the future becomes for these societies what the past is to nonliterate societies. Each adult is expected
to be able to deal with the future more surely than any soothsayer.
The mechanistic demiurge, as the child of rationality, lends support
to a deterministic approach to existence. Machines are knowable,
for they can be assembled and reassembled as necessity requires.
The material from which each part is made can be studied for its
characteristics and its period of action until replacement as necessi-
tated by wear can be accurately calculated. Elapsed time, from the
beginning of some process of manufacture until the product emerges,
is known with great precision. So, too, are distances to markets, distribution systems, anticipated warehousing requirements, shelf life,
and expected durability under a variety of customer-use conditions,
which are calculated as surely as it is accepted that each day the sun
will rise. The mechanistic determinism follows even into the calcula-
tion of how much elapsed time a salesperson ought to require to
begin and complete a sale. All of these and many more examples of
the routinization of everyday life in industrial societies come readily
to mind. The future is considered knowable and, in many facets, determined by the past and present. It is the predictability of that state,
its shape and character, that is of paramount importance for actions
and decisions taken each day. It is perhaps a happy coincidence that
science shares this concern with knowable and predictable futures.

The power of the mechanistic metaphor is nowhere more clearly
observed than in the application of its logic to nonmechanistic oc-
currences, employing often the approach known as science. Organismic processes come to be treated as if they were special cases of

mechanisms. Perhaps this is best exemplified by agricultural production of animal tissues. Production specialists calculate how much food with certain characteristics, fed at certain rates, with certain supplementary aids such as mineral extracts are required to produce a certain number of pounds of animal tissue at a particular rate of gain for specific periods of elapsed time. Reproductive processes are also amenable to such rationalization. While semen has been stored, and animals impregnated mechanically for some time now, so too is the estrus cycle being conceptualized. Now, by the use of certain materials, it is possible to increase the number of offspring produced annually by various domesticated animals through reducing the elapsed time of the ovulatary cycle. Thus time is not wasted by the machine in more efficiently producing its "product." It is irrelevant whether one, as an individual, likes or does not like such aspects of everyday life in modernized societies. What is important is to recognize the presence of the metaphor implicitly underlying many aspects of such societies. These considerations are quite important to the assessment of the trends in leisure participation, to which we now turn our attention.

PREDICTABILITY OF LEISURE BEHAVIOR

Our discussion of leisure has emphasized that it is not unitary. Recreation, leisure, and sport, though occurring in the same society, are not the same. While sharing certain surface similarities, each emerges from differing sources and occurs in differing societies. These basic properties suggest important considerations about the predictability of each. Thus leisure, which is rooted in the biosocial nature of the species, requires different approaches from those used with sport, which is rooted in tradition, particularly martial ritual. In contrast, recreation, the child of modernity and routinization, is most amenable to still other predictive endeavors. Each is predictable, but the nature of the predictability may vary among the three institutions. Yet the concern with predictability arises largely as an anticipated characteristic of the institution of recreation.

Recreation demonstrates especially well the insidious nature of rationality. The routinization of enjoyment ultimately converts the meaning of participation into something quite different. The social organization of recreation requires the prediction of anticipated participation in ways not dissimilar to other market-oriented activities in a society. The desire for prediction and forecasting arises in the efforts to anticipate consumer behavior so that the existing supply will be adequate, and not a single sale will be missed as a result of not having an item in stock. Thus we observe a great deal of attention being given to the prediction of so-called demand by public agencies managing outdoor recreation facilities. The logic is the same, although it is being utilized for the allocation of public monies. What is important is the forecasting as a necessary aspect of the process. As far as we know, there have not been any publicly available studies or reports assessing how accurate the forecasts of participation in outdoor recreation among adults in the United States have been. (This suggests that with respect to publicly provided recreation facilities and programs, forecasting has functions in addition to anticipating demand.) Considerable monies continue to be expended in planning, programming, and development on the basis of futures that are rarely assessed again. Perhaps it is ironic that the present is continually legitimated by the "future"; but this is the case for public recreation. It is the power of this metaphor that produces analytical confusion and that we have attempted to clarify in this book.

The more frequently accepted conceptualization of leisure has been that of discretionary time. Though it tends to be a residual category—that is, a name for what's leftover after all other things have been accomplished—it is peculiarly limited to industrial societies. Occupational endeavors are somewhat different in modernized societies from what they are in other societies. Because of the supposed supremacy of occupation there has been a tendency to follow in the footsteps of a single-factor theory and accept one's occupation as the major determining element of all other aspects of one's everyday life. Our exposition has demonstrated the limits of this view for the understanding of leisure, even in modernized societies. The confusion is exacerbated by assessing discretionary time as a property of individuals, rather than appreciating, as we have suggested, that leisure is a property of social groups and is not conditional upon any particular mode of economic production present in a society. It is these mistakes that have produced the curious outpouring (i.e., leisure as a social problem) in societies where the manufacture of man exists. For whatever the stated reasons such commentators may offer, be it a concern with the perfectability of man, his imputed basic nature and so on, all are but muted pleas engendered by the metaphor of the machine and its insidious meanderings. Time, not programmed, though potentially programmable, ideologically championed, is an uneasy bedfellow for the mechanistic metaphor. But these matters, of interest historically, are unlikely to assist greatly in the understanding of leisure in societies.

Sport has been of considerable interest and concern to observers for some time. Its importance has long been recognized in many societies. Its history is well documented and its functions well cataloged. Sport, rooted as it is in tradition, continues in industrial societies, but it, too, alters in its meanings under the unending and relentless pressures of the metaphor of the machine. The major consequence for sport in modernized societies is its commercialization. It is, as we suggest, the commercialization of ritual with its attendant consequences that are of the greatest magnitude for the meanings of sport as contrasted to recreation and leisure in these societies. Leisure binds individuals to each other uniquely, recreation assists the manufacture of social persons, and sport rewards the subversion of invidious desires for the glory of the collectivity.

This impact of commercialization has important consequences for the place of sport in industrial societies. The distinction between professionals and amateurs becomes of major importance. Generally, professionals are those participants who earn a livelihood from their participation. It is irrelevant whether they earn all or only some of their livelihood from such endeavors; the receipt of any remuneration for participation implies the loss of amateur status for the activity. While it is team sports that are the most widely known examples, many nonteam sports also exhibit the presence of professionals. In recent months one of the most notable examples has been the emergence of tennis as a fully developed professional sport. There are other activities, not usually thought of as competitive sports, that also are undergoing professionalization. For example, while there have always been men and women who made a living as fishermen and guides, it has only been recently that fishing competitions for prize money have developed. Freshwater bass tournaments now occur regularly. Professionals have emerged who make a living participating in these events and who use quite sophisticated fish-finding equipment, costing considerable sums of money. In a similar manner, there are now professionals who compete in casting matches. Almost any activity in which an element of competition can be engendered is a likely prospect for professionalization in a society where the commercialization of labor has emerged.

A further consequence for sport is that it loses its unity as an institution. Recreation draws on sport in the same manner as it draws on leisure. Thus it becomes necessary to distinguish between amateur sport and professional sport before assessing potential trends in the near and not near future. It would be difficult today for the assessment of Napoleon's defeat at Waterloo to have the same ring of truth. The unity of the meaning of sport no longer holds in industrial societies as it did once.

The concern with prediction of behavior, be it leisure, recreation, or sport, arises within the context of the culture emerging in industrialized societies. Each institution differs in ways that suggest the meaning of prediction may be different as well as the appropriateness of the way in which such assessments of futures are to be undertaken. Several additional observations are required before the actual discussion of trends is undertaken.

Unlike sport and leisure, recreation is in the process of completing its legitimation. That is, the acceptance of all the aspects of its institutional configuration remain unclear. Unless one notices at the outset that an analytical distinction must be made among the closely related institutions, great confusion can arise. It is sometimes said that societies in which the Protestant, or work, ethic has held sway do not value leisure. As our analysis has suggested, this is an improper but understandable conclusion. Different sources claim that support for this contention is indicated by (1) the permeability of parklands for various purposes, as by highway rights-of-way and construction, (2) the failure of public bond issues to expand facilities for community recreation, (3) the need to convince the public that recreation is a profession requiring special training and unique application of skills and knowledge, (4) the comparative low rates of expansion of agency budgets for recreation when contrasted to other sectors of governmental activity, (5) the observation that in times of economic fluctuation, recreation-related expenditures are first to be reduced. Although these assertions are often heard they are best interpreted as symbolic of legitimation dilemmas than as refutations of leisure as an institutional force in a society.

The dilemma is real and has consequences for the social organization of recreation in a society. It is unlikely that such problems will be reduced in the near future because there exist functional alternatives for individuals and social groups in sport and leisure. Sportlike activities are tied through physical education into the institution of education in a fairly secure manner. As has been observed, most people in industrial societies do most of their active participation in sport-like activities during childhood. Sportlike activities are an aspect of going to school. Once their school years are over, this participation tends to decline substantially for most people. (These aspects are predictable from what we have indicated about sport as a molder of social persons. Outside of the institution of education, the need for such activity to continue into adulthood tends to decline rapidly). It is perhaps an overstatement to say that should all sportlike components of recreational programs suddenly disappear, the net effect upon adult participation and the legitimation of the institution of sport per se would be negligible. But there seems good analytical reasons to suspect that such might be the case. For the not near future the case may be different.

The differentiation of professional and amateur sport means that a variety of occupational paths now exist, which were not present to the same degree until comparatively recently. It was fairly unusual to hear a child respond to the query of his or her potential adult occupational aspirations with a desire to become a professional athlete. Nowadays it is not as unusual. The implications are that sportlike activities outside of school begin to take on meaning within the institution of professional sport. Hence the source of legitimation undergoes alteration and consequently so, too, does the analytical assessment of futures. This recognition makes contemporary travail over the admission of girls as participants in Little League baseball within the United States of much greater significance than if seen as an aspect solely of the women's rights movement. In another instance the national television coverage of the so-called "Punt, pass, and kick" contests in football for children suggests the rapidity of the transition of the realm of "sports for kids" outside of the educational context from one institutional sphere to another. If careers exist for professionals in sports, then, clearly, there will emerge paths of appropriate socialization for reaching them. But what this may mean for the near and not near future for the institution of recreation may be quite another matter.

The dilemmas of legitimation for recreation arise not only from the competition from sport but also from leisure. As we have suggested, leisure arises partly from the biosocial nature of the species. The ways in which it is manifested are largely cultural. Hence the activities, games, hobbies, and amusements observed during some particular historical epoch tend to differ, yet they remain quite similar as a consequence of socialization. In a similar manner, the locales in which such activities occur are also aspects of socialization. Therefore our attention to the empirical location of leisure activities carries more significance than one might initially assume.

The abode or home is the modal locale of most leisure behavior in contemporary industrial societies or at least in the United States. Participation normally occurs with members of a kin or friendship group. Such events, experiences, and episodes are important for continuing socialization of the young and strengthening of social bonds among all participants. The empirical fact that one engages in softball, has a picnic, makes ceramics, operates a model railroad, gardens, plays a round of bridge or poker, observes wildlife out the window, or schools a dog for obedience is not of overshadowing import. It is the nature of the participation per se that is vital and unchanging.

Recreation draws inevitably upon the previously existing cultural patterns of games, sports, hobbies, amusements, and so on but transfers them into different locales for different reasons. The expectation of recreation as a replacement for the imperatives of leisure and sport are quite limited. Thus while the rationale for the emergence of the institution of recreation may have been patently apparent to its founders, such clarity no longer exists a century later. There are few, if any, activities translated into services that are truly unique to the institution of recreation. Hence political support may decline initially without "damage" to the socializing aspects of leisure. Does this mean that the institution of recreation is to be numbered among those that emerged during a particular epoch only to become memorable in folklore and history? We think not. For as surely as societies and cultures undergo continuing change, so too do institutions. The near future of recreation may be startlingly different from its not near future. Some suggestions of its trajectory are worthy of momentary attention.

An especially interesting phenomenon of the process of industrialization and modernization is the emergence of the institution of retirement. Unlike nonindustrialized societies, adults living an arbitrary number of years are defined as no longer appropriate as participants in gainful employment. They are pensioned off—that is, provided with some sort of income from various sources—but are encouraged not to continue their previous means of livelihood. Within the United States, persons beyond the age of 65 years now constitute approximately 10 percent of the total population. Persons not only live longer but more of them survive to older ages than at any previous known period of time. There are many reasons for this situation: high nutrition, public health measures to reduce epidemics, more widely available and better medical care for individuals, better housing, and so on. In short, the standards of living are higher today for most people than they were previously. The unanticipated consequence is the creation of a social category never previously existing in the society. The first generation of people who have passed their entire lives in this system have yet to reach retirement. So those persons now in the age of retirement were not socialized in a system where this existed. The behavior of these persons may or may not be an accurate indication of the social and cultural makeup of the category as it will exist in approximately another 15 years or so. The importance of the institution of recreation to this cohort may be quite different from what it now is. While recreationists speak today about "special populations" (including the "aged") for which they create a variety of programs, these groupings may become the major population to be served. Why might this be so?

As we have suggested, much leisure behavior occurs in or near the abode of the adult. We have already noted that culture and biology combine to ensure the continuing formation of new social groups and that leisure occupies a unique position in this process. New kin groups are initiated and taste acts as one mechanism for sustaining cultural continuity between groups at a microscopic level. These groups commence as two-person groups, enlarge as offspring are reared, and then decline in number to the original at periods of time now considerably extended prior to the demise of either of the original pair-bonded individuals. The sustaining mechanisms of everyday life act to continually reinforce the particularistic features of existence. While kin ties are sustained, interaction frequency may be altered as grown children move physically greater distances but talk more on the telephone. The demise of friends does not stop the process of friendship formation nor its importance for older persons. Institutions emerge and adapt to cultural and social imperatives. The programs, activities, and concerns of recreation may provide opportunities for interpersonal contacts in such a society with comparatively large numbers of individuals who have normal interests and desires and who lack the problems of enfeeblement for many years. Thus the present state of the legitimation of the institution of recreation may be substantially altered in the remainder of this century.

The concept of "special populations" as employed today in recreation is rather nebulous. It generally is a means of emphasizing that each "population"—be it the aged, the minorities, the children—requires special programming if recreation is to carry out its function as it wishes. Closely allied in this sense are the social service functions, such as unemployment assistance, aid to dependent children, community social work, and so on. Recreation may best be seen as a companion institution to these institutions rather than as an ideologically vital force in the shaping of the lives of children. History will judge the correctness of this interpretation. We turn, finally, to the assessment of the futures of leisure.

We have considered leisure as grounded in the biosocial nature of the species. As such, questions regarding whether there will be more or less leisure in the future of a society are not answerable. Our analysis suggests that as long as there are human beings there will be leisure. No society is possible without it. The number of different activities, the frequency with which participation varies, and the locales where such activities take place will alter but not become greater or smaller in the usual sense of these words. The social organization of leisure will continue to exist analytically distinct from the social organization of work. The rates of change are likely to be different for each, with the former exhibiting greater stability over time than the latter. This is not to say that leisure activities will not undergo change. While we know, from the few studies carried out carefully enough to permit confidence in their data, that in the United States the rank order of the activities discussed in Chapter 2 is quite similar to those found in the earlier studies of "Middletown" and Westchester County, such stability does not mean that significant shifts in the meanings of such activities may not transpire. If an activity loses a locale where participation normatively occurred or acquires a new locale, then its trajectory is likely to vary. Similarly while we operationalize the study of leisure largely by reference to frequency of participation, there is much we do not know. Frequency of participation may or may not be the best way to operationalize the formation of social bonding among people. We do not know the relative weighting of each occurrence in the overall strengthening of these bonds. We do not know much about the mutual effects of participation in one activity with that observed in another. Nor do we know much about the persistence of patterns of participation throughout the lives of individuals nor about the persistence of patterns during a historical epoch. Certain though it is that there remains much to be learned, we know more now empirically about the social organization of leisure for contemporary industrial societies then we have ever known before.

SUMMARY

We have suggested that to approach the question of the future of leisure, recreation, and sport in the usual mode of offering up actuarial estimates of participation for the future presents a somewhat improper form of prognostication. Each has its own emergence in human societies. Each is unique although each arises commonly in the face of the problems of social conduct among conspecifics. Recreation, the most recent emergent, has not yet completed the process of legitimation, hence its future remains problematic. We are comparatively certain that it shall remain as an institution in some industrialized societies. We are less certain as to its precise sociological components. Sport appears to be undergoing further stages in the process of institutional bifurcation. The futures of professional sport and amateur sport though related are likely to be unique in ways not readily assessible. Leisure is ubiquitous to all human social orders as we conceive them. Its content, as with all matters of taste, may vary historically, but its persistence as a major cultural means for meeting an aspect of the one biosocial imperative of the species seems certain—the unique attachment of one individual to another.

AFTERWORD

*Our efforts in this book have been to place the study of leisure
in human societies into a perspective that enables the results to
take their place within the general concerns of contemporary
sociological inquiry. Basically we have argued that human leisure is
not adequately explained by reference to its presumed interconnec-
tions with other institutions found in human societies. Leisure is not
frivolous nor merely another aspect of the playing out of the
determinants of the workaday world. Instead we have argued that it
is an institutional adaptation to an aspect of the biosocial character
of the species Homo sapiens. We have tried to suggest that while
culture as an adaptive mechanism for a species creates considerable
opportunities, it also creates certain dilemmas. The ability to deal
with conspecifics symbolically is, apparently, the dominant advantage of culture. In one sense, an individual can therefore relate
to many more conspecifics (and perhaps other species as well)
through this mechanism than appears possible in its absence. Yet its
power to bewitch the observer is substantial. Culture, its persistence
and emergence as an area of inquiry, constitutes a heady brew. It
is important! But, as we suggest, it cannot provide a complete
understanding of human social orders. Nor should our obvious
enchantment with the biosocial nature of the species be seen as the
excesses of correction often encountered in intellectual dialogue.
To overemphasize one above the other would be no contribution
to discourse. Our attempt has been to suggest how the intersection
of the biosocial and the sociocultural aspects of the species can
contribute to an enlarged understanding of both. If we have per-
suaded the reader to see leisure as worthy of systematic inquiry, as
a phenomenon itself demanding explanation, then more we cannot
ask. Ours has been an attempt at a beginning. Whether it is false
or not, others shall decree.*

REFERENCES

Aldrich-Blake, F. P.G.
1970   "Problems of social structure in forest monkeys." Pp. 79–101 in J. H. Crook (ed.). Social Behavior in Birds and Mammals. New York: Academic.

Anderson, Alan Ross, and Omar Khayyam Moore
1960   "Autotelic folk-models." The Sociological Quarterly 1:203–215.

Anderson, Dewey, and Percy E. Davidson
1943   Ballots and the Democratic Class Struggle. Palo Alto: Stanford University Press.

Anderson, Nels
1961   Work and Leisure. New York: Free Press.

Anderson, W. A.
1936   "Rural youth: activities, interests, and problems." Ithaca: Cornell University Press. Bulletin 649.

Anderson, W. A.
1937   "Rural youth: activities, interests, and problems." Ithaca: Cornell University Press. Bulletin 661.

Anderson, W. A.
1935   "Rural social participation and the family life cycle." Ithaca: Cornell University. Agricultural Experiment Station Memoir 314.

Angrist, Shirley
1967   "Role constellations as a variable in women's leisure activities." Social Forces 45:423–431.

Archibald, Katherine
1947   Wartime Shipyard: A Study in Social Disunity. Berkeley, Calif.: University of California Press.

Archibald, Katherine
1953   "Status orientations among shipyard workers." Pp. 395–402

in Reinhard Bendix and S. M. Lipset (eds.). Class, Status, and Power. New York: Free Press.

Arendt, Hannah
1958   The Human Condition. Chicago: University of Chicago Press.

Avedon, Elliott M.
1974   Therapeutic Recreation Service. Englewood Cliffs, N.J.: Prentice-Hall.

Avedon, Elliott M., and Brian Sutton-Smith
1971   The Study of Games. New York: Wiley.

Axelrod, Morris
1956   "Urban structure and social participation." American Sociological Review 21:13–18.

Azrael, Jeremy R.
1961   "Notes on Soviet urban attitudes toward leisure." Social Problems 9:69–77.

Babchuk, Nicholas, and C. Wayne Gordon
1965   "Voluntary associations and the integration hypothesis." Sociological Inquiry 35:149–162.

Babchuk, Nicholas, and C. Wayne Gordan
1962   The Voluntary Association in the Slum. Lincoln: University of Nebraska Press.

Becker, Howard S.
1963a   Outsiders—Studies in the Sociology of Deviance. New York: Crowell Collier Macmillan.

Bendix, Reinhard
1974   "Inequality and social structure: a comparison of Marx and Weber." American Sociological Review 39:149–161.

Bendix, Reinhard, and Seymour Martin Lipset
1966   Class, Status, and Power. New York: Free Press.

Berger, Bennett M.
1960   Working-Class Suburb: A Study of Auto Workers in Suburbia. Berkeley: University of California Press.

Berger, Bennett M.
1963   "The sociology of leisure." Pp. 21–40 in E. O. Smigel (ed.). Work and Leisure. New Haven: College and University Press.

Bishop, Doyle W., and Massaru Ikeda
1970   "Status and role factors in the leisure behavior of different occupations." Sociology and Social Research 44:190–208.

Blakelock, Edwin H.
1960   "A new look at the new leisure." Administrative Science Quarterly 4:446–467.

Bongartz, Roy
1974   "Question: how do you buy a work of art like this?" Arts

and Leisure Section. The New York Times, August 11, 1974.
1, 19.

Booth, Alan
1972 "Sex and social participation." American Sociological
Review 37:183–192.

Bossard, J., and E. Boll
1963 "Ritual in family living." Pp. 275–280 in M. B. Sussman
(ed.). Sourcebook in Marriage and the Family. Boston:
Houghton Mifflin.

Bottomore, T. B.
1964 "Introduction." Pp. 1–50 in Karl Marx, Selected Writings
in Sociology and Social Philosophy. New York: McGraw-
Hill.

Britt, Steuart H., and Sidney Q. Janus
1941 "Toward a social psychology of human play." Journal of
Social Psychology 13:351–384.

Burch, William R., Jr.
1964 "Observation as a technique for recreation research."
Portland: U.S. Forest Service Research Paper.

Burch, William R., Jr.
1965 "The play world of camping: research into the social
meaning of outdoor recreation." American Journal of
Sociology 70:604–612.

Burch, William R., Jr.
1966 "Wilderness—the life cycle and forest recreational
choice." Journal of Forestry 64:606–610.

Burch, William R., Jr.
1969a "The social circles of leisure: competing explanations."
Journal of Leisure Research 1:125–147.

Burch, William R., Jr.
1971a Daydreams and Nightmares: A Sociological Essay on the
American Environment. New York: Harper & Row.

Burch, William R., Jr.
1971b "Images of future leisure: continuities in changing
expectations." Pp. 160–187 in W. Bell and J. A. Mau (eds.).
The Sociology of the Future. New York: Russell Sage.

Burch, William R., Jr., Merlin Shelstad, and Elizabeth Wallace
1974 "The nature and types of social research on camping and
outdoor education for children and youth— an attempt at
cumulating findings." New Haven: Yale School of
Forestry and Environmental Studies Mimeo.

Burch, William R., Jr., and Wiley Wenger, Jr.
1967 "The social characteristics of participants in three styles of
family camping." Portland: U.S. Forest Service Research
Paper PNW-48.

Burdge, Rabel
1969   "Levels of occupational prestige and leisure activity."
       Journal of Leisure Research 1:262–274.
Bureau of Outdoor Recreation
1967   "The 1965 survey of outdoor recreation." Mimeo.
Bureau of Outdoor Recreation
1970   "The recreation imperative." Washington, D.C.: GPO.
(1974)
Bureau of Outdoor Recreation
1972   "The 1972 survey of outdoor recreation activities: pre-
       liminary report." Mimeo.
Burke, Kenneth
1961   Attitudes Toward History. Boston: Beacon.
Byington, Margaret
1910/ Homestead The Households of a Mill Town.
1974   Pittsburgh: University of Pittsburgh Center for International
       Studies.
Caillois, Roger
1961   Man, Play and Games. M. Barash (trans.). New York: Free
       Press.
Campbell, F. L., J. C. Hendee, and Roger Clark
1968   "Law and order in public parks." Parks and Recreation
       3:28–33, 51–55.
Caplow, Theodore
1954   The Sociology of Work. Minneapolis: University of
       Minnesota Press.
Caplow, Theodore, and Robert Forman
1950   "Neighborhood interaction in a homogeneous commu-
       nity." American Sociological Review 15:357–366.
Carlyle, Thomas
1954   Sartor Resartus—On Heroes and Hero Worship. New
       York: Dutton.
Cassirer, Ernst
1955   The Philosophy of Symbolic Forms. Volume Two: Mythical
       Thought. R. Manheim (trans.). New Haven: Yale
       University Press.
Cheek, Neil H., Jr.
1971   "Toward a Sociology of Not-Work." Pacific Sociological
       Review. 14:245–258.
Cheek, Neil H., Jr.
1972   "Aspects of social age." Unpublished paper presented for
       Rural Sociological Association Annual Meetings.
Chinoy, Ely
1955   Automobile Workers and the American Dream. Garden
       City, New York: Doubleday.

Christ, Edwin A.
  1965   "The 'retired' stamp collector: economic and other func-
         tions of a systematized leisure activity." Pp. 93–112 in
         A. M. Rose and W. A. Peterson (eds.). Older People and
         Their Social World. Philadelphia: F. A. Davis.

Clark, Kenneth
  1961   "Art and society." Harpers 237:74–82.

Clark, Roger N., John C. Hendee, and Frederick L. Campbell
  1971   "Depreciative behavior in forest campgrounds: an ex-
         ploratory study." Portland: U.S. Forest Service Research
         Note PNW-161.

Clarke, Alfred C.
  1956   "Leisure and occupational prestige." American Sociological
         Review 21:301–307.

Clawson, Marion, and Jack L. Knetsch
  1960   Economics of Outdoor Recreation. Baltimore: Johns
         Hopkins Press.

Cohen, Joel
  1971   Casual Groups of Monkeys and Men. Cambridge:
         Harvard University Press.

Cohen, John
  1953   "The ideas of work and play." British Journal of Sociology
         4:312–322.

Coleman, James
  1961   The Adolescent Society. New York: Free Press.

Colvin, Verplanck
  1880   Seventh Report on the Survey of the Adirondack Regions
         of New York to the Year 1879. Albany: Weed, Parsons.

Congalton, A. A., (ed.)
  1954   Hawera—a Social Survey. Hawera, New Zealand: Hawera
         Star Publishing Co.

Cooley, Charles Horton
  1956   Social Organization: The Study of the Larger Mind. New
         York: Free Press.

Cooley, Charles H.
  1964   Human Nature & the Social Order. New York: Schocken.

Coon, Carleton S.
  1962   The Origin of Races. New York: Knopf.

Cramer, M. Ward
  1950   "Leisure time activities of economically privileged
         children." Sociology and Social Research 34:444–450.

Cressman, Elmer W.
  1937   "The out of school activities of junior high pupils in
         relation to intelligence and socio-economic status." State

College: The Pennsylvania State College Studies in
Education No. 20.

Crichton, A., E. James, and J. Wakeford
1962 "Youth and leisure in Cardiff, 1960." The Sociological
Review 10:203–219.

Crook, John Hurrell
1970 "The socio-ecology of primates." Pp. 103–166 in J. H.
Crook (ed.). Social Behavior in Birds and Mammals. New
York: Academic.

Cunningham, K. R., and T. B. Johannis, Jr.
1960 "Research on the family and leisure: a review and critique
of selected studies." Family Life Cordinator 9:25–32.

Davies, Hunter
1974 The Glory Game. New York: St. Martin.

Davis, Fred
1971 On Youth Subcultures: The Hippie Variant. New York:
General Learning Press.

Davis, Kingsley
1937 "The sociolgy of prostitution." American Sociolgical
Review 2:744–755.

Davis, Kingsley
1949 Human Society. New York: Macmillan.

Denney, Reuel
1957 The Astonished Muse. Chicago: University of Chicago
Press.

DeVore, I., (ed.)
1965 Primate Behavior: Studies of Monkeys and Apes. New
York: Holt, Rinehart & Winston.

Dolhinow, Phyllis
1971 "At play in the fields." Natural History 81:66–71.

Dotson, Floyd
1951 "Patterns of voluntary association among urban working-
class families." American Sociological Review 16:687–693.

Dowell, Linus J.
1969 "Recreational pursuits of selected occupational groups."
Research Quarterly 38:719–722.

Drake, Joseph T.
1958 The Aged in American Society. New York: Ronald.

Dubin, Robert
1963 "Industrial workers' worlds: a study of the central life
interests' of industrial workers." Pp. 52–72 in E. Smigel
(ed.). Work and Leisure. New Haven: College and
University Press.

Dulles, Foster Rhea
1965 A History of Recreation: America Learns to Play. 2nd ed.
New York: Appleton.

Dumazedier, J.
1967   Toward a Society of Leisure. New York: Free press.

Duncan, Hugh D.
1962   Communication and Social Order. New York: Bedminster Press.

Duncan, Otis D., Howard Schuman, and Beverly Duncan
1973   Social Change in a Metropolitan Community. New York: Russell Sage.

DuPont, Robert L., and Mark H. Greene
1973   "The dynamics of a heroin addiction epidemic." Science 181:716–722.

Durkheim, Emile
1947   The Division of Labor in Society. G. Simpson (trans.). New York: Free Press.

Durkheim, Emile
1961   The Elementary Forms of Religious Life. J. W. Swain

Duvall, E. M.
1962   Family Development. Philadelphia: Lippincott.

Edwards, Harry
1973   Sociology of Sport. Homewood, Illinois: Dorsey Press.

Eliade, Mircea
1960   Myths, Dreams and Mysteries. P. Mairet (trans.). New York: Harper & Row.

Eliade, Mircea
1963   Myth and Reality. W. R. Trask (trans.). New York: Harper & Row.

Eliade, Mircea
1965   Rites and Symbols of Initiation. W. R. Trask (trans.). New York: Harper & Row.

Embree, John
1939   Suye Mura, A Japanese Village. Chicago: University of Chicago Press.

Ennis, Philip H.
1968   "The definition and measurement of leisure." Pp. 525–572 in E. B. Sheldon and W. E. Moore (eds.). Indication of Social Change: Concepts and Measurements. New York: Russell Sage.

Erikson, Kai T.
1966   Wayward Puritans. New York: Wiley.

Etzkorn, K. Peter
1964   "Leisure and camping: the social meaning of a form of public recreation." Sociology and Social Research 49:76–89.

Evans-Pritchard, E. A.
1940   The Nuer. New York: Oxford University Press.

Fallers, Lloyd A.
　　1966　"Fashion a note on the 'trickle effect'." Pp. 402–405 in
　　　　　R. Bendix and S. M. Lipset (eds.). Class, Status and Power.
　　　　　New York: Free Press.
Ferriss, Albert L.
　　1962　National Recreation Survey. Washington, D.C.: GPO.
Festinger, Leon
　　1957　A Theory of Cognitive Dissonance. New York: Harper &
　　　　　Row.
Field, Donald R.
　　1973　Sociological Dimensions of Leisure Involvement in
　　　　　Water-Based Recreation. Seattle: College of Forest
　　　　　Resources, University of Washington.
Field, Donald R., and Joseph T. O'Leary
　　1973　"Social groups as a basis for assessing participation in
　　　　　selected water activities." Journal of Leisure Research
　　　　　5:16–25.
Firth, Raymond
　　1929　Primitive Economics of the New Zealand Maori. New
　　　　　York: Dutton.
Firth, Raymond
　　1936　We the Tikopia. London: Allen and Unwin.
Foote, Nelson N.
　　1963　"Matching of husband and wife in phases of develop-
　　　　　ment." Pp. 15–20 in M. B. Sussman (ed.). Sourcebook in
　　　　　Marriage and the Family. Boston: Houghton Mifflin.
Fox, J. Charles
　　1903/　The Sports and People of England by Joseph Strutt.
　　1968　Detroit: Singing Tree Press.
Fox, John F.
　　1934　"Leisure-time social backgrounds in a suburban commu-
　　　　　nity." Journal of Educational Sociology 7:493–503.
Freeman, David
　　1972　"Slop art." The New York Times Magazine, November 26,
　　　　　1972: 16, 22, 30, 32.
Friedmann, Georges
　　1961　The Anatomy of Work: Labor, Leisure and the Implications
　　　　　of Automation. New York: The Free Press.
Galbraith, J. K.
　　1958　The Affluent Society, New York: New American Library.
Gans, Herbert
　　1962　The Urban Villagers. New York: Free Press.
Gans, Herbert J.
　　1967　The Levittowners. New York: Pantheon.

Garfinkel, Harold
1967 "Passing and the Managed Achievement of Sex Status in an 'Intersexed' Person, Part 1" in Studies in Ethnomethodology. Englewood Cliffs, New Jersey: Prentice-Hall.

Geertz, Clifford
1972 "Deep play: notes on the Balinese cockfight." Daedalus 101:1–37.

Gerstl, Joel E.
1961 "Determinants of occupational community in high status occupation." Sociological Quarterly 2:37–48.

Gerstl, Joel E.
1963 "Leisure, taste and occupational mileu." Pp. 146–167 in E. Smigel (ed.). Work and Leisure. New Haven: College and University Press.

Goffman, Erving
1959 The Presentation of Self in Everyday Life. Garden City, N.Y.: Doubleday.

Goffman, Erving
1961a Encounters. Indianapolis, Ind.: Bobbs-Merrill.

Goffman, Erving
1961b Asylums. Garden City, New York: Doubleday.

Goffman, Erving
1963a Behavior in Public Places. New York: Free Press.

Goffman, Erving
1963b Stigma. Englewood Cliffs, New Jersey: Prentice-Hall.

Goffman, Erving
1971a Relations in Public. New York: Basic Books.

Goodman, Natalie Cohan
1969 "Leisure, Work and the Use of Time: A Study of Adult Styles of Time Utilization, Childhood Determinants and Vocational Implications." Cambridge: Harvard University E.D.P. Dissertation.

Gottlieb, David
1957 "The neighborhood tavern and the cocktail lounge: a study of class differences." American Journal of Sociology 62:559–562.

Gould, Richard A.
1970 "Journey to Pulykara." Natural History 79:302–317.

Gouldner, Alvin
1970 The Coming Crisis of Western Sociology. New York: Basic Books.

Graham, Saxon
1959 "Social correlates of adult leisure-time behavior." Pp.

331–354 in M. B. Sussman (ed.). Community Structure and Analysis. New York: T. Y. Crowell.

Granovetter, Mark S.
1973   "The strength of weak ties." American Journal of Sociology 78:1360–1380.

Gray, Eugene David
1962   Identification of User Groups in Forest Recreation and Determination of the Characteristics of Such Groups. Ann Arbor: University of Michigan Microfilms.

Green, Arnold W.
1964   Recreation, Leisure, and Politics. New York: McGraw-Hill.

Green, Thomas F.
1968   Work, Leisure, and the American Schools. New York: Random House.

Greenberg, Clement
1953   "Plight of our culture: work and leisure under industrialism." Commentary 16:54–62.

Greist, David A.
1975   "Effects of the social order on human spacing behavior in a national park recreation area." New Haven, Conn.: Yale University PhD Dissertation.

Groos, Karl
1901   The Play of Man. Elizabeth L. Baldwin (trans.). New York: Appleton.

Groos, Karl
1911   The Play of Animals. Elizabeth L. Baldwin (trans.). New York: Appleton.

Hall, Edward T.
1959   The Silent Language. Garden City, New York: Doubleday.

Hall, G. Stanley
1920   Youth. New York: Appleton.

Harlow, H. F., M. K. Harlow, and S. J. Suomi
1971   "From thought to therapy: lessons from a primate laboratory." American Scientist 59:528–544.

Harris, Dale B.
1943   "Relations among play interests and delinquency in boys." American Journal of Orthopsychiatry 13:631–683.

Harris, H. A.
1973   Sport in Greece and Rome. Ithaca: Cornell University Press.

Harry, Joseph
1971   "Work and leisure, situational attitudes." Pacific Sociological Review 19:301–309.

Harry, Joseph, Richard Gale, and John Hendee
1969 "Conservation: an upper-middle class social movement." Journal of Leisure Research 1:246–254.
Havighurst, Robert J.
1957 "Leisure activities of the middle-aged." American Journal of Sociology 22:152:162.
Hawkins, Harold, and James Walters
1952 "Family recreation activities." Journal of Home Economics 44:623–626.
Heberlein, Thomas
1971 "Moral norms, threatened sanctions, and littering behavior." Madison, Wis.: University of Wisconsin PhD Thesis.
Heckscher, August, and Sebastian deGrazia
1959 "Executive leisure." Harvard Business Review 53:6–10, 12, 16, 142–156.
Hendee, John C., and Frederick L. Campbell
1969 "Social aspects of outdoor recreation—the developed campground." Trends 6:13–16.
Hendee, John C., Richard P. Gale, and William R. Catton, Jr.
1971 "A typology of outdoor recreation activity preferences." Journal of Environmental Education 3:28–34.
Hendee, John C., et al.
1968 "Wilderness users in the Pacific Northwest—their characteristics, values, and management preferences." Portland: U.S. Forest Service Research Paper PNW-61.
Henry, Jules
1958 "The personal community and its invariant properties." American Anthropologist 60:827–832.
Hoch, Paul
1972 Rip-off, the Big Game, the Exploitation of Sports by the Power Elite. Garden City, N.Y.: Doubleday.
Hodge, Robert W., and Donald J. Treiman
1968 "Social participation and social status." American Sociological Review 33:722–740.
Hogbin, H. I.
1938 "Social advancement in Guadalcanal." Oceania 8:289–305.
Hoggart, Richard
1963 The Uses of Literacy Harmondsworth. Baltimore: Penguin.
Hollingshead, August B.
1949 Elmtown's Youth. New York: Wiley
Homans, George C.
1950 The Human Group. New York: Harcourt Brace Jovanovich.
Horton, Donald, and Anselm Strauss
1957 "Interaction in audience-participation shows." American Journal of Sociology 62:579–587.

Huizinga, Johann
 1955   Homo Ludens. Boston: Beacon.
Hutchins, H. Clifton, and Edward W. Trecker, Jr.
 1961   "The state park visitor, a report of the Wisconsin park and
        forest travel study." Madison: University of Wisconsin
        Technical Bulletin 22.
Hutchison, Jon
 1973   Outdoor recreation in the Upper Kickapoo Valley. Madi-
        son: University of Wisconsin Institute For Environmental
        Studies Report 6.
Huxley, Aldous
 1939   After Many a Summer Dies the Swan. New York: Harper &
        Row.
Ingham, Alan G., and John W. Loy, Jr.
 1974   "The structure of Ludic action." International Review of
        Sport Sociology 9:23–62.
Ingram, Anne Gayle
 1973   "Delineation of sport sociology—1972." International
        Review of Sport Sociology 8:103–114.
James, H. E., and F. T. Moore
 1940   "Adolescent leisure in a working class district." Occupa-
        tional Psychology 14:132–145.
Jay, Phyllis C., (ed.)
 1968   Primates: Studies in Adaptation and Variability. New York:
        Holt, Rinehart & Winston.
Johnson, Allen
 1972   "Individuality and experimentation in traditional agricul-
        ture." Human Ecology 1:149–160.
Johnson, Sheila K.
 1971   Idle Haven—Community Among the Working-Class
        Retired. Berkeley: University of California Press.
Johnstone, John, and Elihu Katz
 1957   "Youth and popular music: a study in the sociology of
        taste." American Journal of Sociology 62:563–568.
Jordan, Millard L.
 1956   "Leisure time activities of sociologists and attorneys."
        Sociology and Social Research 40:176–178.
Kadushin, Charles
 1966   "The friends and supporters of psychotherapy: on social
        circles in urban life." American Sociological Review
        31:786–802.
Kadushin, Charles
 1968   "Power influence and social circles: a new methodology
        for studying opinion makers." American Sociological
        Review 33:685–699.

Kandel, Denise
    1973   "Adolescent marihuana use: role of parents and peers."
           Science 181:1067–1069.

Kaplan, Max
    1960   Leisure in America: A Social Inquiry. New York: Wiley.

Kasarda, John D., and Morris Janowitz
    1974   "Community attachment in mass society." American
           Sociological Review 39:328–339.

Katz, Elihu
           "Social itinerary of technical change: two studies in the
           diffusion of innovation." Human Organization 20:70–82.

Kaufman, Herbert
    1960   The Forest Ranger. Baltimore: Johns-Hopkins Press.

Kelly, John R.
    1972   "Work and leisure: a simplified paradigm." Journal of
           Leisure Research 4:50–62.

Kenyon, Gerry S.
    1968   "Values held for physical activity by selected urban
           secondary school students in Canada, Australia, England
           and the United States." Madison: University of Wisconsin
           U.S. Office of Education Contract Grant.

King, David A.
    1968a "Characteristics of family campers using the Huron-
           Manistee National Forests." St. Paul: U.S. Forest Service
           Research Paper LS–19.

King, David A.
    1965b "Some socioeconomic comparisons of Huron and Man-
           istee National Forest family campers with market popula-
           tions." Papers of the Michigan Academy of Science,
           Arts, and Letters 50:49–65.

Klausner, Samuel Z.
    1971   On Man in His Environment. San Francisco: Jossey-Bass.

Klessig, Lowell, and James B. Hale
    1972   "A profile of Wisconsin hunters." Madison: Department
           of Natural Resources Technical Bulletin 60.

Kohn, Melvin
    1969   Class and Conformity—A Study in Values. Homewood,
           Illinois: Dorsey Press.

Komarovsky, Mirra
    1946   "The voluntary association of urban dwellers." American
           Sociological Review 11:686–698.

Kohnhauser, Arthur
    1965   Mental Health of the Industrial Worker: A Detroit Study.
           New York: Wiley.

Kottke, Marvin W.
  1975 "A perspective on the camping-involvement cycle." Upper
        Darby, Pennsylvania: U.S. Forest Service Research Paper
        NE–322.
Kummer, Hans
  1971 Primate Societies. Chicago: Aldine.
LaPage, Wilbur F.
  1973 "Growth potential of the family camping market." Upper
        Darby, Pennsylvania: U.S. Forest Service Research Paper
        NE–252.
LaPage, W. F., and D. P. Ragain
  1973 "Family camping trends—an eight year panel study."
        Unpublished report in the files of the N.E. Forest Expt.
        Station, Durham, New Hampshire. Mimeo.
LaPage, W. F., and O. P. Ragain
  1971 "Trends in camping participation." Upper Darby,
        Pennsylvania: U.S. Forest Service Research Paper NE–183.
Leach, Edmund R.
  1967 "Genesis as myth." Pp. 1–13 in J. Middleton (ed.). Myth
        and Cosmos. Garden City, New York: Natural History
        Press.
Lee, Alfred McClung
  1966 Multivalent Man. New York: Braziller.
Lee, Alfred McClung
  1967 "Time budgets in the U.S.A.: problems associated with the
        apparently shrinking American work-week." Prepared for
        Institute v. Sociologica, Universita degli studi di Roma.
        Copy supplied by author.
Lee, Dorothy
  1959 Freedom and Culture. Englewood Cliffs, New Jersey:
        Prentice-Hall.
Lee, Richard B.
  1969 "! Kung Bushman subsistence: an input-output analysis."
        Pp. 47–49 in A. P. Vayda (ed.). Environment and Cultural
        Behavior. Garden City, New York: Natural History Press.
Lee, Richard B., and I. DeVore, (eds.)
  1968 Man the Hunter. Chicago: Aldine.
Lee, Robert G.
  1972 "The social definition of outdoor recreation places." Pp.
        68–84 in William R. Burch, Jr., Neil H. Cheek, Jr., and
        Lee Taylor (eds.). Social Behavior, Natural Resources and
        the Environment. New York: Harper & Row.
Lee, Robert G.
  1973 "Social organization and spatial behavior in outdoor
        recreation." Berkeley, California: University of
        California PhD. Thesis.

Leevy, John R.
1950   "Leisure time of the American housewife." Sociology and Social Research 35:97–105.

Lehman, H. C., and P. A. Witty
1927   The Psychology of Play Activities. New York: Barnes and Co.

Lenski, Gerhard
1966   Power and Privilege. New York: McGraw-Hill.

Lévi-Strauss, Claude
1969   The Raw and the Cooked. J. and D. Weightman (trans.). New York: Harper & Row.

Lewis, Oscar
1958   Village Life in Northern India. New York: Random House.

Liebow, Elliot
1967   Tally's Corner. Boston: Little, Brown.

Linder, Stephan B.
1970   The Harried Leisure Class. New York: Columbia University Press.

Lindesmith, Alfred
1947   Opiate Addiction. Bloomington, Indiana: Principia Press.

Lipset, S. M., and Reinhard Bendix
1959   Social Mobility in Industrial Society. Berkeley: University of California Press.

Lipset, Seymour M., Martin Trow, and James Coleman
1956   Union Democracy. Garden City, New York: Doubleday.

Lipsyte, Robert
1973   "When you lose, you die a little." The New York Times Magazine. September 16:13, 93–102.

Litwak, Eugene
1960a   "Occupational mobility and extended family cohesion." American Sociological Review 25:9–21.
1960b   "Geographic mobility and extended family cohesion." American Sociological Review 25:385–394.
1960c   "Reference group theory, bureaucratic career, and neighborhood primary group cohesion." Sociometry 23:72–84.
1961   "Voluntary associations and neighborhood cohesion." American Sociological Review 26:258–271.

Litwak, Eugene, and J. Fiqueriria
1968   "Technological innovation and theoretical functions of primary groups and bureaucratic structures." American Journal of Sociology 73:468–481.

Litwak, Eugene, and Ivan Szelenyi
1969   "Primary group structures and their functions: kin, neighbors and friends." American Sociological Review 34:465–480.

Loizos, Caroline
 1973 "Play in mammals." Pp. 513–523 in M. W. Fox (ed.).
  Readings in Ethology and Comparative Psychology. Bel-
  mont, California: Wadsworth.

Lowe, Benjamin
 1973 "Relationship of sport and aesthetics." International
  Review of Sport Sociolgy 8:95–101.

Loy, John, and Gerald Kenyon, (eds.)
 1969 Sport, culture and society. New York: Macmillan.

Lucas, Robert C.
 1962 "The Quetico-Superior area: recreational use in relation
  to capacity." Minneapolis: University of Minnesota
  Unpublished Dissertation.

Lucas, Robert C.
 1964a "The recreational use of the Quetico-Superior area." St.
  Paul: U.S. Forest Service Research Paper LS–8.

Lucas, Robert C.
 1964b "Wilderness perception and use: the example of the
  boundary waters canoe area." Natural Resources Journal
  3:394–411.

Lundberg, George A., Mirra Komarovsky, and Mary Alice McInerny
 1934 Leisure: a suburban study. New York: Columbia University
  Press.

Lynd, Robert S., and Helen M. Lynd
 1956 Middletown: a study in modern American culture. New
  York: Harcourt Brace.

Lynes, Russell
 1949 The Taste Makers. London: Hamish Hamilton.

McAuliffe, William E., and Robert A. Goron
 1974 "A test of Lindesmith's theory of addiction: the frequency
  of euphoria among long-term addicts." American Journal
  of Sociology 79:795–840.

MacDonald, M., Carson McGuire, and R. J. Havighurst
 1949 "Leisure activities and socioeconomic status of children."
  American Journal of Sociology 54:505–519.

MacDonald, Marjorie N., and Robert J. Havighurst
 1959 "The meanings of leisure." Social Forces 37:355–360.

McKechnie, George E.
 1974 "The Psychological Structure of Leisure: Past Behavior."
  Journal of Leisure Research 6:27–45.

Mandell, Lewis, and Robert W. Marans
 1972 Participation in Outdoor Recreation—a National Perspective. Ann Arbor: University of Michigan Survey
  Research Center.

Marwell, Gerald
1975   "Why ascription? Parts of a more or less formal theory of the functions and dysfunctions of sex roles." American Sociological Review 40:445–455.

Maslow, A. H.
1954   Motivation and Personality. New York: Harper & Row.

Mass Observation
1970   "Survey of mobile caravanning and camping." London: British Tourist Authority and the Countryside Commission.

Mead, George Herbert
1934   Mind, Self and Society. Chicago: University of Chicago Press.

Merriam, Lawrence C., Jr.
1963   "The Bob Marshall Wilderness Area of Montana, a study in land use." Corvallis: Oregon State University PhD Dissertation.

Meyersohn, Rolf
1963   "Changing work and leisure routines." Pp. 97–106 in E. Smigel (ed.). New Haven: College and University Press.

Miller, S. M., and Frank Riessman
1961   "The working-class subculture: a new view." Social Problems 9:86–97.

Miller, Stephen J.
1965   "The social dilemma of the aging leisure participant." Pp. 72–92 in A. M. Rose and W. A. Peterson (eds.). Older People and Their Social World. Philadelphia: F. A. Davis.

Mills, C. Wright
1951   White Collar. New York: Oxford University Press.

Mills, C. Wright
1953   "Introduction." Pp. vi–ix in Thorstein Veblen. The Theory of the Leisure Class. New York: New American Library.

Mills, C. Wright
1956   The Power Elite. New York: Oxford University Press.

Moore, Joan W.
1961   "Patterns of women's participation in voluntary associations." American Journal of Sociology 66:592–598.

Moore, Wilbert
1951   Industrial Relations and the Social Order. New York: Macmillan.

Moore, Wilbert E.
1963   Man, Time and Society. New York: Wiley.

Morse, Nancy C., and Robert Weiss
1955   "The function and meaning of work and the job." American Sociological Review 20:191–198.

Moss, W. T.
1966 "Forest recreation: a profile." Macon: Georgia Forest Research Council.

Mueller, Eva, and Gerald Gurin
1962 Participation in Outdoor Recreation: Factors Affecting Demand Among American Adults. Washington, D.C.: GPO.

Mumford, Lewis
1967 The Myth of the Machine. New York: Harcourt Brace Jovanovich.

Murdock, George P.
1949 Social Structure. New York: Free Press.

Nash, Roderick
1973 Wilderness and the American Mind. New Haven: Yale University Press.

Neumeyer, Martin H.
1949 Leisure and Recreation. Cranberry, New Jersey: A. S. Barnes.

Nicolson, Harold
1955 Good Behaviour. Boston: Beacon.

Noe, Francis P.
1970 "A comparative typology of leisure in nonindustrialized society." Journal of Leisure Research 2:30–42.

Norbeck, Edward
1971 "Man at play." Natural History Magazine. Special Supplement. 81:48–53.

Ogburn, William F.
1922 Social Change with Respect to Culture and Original Nature. New York: Viking.

O'Leary, Joseph T., Donald R. Field, and Gerard F. Schreuder
1974 "Social groups and water activity clusters: an exploration of interchangeability and substitution." Pp. 195–216 in D. R. Field, J. C. Barrow, and B. F. Long (eds.). Water and Community Development. Ann Arbor: Ann Arbor Science.

Orzack, Louis
1963 "Work as a 'central interest' of professionals." Pp. 73–84 in E. Smigel (ed.). Work and Leisure. New Haven: College and University Press.

Palmer, Edgar Z.
1960 "Recreational aspects of three Nebraska lakes." Lincoln: University of Nebraska Community Study 3.

Pareto, Vilfredo
1966 Sociological Writings. Derick Mirfin (trans.). London: Pall Mall Press.

Parker, Stanley R.
1964 "Type of work, friendship patterns, and leisure." Human Relations 28:215–219.

Parker, Stanley R.
 1965   "Work and non-work in three occupations." Sociological
        Review 13:65–75.
Parker, Stanley R.
 1971   The Future of Work and Leisure. New York: Praeger.
Parsons, Talcott
 1937   Structure of Social Action. New York: McGraw-Hill.
Parsons, Talcott
 1942   "Age and sex in the social structure of the United States."
        American Sociological Review 7:604–616.
Parsons, Talcott
 1951   The Social System. New York: Free Press.
Piaget, Jean, et al.
 1965   The Moral Judgment of the Child. New York: Free Press.
Polanyi, Karl
 1947   "Our obsolete market mentality—civilization must find
        a new thought pattern." Commentary 3:117–123.
Polsky, Ned
 1967   Hustlers, Beats and Others. Chicago: Aldine.
Provinse, J. H.
 1939   "Cooperative rice field cultivation among the Siang Dyak
        of Central Borneo." American Anthropology 39:77–102.
Radosta, John S.
 1974   "Stock-car streaking." The New York Times Magazine,
        June 16:22–29.
Rapoport, Rhona, and Robert N. Rapoport
 1974   "Four themes in the sociology of leisure." British Journal
        of Sociology 25:215–229.
Raser, John R.
 1969   Simulation and Society: An Exploration of Scientific
        Gaming. Boston: Allyn and Bacon.
Reissman, Leonard
 1954   "Class, leisure and social participation." American Socio-
        logical Review 19:76–84.
Richards, A. I.
 1939   Land, Labour and Diet in Northern Rhodesia. London:
        Oxford University Press.
Robb, J. H., and Margaret Carr
 1969   The City of Poriua. Wellington: Department of Social
        Administration and Sociology, Victoria University.
Robb, J. H., and Anthony Somerset
 1957   Report to Masterton. Masterton, New Zealand: Masterton
        Printing Company.
Roberts, John M.
 1962   "Child training and game involvement." Ethnology
        1:166–185.

Roberts, John M., Malcolm J. Arth, and Robert R. Bush
1959 "Games in culture." American Anthropologist 61:597–605.

Roberts, John M., Brian Sutton-Smith, and Adam Kendon
1963 "Strategy in games and folk tales." Journal of Social Psychology 61:185–199.

Roberts, Kenneth
1970 Leisure. Harlow, Essex, England: Longmans.

Robinson, Reginald
1936 "Leisure time activities of children of New York lower west side." Journal of Educational Sociology 9:484–493.

Romano-V, Octavio I.
1974 "Institutions in modern society: caretakers and subjects." Science 183:722–725.

Rothe, Marylou, and Christine Newark
1958 "Homemakers in voluntary community activities." Marriage and Family 20:175–178.

Rottenberg, Simon
1952 "Income and leisure in an underdeveloped economy." Journal of Political Economy 60:95–101.

Sage, George H., (ed.)
1970 Sport and American Society: Selected Readings. Reading. Mass.: Addison-Wesley.

Sahlins, Marshall O.
1968 "Notes on the original affluent society." Pp. 85–89 in R. B. Lee and I. DeVore (eds.). Man the Hunter. Chicago: Aldine.

Salz, Beate R.
1955 "The human element in industrialization in hypothetical case study of Ecuadorean Indians." Economic Development and Cultural Change 4:94–114.

Sapora, A. V., and E. D. Mitchell
1961 The Theory of Play and Recreation. 3rd ed. New York: Ronald.

Schiller, Frederick
1875 Essays, Aesthetical and Philosophical. London: Bell.

Schmitz-Scherzer, R., and W. H. Bierhoff
1974 "Recreational ecology—trends in the use of leisure facilities." Contributions to Human Development 1:91–108.

Schmitz-Scherzer, R., and I. Strödel
1971 "Age-dependency of leisure-time activities." Human Development 14:46–50.

Schmitz-Scherzer, Reinhard
1972 "Freizeitverhalten und sozialer kontext." Zeitschrift für Sozialpsychologie 2:116–125.

Schumpeter, Joseph
   1960   Imperialism and Social Classes. Heinz Nordes (trans.). New York: Meridian.

Schwartz, Barry
   1974   "Waiting, exchange, and power: the distribution of time in social systems." American Journal of Sociology 79:841–870.

Sexton, Patricia Cayo
   1962   "The auto assembly line, an inside view." Harpers 238:197–203.

Shafer, Elwood L.
   1965   "Socioeconomic characteristics of Adirondack campers." Journal of Forestry 63:690–694.

Shanas, Ethel, et al.
   1968   The Social Condition of the Aged. New York: Atherton.

Sidaway, Roger
   1971   "Public pressures on the countryside." Forestry Supplement.

Simmel, Georg
   1950   The Sociology of Georg Simmel, Kurt R. Wolff (trans. and ed.). New York: Free Press.

Simmel, Georg
   1955   The web of group affiliations. Reinhard Bendix (trans.). New York: Free Press.

Simmel, Georg
   1957   "Fashion." American Journal of Sociology 62:541–558.

Slater, Carol
   1960   "Class differences in definition of role and membership in voluntary associations among urban married women." American Journal of Sociology 65:616–619.

Slocum, Walter L.
   1963   "Family culture patterns and adolescent behavior. Pullman: Washington State University Bulletin 648.

Smith, John W.
   1969   Messages of vertebrate communication. Science 165:145: 150.

Sofranko, Andrew J., and Michael F. Nolan
   1972   "Early life experiences and adult sports participation." Journal of Leisure Research 4:6–18.

Sommer, Robert
   1969   Personal Space. Englewood Cliffs, New Jersey: Prentice-Hall.

Spaulding, Irving A.
   1973   "Factors Related to Beach Use." Kingston: University of Rhode Island, Marine Technical Report Series Number 13.

Spencer, Herbert
1870   The Principles of Psychology. London: Williams and
        Norgate.
Stankey, George H.
1972   "A strategy for the definition and management of wilder-
        ness quality. Pp. 88–114 in John V. Krutilla (ed.). Natural
        Environments. Baltimore: Johns Hopkins Press.
Stankey, George H.
1973   "Visitor Perception of Wilderness Recreation Carrying
        Capacity." Ogden, Utah: U.S. Forest Service Research
        Paper INT–142.
Stendler, Celia
1949   "Children of Brasstown." Chicago: University of Illinois
        Bulletin 45.
Stone, C. D.
1963   "Family recreation—a parental dilemma." Family Life
        Coordinator 12:85–87.
Stone, Gregory P.
1955   American sports—play and dis-play. Chicago Review
        9:83–100.
Stone, Gregory P.
1957   "Some meanings of American sport." Pp. 6–29. Columbus,
        Ohio: 60th Annual Meeting College Physical Examination
        Association.
Stone, Gregory P.
1962   "Appearance and the self." Pp. 86–118 in A. M. Rose (ed.).
        Human Behavior and Social Processes. Boston: Houghton
        Mifflin.
Stone, Gregory P.
1972   Games, Sport and Power. New Brunswick, N.J.: Transaction
        Books.
Stone, Gregory P., and Ramon A. Oldenburg
1967   "Wrestling." Pp. 503–532 in Ralph Slovenko and James A.
        Knight (eds.). Motivations in Play, Games, and Sports.
        Springfield, Illinois: C. C Thomas.
Strauss, Anselm
1959   Mirror and Masks. New York: Free Press.
Stumpf, Florence, and Frederick W. Cozens
1947   " Some aspects of the role of games, sports and recrea-
        tional activities in the culture of modern primitive peoples.
        1. The New Zealand Maoris." Research Quarterly 18:198–
        218.
Stumpf, Florence, and Frederick W. Cozens
1949   "Some aspects of the role of games, sports, and recrea-

tional activities in the culture of modern primitive peoples. 2. The Fijians." Research Quarterly 20:2–20.

Sullivan, Harry Stack
1940   Conceptions of Modern Psychiatry. New York. Norton.

Suomi, Stephen, and Harry F. Harlow
1971   "Monkeys at play." Natural History 81:72–75.

Sutton-Smith, Brian
1951   "The meeting of Maori and European cultures and its effects upon the unorganized games of Maori children." Journal of the Polynesian Society 11:93–107.

Sutton-Smith, Brian
1971   "Children at play." Play. Natural History Magazine Special Supplement 81:54–59.

Sutton-Smith, Brian, and John M. Roberts
1964   "Rubrics of competitive behavior." Journal of Genetic Psychology 105:13–31.

Sutton-Smith, Brian, John M. Roberts, and Robert Kozelka
1963   "Game involvement in adults." The Journal of Social Psychology 60:15–30.

Svalastoga, Kaare
1965   Social Differentiation. New York: McKay.

Swados, Harvey
1967   On the Line. New York: Bantam.

Szalai, Alexander
1966   "The multinational comparative time budget research project: a venture in international research cooperation." American Behavioral Scientist 10:1–31.

Szalai, Alexander (ed.)
1972   The Use of Time. The Hague: European Coordination Centre for Research and Documentation in the Social Sciences.

Talmon, Yonina
1972   Family and Community in the Kibbutz. Cambridge: Harvard University Press.

Taves, Marvin, William Hathaway, and Gordon Bultena
1960   "Canoe country vacationers." St. Paul: University of Minnesota Agricultural Experiment Station.

Taylor, G. D., and R. Y. Edwards
1960   "A survey of summer visitors to Wells Gray Park, British Columbia." The Forestry Chronicle 36:346–354.

Taylor, Lee
1968   Occupational Sociology. New York: Oxford University Press.

Terkel, Studs
  1974   Working People Talk About What They Do All Day and
         How They Feel About What They Do. New York: Pantheon.
Thomas, Lawrence C.
  1956   "Leisure pursuits by SES." Journal of Educational Sociology
         29:367–377.
Thompson, Richard
  1964   Race and Sport. London: Oxford University Press.
Thompson, Richard
  1969   "Sport and politics." Pp. 272–286 in John Forster (ed.).
         Social Process in New Zealand, Auckland: Longman Paul
         Ltd.
Tiger, Lionel
  1969   Men in Groups. New York: Random House.
Tiger, Lionel, and Robin Fox
  1971   The Imperial Animal. New York: Holt, Rinehart and
         Winston.
Toffler, Alvin
  1965   The Culture Consumers, Art and Affluence in America.
         Baltimore: Penguin.
Tuite, James
  1975   "In sports, the new poor." The New York Times. January
         5:51.
U.S. National Park Service
  1938   Park Use Studies and Demonstrations. Washington, D.C.:
         GPO.
  1971   North Pacific Border Study—Sociological Studies.
  1972   The Piedmont Study—Sociological Studies.
Veblen, Thorstein
  1953   The Theory of the Leisure Class. New York: New American
         Library.
Wade, Nicholas
  1974   "Bottle-feeding: adverse effects of a Western technology."
         Science 184:45–48.
Walker, Charles R., and Robert H. Guest
  1952   The Man on the Assembly Line. Cambridge, Mass.: Harvard
         University Press.
Wallace, Elizabeth
  1974   "A study of crafts careers." New Haven, Conn.: Yale
         University, Preliminary data analysis for PhD Thesis.
Washburn, Sherwood L.
  1961   Social Life of Early Man. Chicago: Aldine.
Wax, Murray
  1962   "Themes in cosmetics and grooming." American Journal
         of Sociology 33:588–593.

Weber, Max
1947   Theory of Social and Economic Organization. A. M. Henderson and T. Parsons (trans.). Oxford University Press.

Weber, Max
1958a The Protestant Ethic and the Spirit of Capitalism. Talcott Parsons (trans.). New York: Scribner.

Weber, Max
1958b From Max Weber: Essays in Sociology. H. H. Gerth and C. W. Mills (trans. and eds.). New York: Oxford University Press.

Weber, Max
1962   Basic Concepts in Sociology. H. P. Secher (trans.). New York: Citadel.

Weber, Max
1966   "Class, status and party." Pp. 21–27. R. M. Bendix and S. M. Lipset (eds.). Class, Status, and Power. New York: Free Press.

Weiss, Paul
1969   Sport: A Philosophic Inquiry. Carbondale, Illinois: Southern Illinois Press.

Weiss, Robert S., Edwin Harwood, and David Riesman
1971   "Work and automation: problems and prospects." Pp. 545–600 in Robert K. Merton and Robert Nisbet (eds.). Contemporary Social Problems. New York: Hartcourt-Brace Jovanovich.

West, James
1945   Plainville, USA. New York: Columbia University Press.

West, Patrick C., and L. C. Merriam, Jr.
1970   "Outdoor recreation and family cohesiveness: a research approach." Journal of Leisure Research 2:251–259.

White, R. Clyde
1955   "Social class differences in the uses of leisure." American Journal of Sociology 60:145–150.

Whorf, Benjamin Lee
1947   "Science and linguistics." Pp. 111–119 in Theodore M. Newcomb et al. (eds.) Readings in Social Psychology. New York: Holt, Rinehart & Winston.

Whorf, Benjamin Lee
1956   Language, Thought and Reality. John B. Carroll (ed.). New York: MIT, Wiley.

Whyte, William F.
1948   Human Relations in the Restaurant Industry. New York: McGraw-Hill.

Whyte, William Foote
1943   Street Corner Society. Chicago: University of Chicago Press.

Wilensky, Harold
    1963   "The uneven distribution of leisure: the impact of economic growth on 'free time'." Pp. 107–145 in E. Smigel (ed.). Work and Leisure. New Haven: College and University Press.

Wilensky, Harold
    1964   "Mass society and mass culture: interdependence or independence." American Sociological Review 29:173–197.

Wilensky, Harold L.
    1960   "Work, careers and social integration." International Social Science Journal 12:543–560.

Williams, W. M.
    1956   Gosforth: The Sociology of an English Village. New York: Free Press.

Wilson, Edmund O.
    1975   Sociobiology—The New Synthesis. Cambridge: Harvard University Press.

Wilson, Monica
    1967   "Nyakyusa ritual and symbolism." Pp. 147–166 in J. Middleton (ed.). Myth and Cosmos. Garden City, New York: Natural History Press.

Wippler, Reinhard
    1968   Social Determinants of Leisure Behavior. English Summary. Assen: Van Gorcum.

Wippler, Reinhard
    1970   "Leisure behavior: a multivariate approach." Sociologia Neerlandica 6:51–67.

Witt, Peter A., and Doyle W. Bishop
    1970   "Situational antecedents to leisure behavior." Journal of Leisure Research 2:64–77.

Wohlwill, Joachim F., and Daniel H. Carson, (eds.)
    1972   Environment and the Social Sciences: Perspectives and Applications. Washington, D.C.: American Psychological Association.

Wylie, J. A.
    1953   "A survey of 504 families to determine the relationships between certain factors and the nature of the family recreation program." Research Quarterly 24:229–243.

Yancey, William L., David Britt, and Jane Snell
    1971   Patterns of Leisure in the Inner-city. Nashville: Urban and Regional Development Center of Vanderbilt University.

Yoesting, Dean R., and Dan L. Burkhead
    1971   "Sociological aspects of water-based recreation in Iowa." Ames: Iowa State University Sociology Report 94.

Yoesting, Dean R., and Dan L. Burkhead
1973 "Significance of childhood recreation experience on adult leisure behavior: an exploratory analysis." Journal of Leisure Research. 5:25–36.

Young, Bart, Merlin Shelstad, and William Burch
1974 "The use of interpretive media in environmental education." New Haven: Yale University Institution for Social and Policy Studies Working Paper W4–6.

Young, Franklin
1965 Initiation Ceremonies. Indianapolis: Bobb-Merrill.

Young, Michael, and Peter Willmott
1957 Family and Kinship in East London. Harmondsworth: Penguin.

Zuckerman, Solly
1932 The Social Life of Monkeys and Apes. London: Kegan Paul.

INDEX

3 1194 00232 4998

AMERICAN UNIVERSITY LIBRARY